PENTECOSTALISM

PENTECOSTALISM

by John Thomas Nichol

HARPER & ROW, PUBLISHERS

NEW YORK, EVANSTON, AND LONDON

FIRST EDITION

LIBRARY OF CONGRESS CATALOG CARD NUMBER: 66–20782

K-Q

To
My Mother and Father
and
Dorothy's

PENTECOSTAL PIONEERS

Through the battle, through defeat,
moving yet and never stopping,
Pioneers! O Pioneers!
—*Walt Whitman*

Contents

Preface

America is noted for nurturing religious movements. In the nineteenth century she gave birth to Mormonism, Adventism, and Christian Science. At the turn of this century she produced still another one—Pentecostalism, a movement which boldly maintains that a Holy Spirit baptism that is accompanied by the evidential sign of "speaking in tongues" is a normative religious experience available to all Christians. Moreover, Pentecostalism declares that other spiritual graces—the ability to prophesy, to heal, to interpret unknown tongues—ought to be manifested in the life of the contemporary church and in the lives of Christians.

When Pentecostalism first appeared on the American religious scene, some critics prophesied its rapid demise. In 1913, for example, D. A. Hayes, Professor of New Testament at Garrett, predicted: "The present day tongues movement is likely to run its course in a few months or a few years." On the contrary, during the last thirty years Pentecostalism has expanded phenomenally. It has exceeded the rate of growth of most of the so-called main line denominations, causing observers like Henry P. Van Dusen to characterize it as a religious revolution comparable in importance with the establishment of the original Apostolic Church and with the Protestant Reformation.

However, our information about Pentecostalism, which in little more than a half century has emerged from a small decentralized fellowship to a worldwide charismatic movement, has not kept pace with its growth and influence. Because references to Pentecostalism in most church histories, religious encyclopedias, and periodical literature is rather sketchy, it has been necessary to locate and consult rare source materials both here and abroad. Based on these documents—yearbooks, minutes, pamphlets, periodicals, and tracts—and supplemented by firsthand observation—attendance at Pentecostal worship services, revivals, camp meetings, national conclaves, and international conferences—this book presents the first comprehensive survey of worldwide Pentecostalism. First, it reviews those characteristics of faith and practice that are unique to Pentecostalism, that set it apart from other types of Protestant Christianity. Then, it traces modern Pentecostalism from its origin in Topeka, Kansas, in 1901, to its rapid expansion throughout the world. Furthermore, it offers reasons for the widespread extension of Pentecostalism, for its tendency to proliferate, and for the severe opposition which it encountered. In addition, it classifies the scores of groups which comprise contemporary Pentecostalism in America and provides a country-by-country chronicle of many foreign Pentecostal groups about which little or nothing has been written heretofore. Finally, it surveys the most significant trends that have taken place within Pentecostalism since World War II.

Only the historical implications of Pentecostalism will be treated in this book. Facts about its origin, message, and global expansion will be recorded faithfully. Whenever necessary, causes will be studied and facts interpreted; for, as R. L. P. Milburn noted in his Bampton Lectures for 1952, it is this function which distinguishes the historian from the chronicler. What I want to emphasize is that no attempt will be made to inquire into the truth or falsity of the Pentecostal doctrinal claims, which are more properly the province of the theologian or philosopher. Neither will any great effort be made to examine Pentecostalism sociologically or psychologically.

And yet to present a comprehensive history of Pentecostalism is not a simple task. It involves certain risks, not the least of which is caused by the tendency of Pentecostal bodies to come and go, merge and split, and drop old titles for new ones. Rather than attempting to write an exhaustive survey, therefore, I have chosen to be selective, to describe Pentecostalism in terms of representative groups: the large and small, the Negro and white, the American and non-American, the sophisticated and the radical.

Although it is my conviction that this history of Pentecostalism is based on more primary and secondary sources than any other previous work in English, I also realize that, because of the paucity or inaccessibility of many documents, my study is tentative. It is an *avant-propos,* but therein is its value: it has assembled data on which subsequent research may focus and which it may explore more fully.

Finally, it seems only fair to inform the reader that I have been reared in Pentecostalism. However, as a historian I have striven not to allow my heritage or my deeply held convictions to distort this chronicle of the twentieth-century charismatic revival. This book is not intended as an apologetic for Pentecostalism, rather it seeks to portray the Pentecostals as they have been and are—sometimes crassly emotional, too often exhibiting holier-than-thou attitudes, often suspicious of change, anti-intellectual; but, on the other hand, genuinely sincere, vitally enthusiastic, and utterly evangelistic. They are members of a movement that represents a renaissance of Apostolic Christianity. Standing alongside Catholicism and Classical Protestantism as a "Third Force," Pentecostalism commands our attention. It cannot be ignored any longer.

JOHN THOMAS NICHOL

Beverly, Massachusetts
July, 1966

Acknowledgments

The author gratefully acknowledges the kindness of the following publishers in granting permission to reproduce their copyrighted materials in this book:

Advocate Press: *The Pentecostal Holiness Church* by Joseph Campbell.
Augsburg Publishing House: *Speaking in Tongues* by Haakon J. Stolee.
Berea College Press: *Glossolalia* by Ira Jay Martin.
Christian Century Foundation: "New York's Spanish Protestants" by Frederick L. Whitam, "Shock Troops in Chile" by Theo Tschuy, and "What About Oral Roberts?" by W. E. Mann.
Church of God Publishing House: *Evangel Reader, Like a Mighty Army, Pillars of Pentecost,* and *Where the Saints Have Trod* by Charles W. Conn; and *Healing in the Church* by James A. Cross.
College Press: *The Third Force* by Gordon Atter.
Gospel Publishing House: *Suddenly from Heaven* and *What Meaneth This?* by Carl Brumback; *With Signs Following* by Stanley Frodsham; *Upon All Flesh* by Donald Gee; and *The Promise Fulfilled* by Klaude Kendrick.
National Council of the Churches of Christ in the U.S.A.: *Yearbook of American Churches for 1966.*

Scripture quotations are from *The Holy Bible, Revised Standard Version,* copyrighted in 1946 and 1952 and used by permission of the National Council of the Churches of Christ, Division of Christian Education.

Although I cannot make individual acknowledgment to all the people who have aided me in writing this book, my sincere gratitude goes to those historians of Pentecostalism, especially Gordon Atter, Carl Brumback, Joseph Campbell, Charles W. Conn, Donald Gee, and Klaude Kendrick, whose scholarship has made my research easier. I am obliged to pay tribute to George H. Williams, Richard M. Cameron, and the late Raymond W. Albright. By word and deed they taught me that a historian ought to be precise, faithful, and unprejudiced; and that nothing should make him swerve from the way of truth.

Special recognition is also due Howard H. Hunter and Earl Kent Brown for their penetrating yet inspiring criticism of much of this material when it was originally submitted to satisfy the doctoral requirements at the Boston Universty Graduate School.

Nor can I forget the encouragement of Roger Nicole, a friend indeed; the innumerable favors by the librarians at the Andover-Harvard Library, the General Theological Library, the Congregational Library, and the Boston University School of Theology Library; the diligence of my typists—Mary Ann Hawkes and Eleanor Nelson.

Most of all I am indebted to Dorothy, a devoted and understanding wife whose "pleasures are in the happiness of her family," and to Jonathan and Jacqueline for tiptoeing and whispering while dad was working.

PENTECOSTALISM

CHAPTER 1

Pentecostal Faith and Practice

Early in The Acts of the Apostles one reads that a small band of men and women, following Jesus' charge that they tarry in Jerusalem for the promise of the Father—a Holy Spirit baptism—gathered in an upper room and remained steadfastly in prayer. Not too long afterward they became spectator-participants to phenomena which transformed their lives. In addition to hearing a sound come from heaven like the rush of a mighty wind and seeing tongues as of fire, we read that all were filled with the Holy Spirit and began to speak in other tongues, as the Spirit gave them utterance.[1]

These events which occurred on the Day of Pentecost constitute the very core of modern Pentecostal belief and practice. Whatever else may separate them, all Pentecostals agree that like the 120 who had gathered in the upper room, they too must "tarry" and be "endued with power from on high." They take seriously and personally the Petrine challenge to the gathered multitude on the Day of Pentecost:

> Repent, and be baptized every one of you in the name of Jesus Christ for the forgiveness of your sins; and you shall receive the gift of the Holy Spirit. For the promise is to you and to your children. . . .[2]

Very simply, then, the now nearly 8 million Pentecostals bear that name because they are convinced of "the reality of a present-day

[1] Acts 1–2:4.
[2] Acts 2:38–39.

experience for . . . believers such as was received by the early disciples on the Day of Pentecost."[3]

This emphasis upon a recurring experience of Pentecost—with all the attending supernatural phenomena—has earned Pentecostalism and its adherents sobriquets like "Tongues Movement," "Holy Rollers," or "Holy Jumpers." Moreover, those who believe that speaking in tongues is demonically inspired have classified Pentecostalism, together with Mormonism and Spiritism, as anti-Christian. Still others have equated Pentecostalism with the fire-eaters and snake-handlers in the South whose fanaticism puts them, at best, on the periphery of orthodox Christianity.[4] Because of this, Pentecostal writers stress that theirs is a back-to-the-Bible movement and that their experience is scripturally oriented.[5] Says one author: "There is absolutely no evidence during any period of the Pentecostal revival that the people ever considered themselves other than simply, orthodox Christian believers,"[6] who, adds a British pamphleteer, "could heartily subscribe to the Apostles' Creed."[7]

Similarities to Other Protestant Bodies

With the host of churches in the so-called Protestant tradition, the Pentecostals subscribe to the Reformation principles that salvation is a free gift of divine grace apart from deeds and efforts or ecclesiastical sanction; that all Christian believers are priests by virtue of their association in the Church, the Body of Christ, and as such minister to each other in matters of faith; and that the Word of God must be the

[3] Earl P. Paulk, Jr., *Your Pentecostal Neighbor* (Cleveland, Tenn.: The Pathway Press, 1958), p. 61.

[4] Pentecostals repudiate this equation. See Irwin Winehouse, *The Assemblies of God: A Popular Survey* (New York: Vantage Press, 1959), p. 87. Charles W. Conn, *Like a Mighty Army* (Cleveland, Tenn.: Church of God Publishing House, 1955), p. 191, describes how the 23rd Annual Assembly in 1928 formally denounced such aberrational conduct.

[5] Consult Carl Brumback, *What Meaneth This?* (Springfield, Mo.: Gospel Publishing House, 1947), pp. 98–115; and Charles W. Conn, *Pillars of Pentecost* (Cleveland, Tenn.: The Pathway Press, 1956), pp. 22–27.

[6] Conn, *Pillars of Pentecost,* p. 23.

[7] British Pentecostal Fellowship, *What Is This Pentecostal Movement?* (London: Evangel Press, n.d.), p. 10.

norm for faith and practice, and that it is each Christian's right and duty to interpret it for himself.

Beyond this, however, the emphases which are manifested by the Pentecostals would place them in the radical (left) wing of the Reformation. Like their spiritual ancestors, the Anabaptists, Pentecostals declare (1) that the individual as well as the corporate body of believers should seek for and submit to the leading of the Spirit; (2) that there should be a return to apostolic simplicity in worship; (3) that believers ought to separate themselves from the world; (4) that believer's baptism replaces infant baptism; and (5) that believers should look for the imminent visible return of Christ who will set up his millennial reign.

Notice the left-wing-of-the-Reformation nuances in this passage drawn from Gordon Atter's *The Third Force:*

> Within certain Pentecostal circles there are increasing evidences of a trend toward a new and unwholesome emphasis on the externals of form and ceremony. This was the cause of the fall of Israel in the long ago. . . . The truth became well-nigh lost in all of these externals and traditions.
>
> . . . .
>
> The Pentecostal Movement has not altogether escaped this devitalizing trend. Beautiful church buildings, trained choirs, an educated ministry, a well-organized church program are all very fine in their place as long as the Holy Ghost has the pre-eminence. However, there is definitely a danger here.[8]

In matters of doctrine, Pentecostals can be described as Evangelicals whose theology is akin to Fundamentalism,[9] and their writings on both sides of the Atlantic seem to support such a generalization. After reviewing the doctrinal position of his group in Great Britain, Pentecostal historian Donald Gee writes: "In all this it will be seen that Assemblies of God are entirely one with every true evangelical section

[8] Peterborough, Ont.: The College Press, 1962, p. 292.

[9] Fundamentalism is that militant movement which arose after World War I, and was designed to purge American Protestantism of all who refused to subscribe to "orthodox" beliefs, such as biblical inerrancy, virgin birth, atoning sacrifice of Christ's death, literal resurrection, and second coming of Christ. See the most recent work of Louis Gasper, *The Fundamentalist Movement* (Paris: Mouton & Co., 1963), *passim.*

of the Christian Church."[10] Charles W. Conn, a leader in the American Church of God, agrees: "In every point our faith is the historic, fundamental Christian faith, not in creed only but also in practice and living hope."[11]

The theological stance of Pentecostalism in America can be ascertained from the following Statement of Truth adopted by the Pentecostal Fellowship of North America—an organization which was founded in 1948 and which is made up of fifteen of the major Pentecostal bodies.

1. We believe the Bible to be the inspired, the only infallible authoritative Word of God.

2. We believe that there is one God, eternally existent in three persons: Father, Son and Holy Ghost.

3. We believe in the deity of our Lord Jesus Christ, in His virgin birth, in His sinless life, in His miracles, in His vicarious and atoning sacrifice through His shed blood, in His bodily resurrection, in His ascension to the right hand of the Father, and His personal return in power and glory.

4. We believe that for the salvation of the lost and sinful men regeneration by the Holy Spirit is absolutely essential.

5. We believe that the full gospel includes holiness of heart and life, healing for the body and the baptism in the Holy Spirit with the initial evidence of speaking in other tongues as the Spirit gives utterance.

6. We believe in the present ministry of the Holy Spirit by whose indwelling the Christian is enabled to live a godly life.

7. We believe in the resurrection of both the saved and the lost; they that are saved unto the resurrection of life and they that are lost unto the resurrection of damnation.

8. We believe in the spiritual unity of believers in our Lord Jesus Christ.[12]

Except for Article Five, this entire formulation was taken from the

[10] *The Story of the Great Revival* (London: Assemblies of God Publishing House, n.d.), p. 7.

[11] *Pillars of Pentecost,* pp. 26 f.

[12] From a brochure published by the Pentecostal Fellowship of North America, describing its origin, progress, doctrines, and membership. It is available from any member body.

Statement of Faith that was drawn up in 1943 by the National Association of Evangelicals—an organization which many Pentecostal groups initially joined.[13] The ultraconservative nature of their doctrinal statement would obviously preclude any extensive intercourse between the Pentecostals and most of the groups that are affiliated with the National Council or the World Council of Churches. It would ally them, however, with millions of theologically like-minded Evangelicals—a host of Conservative Baptists, Reformed Presbyterians, Wesleyan Methodists, Conservative Congregationalists, and Mennonites.

An even closer kinship exists between Pentecostalism and the Holiness movement from which it evolved. Holiness is generally treated as an outgrowth of the post-Civil War revivals. It was an attempt among certain Methodists to revive an interest in John Wesley's doctrine of sanctification (Christian perfection) because they felt that this emphasis had been neglected by Methodism.[14] Although the movement started under Methodist leadership, it operated on an interdenominational basis with its principal purpose being the stimulation of religious piety as an antidote for the "worldliness" which was thought to prevail in an apostate institutionalized church. William Boardman, an American Presbyterian, and Robert Pearsall Smith conducted meetings all over England which eventually resulted in the emergence of the Keswick movement, conferences for the deepening of the spiritual life.[15] In America the National Holiness movement arose, led by Methodists, appealing to them by the use of media that were fast disappearing in the so-called established churches: namely, the revival meeting, the camp meeting, and holiness literature. The predominant theme that was struck both here and abroad was that "the Christian can attain full holiness (sanctification) only when he abandons all efforts and allows the Holy Spirit to live within him

[13] Gasper, *Fundamentalist*, pp. 28 f., reprints the NAE Statement of Faith which, he says, reiterates in its seven points five of the famous "Five Articles of Fundamentalism."

[14] Elmer T. Clark, "Holiness Churches," *Twentieth Century Encyclopedia of Religious Knowledge*, ed. Lefferts A. Loetscher (Grand Rapids, Mich.: Baker Book House, 1955), I, 520 f.

[15] H. Shelton Smith and others, *American Christianity* (New York: Charles Scribner's Sons, 1963), II, p. 313.

the life of Christ."[16] When the Spirit makes His abode within, it will be manifested by the believer's experiencing a definite emotional reaction. This is his baptism in the Spirit—his "second blessing."[17]

Needless to say various holiness-antiholiness segments developed; controversy and recriminations ensued. In 1894, Methodist bishops, who had been viewing the mounting tensions with alarm, issued a pastoral letter which enunciated their disaffection for the holiness contingent.[18] It became necessary for these holiness bands to withdraw and to form independent religious bodies which exist today under such names as: Church of the Nazarene, Pilgrim Holiness Church, and Church of God (Anderson, Indiana).

Additional fragmentation occurred within the Holiness movement. Some felt that the experience of sanctification (or baptism with the Holy Spirit, or "second blessing") was either an instantaneous total cleansing from sin or an abiding devotion to God. At most, the experience might be attended by boisterous praying, great bodily exercise, or vociferous and constant shouting.[19] However, others were convinced that the same experience would be certified by some supernatural sign—a vision, dream, speaking in tongues.[20] This latter group, which has been dubbed by contemporary scholars as the left wing of the Holiness movement,[21] was destined to become the Pentecostal movement.

Many Pentecostals readily acknowledge their indebtedness to the Holiness movement. The following preamble to a resolution relative to reaffirming the standard of holiness among the Churches of God (Cleveland, Tennessee) illustrates this fact:

> The foundation of the Church of God is laid upon the principles of

[16] *Ibid.*

[17] Sanctification, or the "second blessing," is an experience subsequent to and distinct from justification or conversion, among holiness people. Its effect is the eradication of natural depravity or inbred sin. See Elmer T. Clark: *The Small Sects in America* (rev. ed.; Nashville: Abingdon Press, 1959), pp. 59 f.

[18] For an excerpt see F. E. Mayer, *The Religious Bodies of America,* 4th ed., revised by Arthur Piepkorn (St. Louis: Concordia Publishing House, 1961), pp. 314 f.

[19] Timothy L. Smith, *Called Unto Holiness* (Kansas City, Mo.: Nazarene Publishing House, 1962), p. 316.

[20] *Ibid.*

[21] Clark, "Holiness," p. 864; and Mayer, *Religious Bodies,* p. 313.

Biblical Holiness. Even before the Church experienced the outpouring of the Holy Ghost, its roots were set in the holiness revival of the past century. It was, and is, a holiness church—holiness in fact and holiness in name.[22]

The legacy of the Holiness movement to Pentecostalism has been rather sizable. As Donald Gee points out: "Many of the first Pentecostal leaders had originally been in the Holiness Movement."[23] A number of Holiness churches in the South took the stand that speaking in tongues was the outward sign of a Spirit baptism and joined the newly emerging Pentecostal movement. Among these were the Church of God (Cleveland, Tennessee) and the Pentecostal Holiness Church. Ideologically, the Holiness movement contributed these emphases which have become the very core of Pentecostalism: (1) that there is a blessing to be sought and to be received subsequent to and distinct from conversion; (2) that one must seek to be led by the Spirit in all the affairs of life; (3) that revivals and camp meetings ought to be utilized for the purpose of winning converts and rejuvenating the spiritual lives of the faithful; (4) that believers should maintain a vibrant hope in the imminent return of Christ; and (5) that one ought to forsake the world and shun all manifestations of "worldliness"—amusements, jewelry, use of cosmetics, luxury.

Despite the rather close similarity in so many areas, the great gulf which separates most Protestants from the Pentecostals is the stress which the latter put on what they call the "full gospel"—especially the teaching concerning one's experiential encounter with the Holy Spirit, as well as the emphasis on healing.

Pentecostal Distinctives

Like the Holiness movement from which they emerged, Pentecostals do not feel that they have created any new doctrine or standards. By preaching the "full gospel," they believe that they have simply been re-emphasizing old doctrines: (1) the biblical em-

[22] *Church of God Minutes, 1962* (Cleveland, Tenn.: Church of God Publishing House, 1962), p. 182.

[23] *The Pentecostal Movement* (London: Elim Publishing House, Ltd., 1949), p. 6.

phasis on salvation and justification by faith which the Reformers had revived; (2) the doctrine of the premillennial return of Christ which John Nelson Darby and the Plymouth Brethren had preached so vigorously in the nineteenth century;[24] (3) the stress on divine healing which had resulted from the teaching and evangelistic efforts of A. J. Gordon, a Baptist, A. B. Simpson, a Presbyterian, and John Alexander Dowie of Zion, Illinois;[25] and (4) the doctrine which had been proclaimed by a host of holiness people but which now appeared to be vouchsafed to Pentecostals—that of the Holy Spirit whose baptism empowers a Christian to live victoriously and to witness effectively, and whose gifts enable a Christian believer to perform the supernatural; providing him, as one Pentecostal expressed it, with "a spiritual capacity far mightier than the finest natural abilities could ever supply."[26]

A Baptism with the Holy Spirit. Every Pentecostal believes in the reality of a present-day experience for believers such as was received by the early disciples on the Day of Pentecost (Acts 2:4).[27] For the Pentecostal this experience is scriptural; it is called the baptism with the Holy Spirit: it is an experience subsequent to conversion; and the initial evidence of having received the Pentecostal baptism is that a person under the Spirit's influence speaks in a language hitherto unknown.[28]

It is the view of Pentecostals that they have the strongest warrant in the Bible for seeking a postconversion blessing. First, they believe

[24] Kenneth Scott Latourette, *A History of Christianity* (New York: Harper & Row, 1953), p. 1185.

[25] Stanley Horton, *Into All Truth* (Springfield, Mo.: Gospel Publishing House, 1955), p. 143.

[26] Donald Gee, *Concerning Spiritual Gifts* (Springfield, Mo.: Gospel Publishing House, 1937), p. 15.

[27] Paulk, *Your Pentecostal Neighbor,* p. 61.

[28] There is a prolific literature on this in Pentecostal circles. Some of the better known writings are given here alphabetically, not in terms of merit: Carl Brumback, *What Meaneth This?;* Harold Horton, *The Gifts of the Spirit* (London: Assemblies of God Publishing House, 1962); Ray H. Hughes, *What Is Pentecost?* (Cleveland, Tenn.: The Pathway Press, 1963); Frank W. Lemons, *Our Pentecostal Heritage* (Cleveland, Tenn.: The Pathway Press, 1963); and Ralph M. Riggs, *The Spirit Himself* (Springfield, Mo.: Gospel Publishing House, 1949).

that the experience of a Holy Spirit baptism was foretold by the prophets of the Old Testament.[29] Special emphasis is placed on the prophecies of Joel to which Peter referred on the Day of Pentecost when he attempted to explain the supernatural manifestations to astonished onlookers. When they asked, "What does this mean?" Peter's response was:

". . . but this is what was spoken by the prophet Joel: 'And in the last days it shall be, God declares, that I will pour out my Spirit upon all flesh, and your sons and your daughters shall prophesy, and your young men shall see visions, and your old men shall dream dreams; yea, and on my menservants and my maidservants in those days I will pour out my Spirit; and they shall prophesy.' "[30]

Moreover, Pentecostals view many New Testament statements made by Jesus and John the Baptist as pointing toward the time when a baptism with the Holy Spirit would be a reality.[31] The following key phrases which are quoted time and again among Pentecostals are taken from the last of these prophecies, spoken by Jesus just before the ascension: "but before many days you shall be baptized with the Holy Spirit"; "you shall receive power when the Holy Spirit has come upon you"; "you shall be my witnesses."[32]

All Pentecostals believe that the aforesaid prophecies and promises were fulfilled on the Day of Pentecost. More important, however, they are persuaded that the outpouring of the Holy Spirit on the Day of Pentecost was not just for that time or for the Apostolic community. Pentecost is for them a relevant, recurring phenomenon.[33] Unique too with the Pentecostals is the view that the reception of the Spirit is signified by the phenomenon of speaking in tongues. It is this principle which distinguishes them from the so-called historic Christian churches, and they are well aware of it.

The chief, and perhaps only, justification that the Pentecostal Movement has for its separate existence from the other denominations, is the

[29] See a pamphlet by Henry H. Ness, *The Baptism with the Holy Spirit* (Hayward, Calif.: Evangelism Crusaders, Inc., n.d.), pp. 5–8.

[30] In Acts 2:16–18; the author is citing Joel 2:28–32.

[31] Cf. Luke 3:16; 11:13, 24:49; John 7:37–39, 14:16, 15:26; Mark 16:17.

[32] The full context is found in Acts 1:4–8; cf. Luke 24:49.

[33] P. C. Nelson, "Answers to Questions Concerning the Baptism in the Spirit," *Pentecostal Evangel,* XXXIV (Sept. 21, 1946), 8.

claim to possess the like gift [speaking in tongues] as at the beginning [Apostolic era].

. . . .

The great stumbling block in the Movement is, of course, the manifestation of "other tongues." If only this obstacle could be overcome, many orthodox sections of the Christian Church would be pleased to have greater fellowship with Pentecostal believers.[34]

And yet the Pentecostals will not retreat from what they feel is a biblical basis for their position. In their expositions they assert that "tongues" were an evidence of the Holy Spirit's descent on the Day of Pentecost (Acts 2:4); "tongues" were in evidence when the Holy Spirit was poured out on those who gathered in the house of Cornelius, persuading Peter that God had extended his Spirit to the Gentiles (Acts 10:46); "tongues" were in evidence when Paul laid hands upon the believers at Ephesus (Acts 19:1–7). Although there is no mention of tongues in the narrative concerning Paul's conversion (as recorded in Acts 9:17), in his Corinthian letter he writes: "I thank God that I speak in tongues more than you all" (I Cor. 14:18). Pentecostals conclude, therefore, that whenever the charismatic impartation of the Holy Spirit is described, the outward expression is an ecstatic speaking in a language that the person had never learned.[35]

Finally, Pentecostals are convinced that there is enough evidence from post-Apostolic times to their own experiential involvement with the phenomenon to demonstrate that "tongues" have never completely disappeared from the Church.

It is a commonplace of Church History that the special phenomena now associated with the Pentecostal Movement have occurred again and again during periods of spiritual revival and enthusiasm. A long list of such happenings could be cited, but it will be sufficient to quote such an acknowledged authority as the *Encyclopaedia Britannica* . . . that the Glossolalia (or speaking with tongues), "recurs in Christian revivals in every age; e.g., among the mendicant friars of the thirteenth century, among the Jansenists and early Quakers, the converts of Wesley and

[34] Howard Carter, "The Pentecostal Movement," *Pentecostal Evangel*, XXXIV (May 18, 1946), 3, 7, 8.

[35] Myer Pearlman, *Knowing the Doctrines of the Bible* (Springfield, Mo.: Gospel Publishing House, 1937), p. 313.

Whitefield, the persecuted Protestants of the Cevennes, and the Irvingites."[36]

But what is the precise nature of these glossolalic utterances? Some critics have judged them to be "gibberish," "the babblings of fanaticism," "satanically inspired," "childish prattle which should have been sloughed off upon one's becoming more mature . . . an infantilism thrusting itself into the period of maturity," "hysteria," or "a 'temporary regression' giving people an opportunity for 'stylized primitivizations' while at the same time offering opportunities for temporary identifications with heroes of the faith who reportedly have had similar experiences."[37]

One of the most lucid responses to such estimates has been written by an articulate Church of God executive, Charles W. Conn:

> When the disciples first spoke in tongues it was in clear, precise, understandable languages. Those gathered in Jerusalem heard the gospel proclaimed in their own tongues. The speaking was not in unintelligible gibberish. . . . God has not yet stooped to repetitious and meaningless banality. Gibberish is not the language of the Spirit! . . . The unknown tongue is not the stammering of excited vocal organs, but rather the clear utterances of spiritual ecstasy. When the Spirit speaks through you, it will be exalted praise and convicting exhortation. . . .[38]

Harold Horton, a British Pentecostal, explains the nature of *glossolalia* as "a supernatural utterance by the Holy Spirit in languages never learned by the speaker—not understood by the mind of the speaker—seldom understood by the hearer." Tongues speaking, he goes on to say, is a

> manifestation of the mind of the Spirit of God employing human speech organs. When man is speaking with tongues, his mind, intellect, under-

[36] Gee, *The Pentecostal Movement,* p. 9. It must be noted that when one checks the primary sources, there are few data to support the contention of the *Britannica* or Gee who repeats the claim. Except for a clear-cut evidence that *glossolalia* had manifested itself among the Irvingites and, perhaps, sporadically among the Camisards, there is little else that the writer has been able to document.

[37] See "The New Pentecostalism" by Russell T. Hitt. This is a reprint of an article which originally appeared in the magazine, *Eternity* (Philadelphia: Evangelical Foundation, Inc., 1963); also G. B. Cutten, *Speaking with Tongues* (New Haven: Yale University Press, 1927), and D. A. Hayes, *The Gift of Tongues* (New York: Eaton and Mains, 1913).

[38] *Pillars of Pentecost,* p. 57.

standing are quiescent. It is the faculty of God that is active. Man's will, certainly, is active, and his spirit, and his speech organs; but the mind that is operating is the mind of God through the Holy Spirit.[39]

While there are testimonies from some Pentecostals that they spoke in a recognizable (to somebody present who could recognize it) yet heretofore unlearned language,[40] this seems to be the exception.[41] Speaking in tongues is ordinarily in an "unknown tongue"; that is why the uninitiated often characterize it as "gibberish" or "babbling." It is also why Pentecostals, following Paul's admonition to the Corinthian church, have rules that order the congregational use of the gift: (1) people must have knowledge of what is being said; therefore, if there has been speaking in tongues, there must also be an interpretation of the "unknown tongue";[42] (2) subordinate "words in a tongue" to "words with [the] mind"; (3) "let . . . only two or at most three" speak in a tongue, and "let one interpret";[43] and (4) "let all things be done decently and in order."

Because of the many confusions that often arise regarding the principles and practices of the Pentecostals, it is necessary to underscore the fact that they make a sharp distinction between the ecstatic

[39] Cited in Brumback, *What Meaneth This?* p. 129.

[40] A. G. Ward in "The Sign of Tongues," *Christ's Ambassadors Herald* (Aug., 1947), p. 18. While addressing the Indians of the Fisher River Reservation (near Winnipeg) through an interpreter, the writer burst forth speaking in their language for a while. On another occasion it was German.

[41] "We vigorously object to the teaching that this was the primary purpose of tongues in the early church. It was the exceptional and not the usual manifestation of tongues in those days, and likewise in its subsequent manifestations." Brumback, *What Meaneth This?* p. 36.

[42] I Cor. 14:13–40; see Pearlman, *Knowing Doctrines,* pp. 327–330.

[43] According to Pentecostal apologists, the interpretation of tongues (an illustration of which appears on p. 14) may take place in different ways, the most common of which is the following: After a glossolalic utterance, the meaning is comprehensively interpreted, but not translated verbatim. The one who interprets is just as much "in the Spirit" as the "tongue speaker" was before him; therefore, he is impelled to speak the message that "God gives him." Such a "message" is likely unknown to him at the time that he begins. Like *glossolalia,* then, interpreting tongues is a "gift." It is necessary to note that a few Pentecostals admit that the "gift of interpretation" may be abused. The interpreter may give vent to conscious feelings and criticize his fellows. In the guise of inspired utterance, he makes declarations which otherwise he would be reluctant to make. Cf. Nils Bloch-Hoell, *The Pentecostal Movement* (Oslo: Universitetsforlaget, 1964), pp. 145–147; and Horton, *The Gifts of the Spirit,* pp. 166–176.

utterances which are recorded in Acts and the tongues phenomena related by Paul in I Corinthians 12–14. In referring to the former, they employ the term "evidence" or "sign"; in referring to the latter, the word "gift" is used.[44] In Pentecostal thought, the two are identical neither in purpose nor use. Tongues in Acts, they explain, are "to make manifest to recipient and onlooker that the Holy Ghost had been given."[45] They are always the direct result of a person's being filled with the Spirit. In the Corinthian narrative, on the other hand, the "gift" of tongues has as its sole purpose the personal edification of the speaker, or, when coupled with interpretation, the edification of the hearers.[46] To summarize, a person who is baptized with the Holy Spirit will always signify this by speaking in tongues; thereafter, he may never so speak again; he may enjoy the devotional use of tongues (I Cor. 14:18); or he may possess the gift of tongues, one of the nine gifts of the Spirit, and use it for the edification of the church (I Cor. 12:10). Such a manifestation is to be followed by an interpretation (I Cor. 14:27–28).

Over the years some rather bizarre descriptions have been written of meetings in which people have been baptized in the Spirit and in which *glossolalia* have been in evidence.[47] But how do the Pentecostals who have experienced these phenomena describe them? Here, in part, are some recollections of Pastor Jonathan Paul, the early leader of German Pentecostalism:

> In this way a wonderful language arose in sounds that I had never

[44] Brumback, *What Meaneth This?* pp. 261–272; and W. T. Gaston, "The 'Sign' and the 'Gift' of Tongues," *Pentecostal Evangel* (n.d.), pp. 5, 11, 13. Furthermore, Pentecostals make no distinction of meaning with regard to any of the following phrases: "new tongues" (Mark 16:17), "other tongues" (Acts 2:4), and "unknown tongues" (I Cor. 14:2). "These," says Brumback, "are merely different ways of saying exactly the same thing. The believer is given supernatural utterance by the Holy Spirit in tongues that are 'new' to his lips, 'other' than his own native tongue, and 'unknown' to him in the sense that he is entirely unacquainted with them. . . ."

[45] Brumback, *What Meaneth This?* p. 262.

[46] *Ibid.*, p. 266.

[47] See A. Kampmeier, "Recent Parallels to the Miracle of Pentecost," *Open Court,* XXII (Aug., 1908), 492–499; Duncan Aikman, "The Holy Rollers," *American Mercury,* XV (October 1928), 189–191; Haakon J. Stolee, *Speaking in Tongues* (rev. ed.; Minneapolis: Augsburg Publishing House, 1963), pp. 64–71.

spoken before. I had the impression according to the tones, that it might be Chinese. Then came an entirely different language with an entirely different position of the mouth and wonderful sounds . . . I do not know how long I spoke thus—surely some minutes. Then I had to break out in German in praise and worship of my God. I was sitting during all this; nevertheless my body was shaken by a great power, though in no wise unpleasant or painful.[48]

From the April, 1961, issue of *Pulpit,* in an article written by Rev. James R. Brown, we glean this account:

As I meditated and prayed the Holy Ghost came upon me. Deep within, I began to magnify the Lord. Soon there came from my lips a language I had never known or uttered. A warm fragrant oil, it seemed, was poured over me. I found a place of rest in God that I had never experienced until that time.[49]

Samples of *glossolalia,* because it is an oral phenomenon, are rather difficult to reproduce. A few years ago, *Time* ran a feature story on speaking in tongues and included a short reproduction of a glossolalic manifestation which had been observed in a Van Nuys, California, meeting. Reduced to writing it looks like this: *"Da sheontee konomeki no sienti holay coriente no sheonte mees. . . ."* It was subsequently interpreted, continues the *Time* reporter, as: "The Lord thy God says unto thee that he is here in the midst of thee . . . When you pray, fear not. He is with you always, and his love surrounds you like a fleecy cloud. Thus saith the Lord."[50]

Granting the actuality of the charismatic experience, what is the value or the purpose of being filled with the Spirit? The Pentecostal's response is:

As we humble our proud spirits and allow the Holy Spirit to speak through us in a language unfamiliar to our rational minds, we are making a step of consecration toward God. We are allowing Him to have His way with us rather than having our own way. . . . The relinquishing of our tongue to God is, then, the first step toward the Spirit-directed life.[51]

[48] Cutten, *Speaking with Tongues,* p. 127.

[49] Quoted in Ness, *The Baptism,* p. 26. For other descriptions see "When I Received the Baptism" in *Christ's Ambassadors Herald* (May, 1941), pp. 10–11; also Stanley Frodsham, *With Signs Following* (rev. ed., Springfield, Mo.: Gospel Publishing House, 1941), *passim.*

[50] "Speaking in Tongues," *Time,* LXXVIII (Aug. 14, 1960), 55–56.

[51] *Why Tongues?* (Van Nuys, Calif.: The Blessed Trinity Society, n.d.), p. 8.

The view of P. C. Nelson, veteran Pentecostal apologist, is that the Spirit baptism is God's way of compensating for a believer's lack of knowledge, understanding, courage, and patience.[52]

A lead editorial in one of the largest Pentecostal monthlies suggests that the purpose of the Pentecostal experience is to obtain power to witness.[53] C. M. Ward, nationally known Pentecostal evangelist, believes that speaking in tongues is an evangelistic weapon; he quotes the Bible: "Tongues are a sign to them that believe not."[54]

For the Pentecostal, contrary to the bulk of popular opinion, speaking in tongues is not the final goal of one's religious experience; it is, rather, a commencement—a beginning of a new kind of Christian living that is empowered and graced by one of the nine gifts of the Spirit: discernment of error, power over demonic influences, ability to heal and work miracles, unusual wisdom, and so forth.

Deliverance from Sickness. Only in recent decades have non-Pentecostal churches renewed their interest in the treatment of physical illness by spiritual means. The General Assembly of the Presbyterian Church, U. S. A. appointed a commission to explore this field. In its 1957 report a preliminary committee observed that the ministry of healing was being performed by small groups who had been used by God as the channel of His healing power; by the ministry of clergy and laity, supported by the faith and prayers of the Christian community; and through prayer groups interceding for the sick.[55] *Sharing,* a monthly journal of Christian healing, lists approximately 400 churches (not denominations) in the United States which have services where members of the clergy lay hands on the sick and pray for their recovery.[56]

From the very beginning of the Pentecostal movement, however,

[52] Nelson, "Answers to Questions," *Pentecostal Evangel,* XXXIV (Sept. 21, 1946), 12.

[53] "The Purpose of the Pentecostal Enduement," *Pentecostal Evangel,* XXIV (Dec. 5, 1936), 1, 10, 11.

[54] "The Value of Tongues," *Pentecostal Evangel,* XLVI (Jan. 26, 1958), 4, 20.

[55] Gordon T. Scoville, "The Light That Heals," *Pentecostal Evangel,* XLV (Jan. 13, 1957). A reprint from *Presbyterian Life.*

[56] Robert C. Cunningham, "Healing Waters," *Pentecostal Evangel,* XLIX

the doctrine of divine healing has remained as one of its cardinal truths—an important facet of its "full gospel" message. Healing has been preached and practiced because Pentecostals believe that deliverance from physical sickness is provided for in the atonement and is the privilege of all believers.[57]

To be brief, the Pentecostal view of healing is developed from the promise that "if the fall of man brought sickness, the redemption of Christ should bring a remedy."[58] But how is healing effected? One, by the laying on of hands. Pentecostals interpret Mark 16:18 literally: "They [believers] will lay their hands on the sick; and they will recover." In addition, one must adhere to the procedures outlined in the letter of James (5:14–18): The afflicted person is obliged to call the elders of the church who will come, pray for him, anoint him with oil, and encourage him to confess his sins, if he is guilty of any. Finally, there is a practice of applying to the ailing person handkerchiefs or aprons that had been prayed over, as described in Acts (19:12).

Pentecostal magazines are filled with articles which have been written by people, testifying that they have been healed of cancer and paralysis,[59] tuberculosis,[60] mental illness,[61] severe burns,[62] and a host of other illnesses—mild and serious.

One of the dilemmas that periodically confront Pentecostals is that some people who desire healing are not healed. A typical response to

---

(Nov. 12, 1961), 2, 30. Most of these churches are Episcopal; there are also a number of others—Methodist, Presbyterian, Evangelical and Reformed, Baptist, Augustana Lutheran, and United Church of Christ—on the list.

[57] For extensive Pentecostal discussions see: James A. Cross, (ed.), *Healing in the Church* (Cleveland, Tenn.: The Pathway Press, 1962); Gordon Lindsay, *Bible Days Are Here Again* (Shreveport, La.: Private Printing, 1949); Milton A. Tomlinson, *Basic Bible Beliefs* (Cleveland, Tenn.: White Wing Publishing House, 1961); Fred H. Squire, *Divine Healing Today* (London: Victory Press, 1954).

[58] Harvey McAlister, "The Reasonableness of Divine Healing," *Pentecostal Evangel* (n.d.), pp. 3, 4.

[59] Cross, *Healing*, pp. 109–141.

[60] *Ibid.*

[61] Robert W. Cummings, "The Healer of Mental Sickness," *Pentecostal Evangel* (n.d.), pp. 5, 10–12.

[62] G. W. Hardcastle, Jr., "The Human Torch," *Pentecostal Evangel*, XLV (Apr. 7, 1957), 8, 9, 29.

this seemingly incongruous situation is that a doctrine of divine healing in the work of the atonement must leave a place for permitted sickness as an expression of divine wisdom or divine purpose, inscrutable though it may be.[63] That God does not

> always heal now, but sometimes reaches His ends with His children on the way of bodily weakness and even sickness, can be seen in the apostle Paul himself and some of his co-workers [Timothy, Trophimus]. . . . These examples are reminders that all healing is in the end a gift of God's sovereign mercy and compassion.[64]

The manifestations of speaking in tongues together with other charismatic gifts, and the practice of divine healing are the distinctive characteristics of Pentecostalism. Beyond them, the impression of the preceding paragraphs notwithstanding, Pentecostals are *not* alike.

[63] Sometimes healing is withheld as a test of faith; or, God permits sickness or affliction as a chastisement owing to sin or disobedience; or, owing to a lack of faith on the part of the Christian; or, to further His plan, as in John 9. See Squire, *Divine Healing,* p. 48.

[64] Leonhard Steiner, "Divine Healing in God's Plan of Redemption," *Pentecostal Evangel,* XLVII (May 24, 1959), 5–6, 13.

CHAPTER 2

Antecedents of Modern Pentecostalism

There is some disagreement among Pentecostal scholars as to where, when, and under whose leadership the Pentecostal movement began. For example, Charles W. Conn cites in 1896 revival in Cherokee County, North Carolina, which was led by William F. Bryant, a layman. During that revival, Conn reveals, some of the worshipers were "so enraptured with the One to whom they prayed that they were curiously exercised by the Holy Spirit," speaking in languages unknown to those who heard the ecstatic utterances. And, Conn emphasizes, "this happened in 1896—ten years before the outpouring of the Holy Ghost in California, which is popularly regarded as the beginning of the modern Pentecostal Movement."[1]

Klaude Kendrick views those phenomena in the Southeast as isolated instances, and recommends that "a narrative of modern Pentecost should begin with Charles Fox Parham,"[2] the director of Bethel Bible College, in Topeka, Kansas. It was here, on January 1, 1901, that the Pentecostal blessing fell and as in Apostolic times students spoke in other tongues.[3]

Donald Gee makes the point that "it is usual . . . to connect the appearance of the Pentecostal Movement as such, with the remarkable

[1] *Like a Mighty Army,* pp. 18–27.

[2] *The Promise Fulfilled: A History of the Modern Pentecostal Movement* (Springfield, Mo.: Gospel Publishing House, 1961), pp. 36 f.

[3] Parham, "The Latter Rain," *The Apostolic Faith,* XXVIII (Apr., 1951), 3, 4, 13.

meetings in the old Asuza [*sic*] Street Mission of Los Angeles, California, that continued throughout 1906."[4]

However, all Pentecostals appear to agree on one fact: that the Pentecostal experience is not a religious innovation, and that in one form or another it has manifested itself throughout the history of the Christian Church.[5]

One reads about the occurrences and spread of speaking in other tongues in the Apostolic Church primarily from Lucan and Pauline writings. After the initial outburst in Jerusalem on the Day of Pentecost, one can trace its appearance at Caesarea,[6] Ephesus,[7] and Corinth,[8] a city in which the prophet, healer, and speaker in tongues were—one would gather from the tone of St. Paul's letter—abnormally active. As a matter of fact, he seems to want to suppress their exuberances: there must be no speaking in tongues unless they be interpreted; not more than three glossolalists should speak during a public worship service; a tongues speaker should refrain from publicly demonstrating his gift, although he may practice it privately for his own spiritual edification.[9]

As one studies the post-Apostolic age, he realizes that "Pentecostal" manifestations were becoming rare and were being viewed with some misgiving by those in authority. Perhaps, as Dr. Ira J. Martin of Berea College suggests:

> Paul's drastic treatment and discipline of the [Corinthian] glossolalists so curtailed the manifestation of tongue-speaking that only scattered references can be found in the post-Apostolic period and the succeeding period of the Church Fathers.[10]

Another suggestion is that the use of the *charismata* had degenerated into an abuse. "Prophesying," writes Lindsay Dewar, "had sunk to a

[4] *The Pentecostal Movement,* p. 11.

[5] This view is held by non-Pentecostals like Mayer, *Religious Bodies,* p. 315; and Horton Davies, *Christian Deviations* (London: SCM Press, Ltd., 1961), p. 86.

[6] Acts 10:44–48.

[7] Acts 19:1–7.

[8] I Cor. 12–14.

[9] I Cor. 14:26–40.

[10] *Glossolalia in the Apostolic Church* (Berea, Ky.: Berea College Press, 1960), p. 66.

low level and had become the instrument of cheats and humbugs."[11] The view of C. Anderson Scott is that "tongues" ceased because they were of little value to the religious community.[12]

Whatever the reason, it is quite clear that the spontaneous ministry of prophecy, tongues, and signs—regarded by the early Christians as immediately authorized by the divine action of the Holy Spirit, the bestower of these "gifts"—was being superseded by a permanently appointed "official" ministry of presbyter-bishops of Apostolic appointment and having essentially sacramental and disciplinary ministration.[13] In short, while the charismatic gifts did not disappear entirely, they were incompatible with the regular order of the liturgical service; therefore they soon dropped out of it.[14]

It was against this tendency to organize, to supersede the order of the prophets by the episcopate, to minimize the supernatural work and direction of the Holy Spirit, that Montanus (A.D. 156) undoubtedly fought. He called upon his followers to live in a state of frequent ecstasy and vision. That he set a good example is evident by this report of his actions. Eusebius records that

> he became beside himself, and being suddenly in a sort of frenzy and ecstasy, he raved, and began to babble and utter strange things, prophesying in a manner contrary to the constant custom of the Church which had been handed down by tradition from the beginning.[15]

Except for a somewhat ambiguous reference in Irenaeus (*ca.* A.D. 130)[16] and Tertullian (*ca.* A.D. 160)[17] little more remains in patristic

[11] *The Holy Spirit and Modern Thought* (New York: Harper & Brothers, 1959), p. 92.

[12] In B. H. Streeter (ed.), *The Spirit* (New York: The Macmillan Company, 1919), p. 149.

[13] John Lawson, *A Theological and Historical Introduction to the Apostolic Fathers* (New York: The Macmillan Company, 1961), p. 66.

[14] Louis Duchesne, *Early History of the Christian Church* (London: John Murray, 1950), I, 36.

[15] *Ecclesiastical History,* V:16, 7: in Philip Schaff (ed.), *A Select Library of the Nicene and Post-Nicene Fathers,* 2d ser. (New York: Charles Scribner's Sons, 1890), I, 231.

[16] "Wherefore, also, those who are in truth the disciples, receiving grace from Him, do in His name perform [miracles]. . . . Some do certainly and truly drive out devils. . . . Others have foreknowledge of things to come; they see visions and utter prophetic expressions. Others still, heal the sick by laying their hands upon them." *Against Heresies,* II:32, 4; in Alexander Roberts

literature concerning Pentecostal gifts in the second century.

By the time of Chrysostom (345–407) the *charismata,* especially speaking in tongues, seem to have disappeared almost entirely. The concept of speaking in another (unknown) tongue was replaced by the medieval view that certain saints like St. Francis Xavier, St. Vincent Ferrier, St. Anthony of Padua, St. Pachomius, and St. Hildegard received a supernatural gift of language which they were able to use in their missionary work among strange people.[18] This rather unique interpretation resulted from certain patristic commentators like Origen who advanced the view that the *glossolalia* on the Day of Pentecost was a permanent endowment of the Apostles with a miraculous knowledge of all those foreign languages in which they were to preach the gospel.[19]

From the fifth century until the Reformation the manifestations which had been so prominent in early Christianity were virtually non-existent. To be sure, there are accounts of a variety of "pneumatics" or "Spirituals" who declaimed against the worldliness of the clergy, the hyperinstitutionalism; and who were themselves rather quick to respond to what they thought were the direct impulses of the Holy Spirit. But not one person seems to have possessed the charismatic gifts described by Luke and Paul.

The history of the Christian Church since the Reformation does contain some evidences of a revival of interest in and practice of "Pentecostal" gifts. Ira Martin suggests that since the Reformation brought the Bible to the common man and preached the need to recover and reproduce the character of first-century faith and practice, the reappearance of the supernatural gifts of the Holy Spirit was in-

---

(ed.), *The Ante-Nicene Fathers* (New York: Charles Scribner's Sons, 1926), I, 409.

[17] In his dispute with Marcion, he demands that the latter produce a psalm, a vision, a prayer—only let it be by the Spirit in an ecstasy, that is, in a rapture: "Now all these signs (of spiritual gifts) are forthcoming from my [Tertullian's] side without any difficulty." *Against Marcion,* V:8; in *ibid.,* II, 447.

[18] Cf. Alexander Mackie, *The Gift of Tongues* (New York: George H. Doran Co., 1921), p. 28; and Cutten, *Speaking with Tongues,* pp. 37–47.

[19] Dawson Walker, *The Gift of Tongues* (Edinburgh: T. & T. Clark, 1906), pp. 15 ff. The author observes that after Origen this view was reflected in the writings of Gregory of Nazianzus, Jerome, Augustine, and Gregory of Nyssa.

evitable.[20] Be that as it may, the facts are that *glossolalia* reappeared infrequently among the Radical Anabaptists in sixteenth-century Germany,[21] and the Camisards and Jansenists in seventeenth-century France.[22]

In mid-eighteenth-century America, the gift of tongues was most prolific among the Shakers. Frequent statements appear in the *Testimonies of the Life, Character, and Revelations of Mother Ann Lee*[23] to the effect that the controversial prophetess was often found singing or praying in an unknown tongue. Thomas Brown, author of *An Account of the People Called Shakers,* makes the following comment on the gift of tongues among Shakers:

> Respecting such as speak in an unknown tongue, they have strong faith in this gift; and think a person greatly favoured who has the gift of tongues; and at certain times, when the mind is overloaded with a fiery, strong zeal, it must have vent some way or other; their faith, or belief, at the time being in this gift, and a will strikes the mind according to their faith; and then such break out in a fiery, energetick manner, and speak they know not what, as I have done several times.[24]

During the early decades of the nineteenth century, the Irvingite movement arose in England. The best summary of its background is provided by P. E. Shaw,[25] who writes that religion was at a low ebb and the popular feeling was that the only hope for the Church was divine intervention. Many commenced to pray for an outpouring of the Holy Spirit; clergy and laity concentrated on prophetic texts such as Isaiah 32:15 and Joel 2:23; tracts and literature appeared on the subject of the Holy Spirit; conferences convened. "Men were vaguely feeling toward something higher."[26]

In the year 1830, in Port Glasgow, Scotland, there occurred an out-

[20] *Glossolalia,* pp. 66 f.

[21] George H. Williams, *The Radical Reformation* (Philadelphia: The Westminster Press, 1962), pp. 133, 443.

[22] Cf. Mackie, *Gift of Tongues,* pp. 72–81; and Cutten, *Speaking with Tongues,* pp. 51–59.

[23] Mackie, p. 117; citing *Testimonies,* xxiii:12, pp. 163 f.

[24] Mackie, *Gift of Tongues,* p. 122; citing Brown's book (Troy, N.Y., 1812), pp. 152–3.

[25] *The Catholic Apostolic Church* (New York: King's Crown Press, 1946).

[26] *Ibid.,* p. 25.

burst of tongues speaking and some instances of healing.[27] Dr. Thompson, a member of Edward Irving's Regent Square congregation, went to Scotland to witness the supernatural proceedings. Soon after his return to London and his confirmation of the extraordinary events, many Christians, including members of Irving's church, began to pray for a similar outpouring of the Holy Spirit.

According to the best sources,[28] although Edward Irving "was not called to be an Apostle, nor were prophetic gifts given to him or recognized in him,"[29] he did function as a sort of John the Baptist, introducing a new era in which spiritual gifts would flourish. Shaw is doubtless right in claiming that Irving's immense prestige "gave recognition to the 'tongues' and 'prophesyings' and made both of them respectable as far as that was possible."[30] In any case, disregarding the persistent advice of his trustees, the Kirk Session, and the Presbytery of London, Irving would not (he felt in his innermost being that he could not) forbid tongues speaking in his church. Rumor, criticism (even the *Times* of London involved itself editorially), and an intransigent Irving caused the Regent Square Church to be closed to the minister and the charismatics among his congregation.

On October 19, 1832, the Exhibition Hall off Oxford Street was acquired and made into a church. Needless to say, "Pentecostal" manifestations occurred at the opening meeting and continued thereafter. As a matter of fact, the "Gifted Prophets" and the new order of "Apostles," among whom Irving was not numbered, took over the church, subjecting their minister to their prophetic utterances and rulings, and even interrupting his sermons and the administration of the ordinances with their charismatic outbursts.[31]

[27] While some writers feel that many of the so-called "gifts" among the Irvingites were spuriously concocted, others like Maurice Barnett, *The Living Flame* (London: The Epworth Press, 1953), p. 132, think that the gifts of tongues and of healing being exercised by James and George MacDonald of Port Glasgow—men of unimpeachable character, calmness, and understanding—were genuine.

[28] Shaw, *Catholic Apostolic*, p. 58; cf. "Irving and the Catholic Apostolic Church" in James Hastings (ed.), *Encyclopedia of Religion and Ethics* (New York: Charles Scribner's Sons, 1928), VII, 422 f.

[29] *Ibid.*, p. 58.

[30] *Ibid.*, p. 56.

[31] *Ibid.*, pp. 52–55.

There are some rather striking similarities between the Irvingites and the Pentecostals who flourished seventy years later. First, it is believed that the Irvingites thought that the occurrence of *glossolalia* among them was of the same nature as that which took place on the Day of Pentecost. To them, speaking in tongues was an evidence of Spirit baptism.[32] Second, the Irvingites seem to have regarded such an experience as a prerequisite for obtaining one of the nine gifts of the Spirit.[33] Third, the Irvingites insisted that the *charismata,* as manifested at Pentecost and in the Apostolic Church, were a permanent possession of the Church, withheld because of the unfaithfulness of Christian believers.[34] Fourth, Edward Irving and his charismatic followers were expelled from the Presbyterian Church and were forced to establish a new denomination, the Catholic Apostolic Church.

At the same time that the Irvingites were flourishing in England, the gift of tongues was being manifested in the United States among the Mormons,[35] the "Gift Adventists" who met in Ashdod, Massachusetts,[36] and various groups of people in the mountains of Tennessee and North Carolina. But these were more or less isolated instances, nothing like the plethora of Pentecostal phenomena which literally flooded the religious world of the twentieth century.

[32] *Idem.*

[33] P. G. S. Hopwood, *The Religious Experience of the Primitive Church* (Edinburgh: T. & T. Clark, 1936), p. 158.

[34] Cutten, *Speaking with Tongues,* p. 94. This rather long excursus on the Irvingites is presented because the source materials regarding them provide the most careful observations we have about speaking in tongues and prophesying in any period prior to the emergence of "modern" Pentecostalism.

[35] Cutten, *Speaking with Tongues,* p. 10.

[36] Carl Brumback, *Suddenly from Heaven* (Springfield, Mo.: Gospel Publishing House, 1961), pp. 12 f.; and Atter, *Third Force,* p. 18.

CHAPTER 3

The United States: Birthplace of Twentieth-Century Pentecostalism

Spiritual stagnation, moral lethargy, and theological and practical problems haunted American Protestantism in the years following the Civil War. While many churches experienced substantial gains in membership, this did not signify spiritual health. Never before in this country's history, notes Clifton Olmstead, had the Church been stronger in membership and weaker in spiritual soundness.[1] Churches which had been revivalistic before the war began to ignore the worth of an emotional experience. Darwin's *Origin of Species* and *The Descent of Man* challenged the traditional orthodox theories of man's origin, producing sharp cleavages between believers and dividing churches. The "new criticism" attacked some of the fundamentals of faith as reposited in the Bible; many were appalled that "the sacred citadel of divine authority was being invaded by impious hands."[2]

The Church, keeping pace with the nation, became increasingly wealthy and institutionalized. It began doing away with the so-called "crudities" of religion—the unimposing wooden churches were razed, and magnificent brick sanctuaries replaced them; the "mourner's bench" was abandoned; spirited congregational singing was supplanted

[1] *History of Religion in the United States* (Englewood Cliffs, N.J.: Prentice-Hall, 1960), pp. 447–451. See also *The Rise of the City, 1873–1898* (Vol. X of the *History of American Life Series,* ed. A. M. Schlesinger and others. 12 vols.; New York: The Macmillan Company, 1957), p. 344.

[2] Smith, *American Christianity,* II, p. 217.

by a robed choir; cushions adorned pews; "shouting" Methodists became hushed; a seminary-trained minister replaced the "lay" preacher whose credentials were his "call" and his fervor. In short, writes William Warren Sweet, the popular churches once known as the poor man's churches were transformed into churches of the upper middle class.[3]

People of limited means began to feel more and more out of place; they complained that "heart religion" was disappearing.

To counteract the religious inertia, the cold formalism—"modernism" the Holiness folk called it—many gave themselves to prayer, fasting, heart-searching, and attendance at various Bible and prophetic conferences. They desired "to ascertain God's thought for the closing of the Church Age."[4] At these conferences, one of the topics that was stressed concerned God's promise to pour out His Spirit in the last days. Many believers had already decided that the last days were upon them; therefore, they commenced to await an outpouring of the Spirit. The expository preaching of men like Yale-and-Leipzig-trained Reuben A. Torrey encouraged them.

> The baptism with the Holy Spirit is an operation of the Holy Spirit distinct from and subsequent to His regenerating work . . . an impartation of power, and the one who receives it is fitted for service. [Such an experience was] not merely for the Apostles, nor merely for those of the apostolic age, but for "all that are afar off, even as many as the Lord our God shall call." . . . It is for every believer in every age of the Church's history.[5]

Outburst of Pentecostalism in Topeka, Kansas (1901)

Charles Fox Parham was one of those who believed that if the complacent, prosperity-ridden, coldly formalistic Church and its members were to be reached, an enduement of the Spirit would be necessary. Born in Muscatine, Iowa, on June 4, 1873, Parham had been a lay preacher in the Congregational Church by the time that he was fifteen. Later he was associated with the Methodists from whose ranks

[3] *The Story of Religion in America* (New York: Harper & Row, 1939), pp. 345–352.

[4] Brumback, *Suddenly from Heaven,* p. 7.

[5] Quoted in Kendrick, *Promise Fulfilled,* p. 47.

he withdrew to join the rapidly expanding Holiness movement.[6] Parham was convinced "that while many had obtained real experiences in sanctification . . . there still remained a great outpouring of power for Christians."[7]

According to his own testimony, he also believed that the narrative concerning *glossolalia* in Acts 2 meant a gift of languages; therefore, he advised his students at Bethel Bible College

> that if God had ever equipped His ministers in that way He could do it today. . . . Anybody today ought to be able to preach in any language of the world if they had horse sense enough to let God use their tongue and throat.[8]

Parham had opened this school in Topeka in October, 1900. He charged no tuition, running it on the "faith home" policy that had been conceived by the Holiness-Healing groups of the late nineteenth century, namely, that infirm persons would not be charged for services or entertainment while residing in "homes" that had been established to provide instruction in faith healing. Such retreats operated literally on "faith" that God would provide all material requirements through the freewill, unsolicited gifts of interested Christians. Here are Parham's words:

> No one paid board or tuition, the poor were fed, the sick were entertained and healed, and from day to day, week to week, and month to month, with no sect or mission or known source of income back of us, God supplied our every need, and He was our all sufficiency in all things.[9]

Late in December, 1900, Parham had to go to Kansas City. Before departing, he instructed each of his students to study the Bible individually and to see if there were some sort of special witness to the fact that a person has been baptized with the Holy Spirit. When he returned and reconvened the students, they informed him that on each occasion in Apostolic times when the Holy Spirit baptized believers, there was an outward manifestation—speaking in tongues. From that moment, each member of the college family determined to

[6] A fine survey of Parham's life and theology appears in Kendrick, *ibid.*, pp. 37–64.

[7] *Ibid.*, p. 47.

[8] Parham, "Latter Rain," p. 3.

[9] *Idem.*

pray and to look for an experience that would square with those recounted in Acts.

On New Year's Eve, as Parham relates the incident, some seventy outsiders and forty students gathered for the traditional "Watch Night" service. A Miss Agnes Ozman asked that hands be laid upon her so that she might receive the Holy Spirit. After repeated entreaties, Parham consented.[10] He placed his hands upon her head and prayed.

> I had scarcely repeated three dozen sentences when a glory fell upon her, a halo seemed to surround her head and face, and she began speaking in the Chinese language, and was unable to speak English for three days.
>
> Seeing this marvelous manifestation of the restoration of Pentecostal power, . . . we decided as a school to wait upon God. We felt that God was no respecter of persons and what He had so graciously poured out upon one, He would upon all.[11]

This event was significant not because Miss Ozman had spoken in tongues, for there had been sporadic outbursts of *glossolalia* throughout the history of the Church. In each of these cases, however, the phenomenon was considered to be nothing more or less than the reception of one of the gifts of the Spirit referred to in Pauline literature (I Cor. 12:1, 4, 31; and 14:1, 39). The importance of these events in Topeka is that for the first time the concept of being baptized (or filled) with the Holy Spirit was linked to an outward sign—speaking in tongues. Henceforth, for the Pentecostals the evidence that one has been "filled wth the Holy Spirit" is that he will have spoken in other tongues.[12]

Following Miss Ozman's "Pentecostal experience," classes were suspended. During the month of January, 1901, the whole student body engaged in prayer, believing that what God had done for her He would do for them. Soon the majority of them,[13] including the Rev.

[10] Perhaps Parham's reluctance was due to modesty, for he himself had not yet been "filled with the Spirit."

[11] Parham, "Latter Rain," p. 4.

[12] This decision to seek for a Holy Spirit baptism with the expectation of speaking in tongues, says J. Roswell Flower, was a momentous one. "It . . . made the Pentecostal Movement of the Twentieth Century." See his "Birth of the Pentecostal Movement," *Pentecostal Evangel,* 38 (Nov. 26, 1950), 3. For decades Flower was General Secretary of the Assemblies of God.

[13] Of the forty students enrolled at Parham's school, twelve held ministerial

Mr. Parham, were able to testify that they had experienced a Spirit baptism and had spoken in "other tongues." Feeling uniquely empowered, many immediately went into evangelistic and missionary work.[14]

A sense of urgency impelled Parham and his followers. The recurrence of Pentecost in Topeka had definite prophetic overtones for them. They were familiar with the prophecies of Joel ("in the last days . . . I will pour out my spirit"); they had experienced the supernatural outpouring, *ergo* these must be the last days. Hence they felt constrained to preach the gospel to every creature. The Lord was at hand, the day was far spent, night was near. That which ought to be done for God must be done quickly.[15]

Initially, however, the Parhamites were not successful. Two years of privation, persecution, and frustration followed the Topeka revival. Mr. and Mrs. Parham, together with a few students (among them, Agnes Ozman), set out for Kansas City, the first step in a projected tour of the United States and Canada. But their revival efforts in Kansas City proved to be a dismal failure. This outcome was attributed to severe criticism by the established churches, on the one hand, and to unfavorable newspaper publicity, on the other. This was a harbinger of events in the immediate future, when Parham "was to find no wide acceptance of his new 'experience' for several years."[16] Other revival meetings in Lawrence, Kansas, were equally abortive.

During this time Parham was also forced to close Bethel and move

---

credentials with Methodist, Friends, or Holiness Churches. See Frodsham, *With Signs Following* p. 10.

[14] Pentecostals have always equated the impartation of the Holy Spirit with the reception of power, a dynamic to assist them to witness more effectively. They never considered it to be a superfluous mystical experience that was given to titillate the seeker. This may account for the variegated and potent evangelistic-missionary efforts in which Pentecostals engaged from the very outset.

[15] This attitude has never changed. As recently as 1959 Winehouse (*Assemblies of God,* pp. 193 f.) quotes a Pentecostal spokesman as saying: "It is our obligation to tell all men everywhere of the salvation which He has provided. To give people a last chance to come into the ark of safety before the storm. The baptism of the Holy Spirit . . . provides a motive, the urgency and the power with which we are qualified to carry the gospel to the ends of the earth."

[16] Kendrick, *Promise Fulfilled,* p. 55.

to Kansas City, only to encounter opposition and persecution there. He writes:

Both the pulpit and the press sought to utterly destroy our place and prestige, until my wife, her sister and myself stood alone. Hated, despised, counted as naught, for weeks never knowing where our next meal would come from, yet feeling that we must maintain the faith once for all delivered to the saints. When we had car fare we rode, when we didn't we walked. When buildings were closed to us we preached on the street.[17]

Charles Parham's fortunes did not change until he was invited to conduct a revival campaign in Galena, Kansas. The events which led to the invitation were as follows. Mary A. Arthur of Galena was, by her own testimony, an ill person:

I was afflicted with dyspepsia for fourteen years, also with prolapsus, hemorrhoids, and paralysis of the bowels, but my greatest distress was in my eyes. My right eye was virtually blind from birth, and my left eye was suffering from inflammation and nerve strain.[18]

She had sought the help of oculists, allopathy, homeopathy, osteopathy, Christian Science, and her pastor—all to no avail. In despair, Mrs. Arthur went to Eldorado Springs, Missouri. Parham was there at the same time (August, 1903), preaching and teaching divine healing. She attended one of his meetings, received prayer for her physical condition, and returned to Galena, testifying that she had been completely cured. When one of her friends was also healed of an alleged cancerous tumor, some people in the town became alert to the miraculous quality of this new "Pentecostal" ministry of Parham's and invited him to conduct meetings in Galena.

Charles Fox Parham arrived in late October and commenced to preach in the Arthur home. The crowds became so great that a tent was pitched on an adjacent lot. Inclement weather forced them to occupy the Grand Leader building on Main Street until mid-January, 1904. During the nearly three months of revival meetings, the news of the supernatural happenings spread far and wide. The Cincinnati *Inquirer,* for instance, ran a feature story in its January 27, 1904, issue from which the following are excerpts.

[17] *Ibid.,* p. 56.
[18] Quoted in Brumback, *Suddenly from Heaven,* pp. 26 f.

Almost three months have elapsed since this man [Parham] came to Galena and during that time he has healed over a thousand people and converted more than 800. . . . During the services there have been as many as 50 people at the altar at one time seeking to be restored in soul and body. Here people who have not walked for years without the aid of crutches have risen from the altar with their limbs so straightened that they were enabled to lay aside their crutches, to the astonishment of the audience.

These cures, they claim, are effected solely through prayer and faith. Nothing else is done, though Mr. Parham often lays his hands upon the afflicted one while the devotions are going on. . . .

Here women who have formerly lived for society and gaiety kneel beside some fallen sister and endeavor to point her heavenward, and here the "followers" receive what they term "the Pentecost," and are enabled to speak in foreign tongues, in languages with which they are, when free from this power, utterly unfamiliar. This alone is considered one of the most remarkable things of the meetings.[19]

After the Galena campaign, Parham's evangelistic efforts continued to be so successful that by 1905 "Pentecostal" or "Full Gospel" meeting places existed in the towns of Columbus, Melrose, and Baxter Springs, Kansas; in Joplin, Missouri; and in Orchard,[20] Houston, and Galveston, Texas. It is estimated that by the winter of 1905, Texas alone had 25,000 Pentecostal believers and about 60 preachers—all the direct result of Parham's consecrated efforts.[21]

From Texas, small bands of Pentecostals fanned out through Alabama and west Florida, "bringing the full-gospel message in 'one-night stands' to families in their homes in 1905 and 1906."[22] From Texas too would come the key figure in the world-famous (among Pentecostals) Los Angeles revival—William J. Seymour.

As an adjunct to his Houston campaign in 1905, Parham established a Bible school, patterned after the one he had directed in Topeka. It was operated on a "faith" basis: no tuition was charged; students were

[19] Quoted in Kendrick, *Promise Fulfilled,* p. 59.

[20] No longer on the Texas map, this town was situated about 45 miles from Houston.

[21] Some Pentecostals maintain that the impact of the Galena revival more than any other reason, perhaps, caused the tri-state region (Kansas, Missouri, and Texas) to become an early Pentecostal stronghold. Consult Kendrick, *Promise Fulfilled,* p. 63, and Frodsham, *Signs Following,* p. 29.

[22] Brumback, *Suddenly from Heaven,* p. 33.

obliged to assist in doing the chores and in maintaining the plant; the Bible was the only textbook; Parham was sole lecturer, presenting lessons on such topics as repentance, conversion, consecration, sanctification, healing, the Holy Spirit in His different operations, prophecy (especially emphasizing the Book of Revelation) and "other practical subjects."[23] Among his students was a Negro Holiness preacher, William J. Seymour, who, while not yet having spoken in tongues, was, nevertheless, convinced that such an experience was both biblical and necessary.

While visiting Houston, Neeley Terry, a Negro, received the much-publicized Holy Spirit baptism. Upon returning to her home in Los Angeles, she recommended that the members of the Nazarene mission on Santa Fe Avenue call Seymour to be the associate pastor. An invitation was issued, and Seymour accepted, unaware that his transfer to Los Angeles would involve him in events that would have international implications.

The Renowned Azusa Street Revival (1906)

As a text for his first sermon before the California congregation, William J. Seymour selected Acts 2:4. He preached about the new Pentecostal experiences to which he had been exposed in Houston, emphasizing the fact that every person who was truly baptized in the Holy Spirit would react as the disciples did on the Day of Pentecost, namely, speak in tongues. From what little source material[24] is available, one learns that Julia Hutchins, with whom Seymour was to be associated, was offended by the sermon. She believed, as most Holiness people did at that time, that she had been baptized with the Holy Spirit; and here was a stranger informing her and the congregation that it had merely been an experience of sanctification, that she did not really possess the Spirit in his "fullness," and that she needed an additional sign—tongues. When Seymour returned for the afternoon service, he found the door bolted. What to do?

[23] Kendrick, *Promise Fulfilled,* p. 63.
[24] *Ibid.,* pp. 64 f.

Richard and Ruth Asberry, who were related to Neeley Terry, invited the ousted preacher to conduct worship services in their home at 214 Bonnie Brae Street. There on April 9, 1906, seven seekers received the Holy Spirit baptism and commenced to speak in tongues.[25] The records state that for three days and nights they shouted and praised God.[26] People began to come from everywhere, forcing Seymour and his followers to procure an old frame building (once a Methodist church) on Azusa Street in the industrial section of Los Angeles. The building supplies that cluttered the hall were pushed aside; planks were placed upon empty nail kegs to provide seating space for the multitudes which came at ten o'clock in the morning (and often remained until three o'clock on the following morning),[27] seeking salvation, sanctification, the Holy Spirit baptism, or healing.

The Apostolic Faith Gospel Mission on Azusa Street was certainly unpretentious, but so also was its leader, William J. Seymour. Arthur Osterberg, who was introduced to Pentecostalism at the Azusa Street Mission, gave the following description of the one-eyed Negro preacher to a Los Angeles *Times* reporter in 1956:

> He was meek and plain spoken and no orator. He spoke the common language of the uneducated class. He might preach for three-quarters of an hour with no more emotionalism than that there post. He was no arm-waving thunderer, by any stretch of the imagination.[28]

Frank Bartleman, a contemporary of Seymour's who often occupied the platform with him, adds this to our vignette of the man:

> Brother Seymour generally sat behind two empty shoe boxes, one on top of the other. He usually kept his head inside the top one during the meeting, in prayer. There was no pride there.[29]

Of his first meeting with Seymour on March 26, 1906, Bartleman wrote somewhat tersely: "He was a colored man, very plain, spiritual,

[25] Stanley Horton, "Pentecostal Explosion," *Pentecostal Evangel,* L (Oct. 7, 1962), 8 f.

[26] "How Pentecost Came to Los Angeles," *Pentecostal Evangel,* XLIV (Apr. 8, 1956), 4 f.

[27] "Pentecost 39 Years Ago," *Pentecostal Evangel,* XLIII (Apr. 7, 1945), 5.

[28] Quoted in Brumback, *Suddenly From Heaven,* p. 37.

[29] *How Pentecost Came to Los Angeles* (Los Angeles: Privately Printed, 1925), p. 58.

and humble. He attended the meetings at Bonnie Brae Street. He was blind in one eye."[30]

There was no doubt that the religious community in Los Angeles was in the throes of a spiritual awakening. But this event had been anticipated for some time by men like Dr. Joseph Smale and Elmer K. Fisher, pastors respectively of the First Baptist Church in Los Angeles and Glendale. One year before the Azusa Street revival, Smale had returned from Wales, where he had witnessed the stirring religious awakening led by Evan Roberts. He admonished his California congregation to seek for a similar revival, but the officials of the church objected. Smale resigned and proceeded to organize the New Testament Church. After preaching a series of sermons on the Holy Spirit and the need for revival that disturbed his board of deacons, Fisher likewise resigned. Soon thereafter he received the Holy Spirit baptism at Dr. Smale's newly organized church and became associated with Seymour at the Apostolic Faith Gospel Mission on Azusa Street.

Azusa Street became a veritable Pentecostal mecca to which pilgrims from all over the world came and from which the news of supernatural signs and wonders was broadcast.[31] It is hard to explain its magnetism, especially as one reads Frank Bartleman's diary entries:

> No subjects or sermons were announced ahead of time, and no special speakers for such an hour. No one knew what might be coming, what God would do. All was spontaneous, ordered of the Spirit. We wanted to hear from God. . . . In that old building with its low rafters and bare floors, God took strong men and women to pieces, and put them together again, for His glory. It was a tremendous overhauling process.[32]

Perhaps a clue to the mission's attraction may be found in the frequently recurring clauses which echo throughout Bartleman's narrative: "We wanted God." "We wanted to meet God." It was not so much the meeting place, then, as the fact that those who went there expected to receive spiritual help. And in some inexplicable yet ex-

[30] *Ibid.*, p. 43.
[31] Horton, "Pentecostal," p. 9.
[32] Bartleman, *How Pentecost Came,* pp. 58 f.

citingly real way they did, and the supernatural encounter propelled them northward, eastward, southward.

Florence Louise Crawford was a twice-married mother of two when in 1906 she attended the Apostolic Faith Gospel Mission.[33] As she sat in one of the services, she relates that

> A sound like a rushing, mighty wind filled the room, and I was baptized with the Holy Ghost and fire. Rivers of joy and love divine flooded my soul. God also gave me the Bible evidence of receiving this experience in letting me speak in another language. . . . But the greatest joy in my heart was the knowledge that I received power to witness for Christ, power to tell others what great things God can do in a human life.[34]

In addition to this impartation of the Holy Spirit, Mrs. Crawford was healed of eye defects, lung trouble, and a childhood injury which had forced her to wear surgical supports. Of this event she says: "Once diseased from the crown of my head to the soles of my feet, I now was made sound and well through the blood of Jesus. The Christ of Calvary touched my body and made me whole."[35]

Sustained by these two remarkable experiences, Mrs. Crawford embarked on an evangelistic career which began in Los Angeles and which took her to the principal cities of the Pacific Northwest and as far east as Minnesota. From here she returned to Portland, Oregon, establishing her headquarters there on Christmas Day, 1906. From that day forward The Apostolic Faith has been known as "the church without a collection plate." In keeping with the tradition which had been utilized by Parham, the organization operated on a "faith" basis, and officials testify to its effectiveness: "Freewill offerings and tithes have met every need, and God has supplied adequate funds to forward this world-wide evangelistic work."[36] The Apostolic Faith never got any larger than its present 42 churches serving 4,764 members.[37] Because of its evangelistic efforts, however, it has exerted an influence far beyond its size.

[33] "Camp Meeting Apostolic Faith," *Time,* XXVI (Aug. 19,1935), 34.

[34] *A Historical Account of The Apostolic Faith* (Portland, Ore.: The Apostolic Faith Publishing House, 1965), p. 59.

[35] *Ibid.,* p. 61.

[36] *Ibid.,* p. 64.

[37] Benson Y. Landis (ed.), *Yearbook of American Churches for 1966* (New York: National Council of the Churches of Christ in the USA, 1966), p. 14.

William H. Durham, who later became an outstanding Pentecostal leader in Chicago, traveled to Los Angeles in 1907 as a skeptic. He returned as an ardent proponent of speaking in tongues and a Holy Spirit baptism. The supernatural experiences which had overwhelmed him at the Azusa Street Mission revolutionized his ministry at the modest mission on North Avenue. "People began to come in considerable numbers. Soon our little place would not hold them. . . . We had meetings every night—sometimes all night."[38] At some services there were as many as twenty-five ministers from out of town "tarrying for the gift of the Holy Spirit." One of these men was A. H. Argue, who was to carry the message of Pentecostalism to his native Canada (Winnipeg).[39] Another was Eudorus N. Bell of Fort Worth, who subsequently became the first chairman of the Assemblies of God.

Scores of recent immigrants, especially Italians and Persians, also received the Pentecostal "infilling" at Durham's mission. Some of the Persians returned to "the old country" to evangelize it.[40] Louis Francescon, one of the Italians, traveled throughout the United States, establishing small cells of Pentecostals. Eventually he went to South America, while some of his colleagues went back to their native land to establish works in Rome (1908), Turin (1910), and Milan (1910).[41]

The spread of Pentecostalism throughout the Southeast was likewise the handiwork of two more Azusa Street products—G. B. Cashwell

[38] William H. Durham, "A Glimpse of a Gracious Work in Chicago," *Word and Work,* XXXII (May, 1910), 154. Later in this article (p. 156) Durham wrote: "We put in a baptistry two years ago, and about 800 people have been immersed in two years, and still we have from one to three baptismal services almost every week."

[39] Earlier (1906), another Canadian, R. E. McAlister, having received the Spirit baptism in Los Angeles, returned to Ottawa to conduct an outstanding revival. One of the workers, Mrs. C. Baker, who became a convinced Pentecostal, went to Montreal to open a mission among the French-speaking populace. See Atter, *Third Force,* pp. 35–42.

[40] Frodsham, *Signs Following,* p. 45.

[41] Joseph Fiorentino, "A Summary of the Italian Pentecostal Movement in the United States and Abroad" (an unpublished monograph given to me by Rev. Mr. Fiorentino, an instructor at Zion Bible Institute in East Providence, R.I.), pp. 3–5.

and Charles H. Mason. Cashwell conducted extremely successful revival meetings in Tennessee, North Carolina, Georgia, and Florida. It was during one of these campaigns that A. J. Tomlinson who was to be the influential leader of the Church of God (Cleveland, Tennessee) for more than a decade, received his Spirit baptism.

> On Sunday morning, January 12, [1908] while he [Cashwell] was preaching, a peculiar sensation took hold of me, and almost unconsciously I slipped off my chair in a heap on the rostrum at Brother Cashwell's feet. I did not know what such an experience meant. My mind was clear, but a peculiar power so enveloped and thrilled my whole being that I concluded to yield myself up and await results. I was soon lost to my surroundings as I lay there on the floor, occupied only with God and eternal things.[42]

Church of God historian, Charles W. Conn, adds that Tomlinson testified to speaking in about ten unknown languages on that occasion.[43] Moreover, it was during Cashwell's revival campaign in Dunn, North Carolina, that many Fire-Baptized Holiness people—including J. H. King, who would become Bishop of the Pentecostal Holiness Church—accepted the Pentecostal message and the experience of speaking in tongues.[44]

Like Cashwell, Charles H. Mason returned from Los Angeles a Spirit-filled man. This Negro man of God, who had been reared by parents who were formerly slaves, commenced a ministry in Memphis, Tennessee, which was to mushroom into a movement of 4,000 churches and nearly 500,000 adherents—one of the largest Negro Pentecostal bodies in the world,[45] The Church of God in Christ.

From the foregoing, it is rather easy to see that the Azusa Street revival was responsible for the emergence of Pentecostalism in various areas of the United States and Canada. However, one outburst of Pentecostal phenomena which cannot be attributed directly to West Coast influence is the charismatic revival that occurred within the Christian and Missionary Alliance.

[42] Conn, *Like a Mighty Army,* p. 85.
[43] *Idem.*
[44] Kendrick, *Promise Fulfilled,* p. 180.
[45] Landis, *Yearbook,* p. 36.

The Disruptive Effects of Pentecostalism in the Northeast

Dr. A. B. Simpson started the Christian and Missionary Alliance (1887) in order to encourage the preaching and practice of what he called "the four-fold gospel," one of the four major tenets being a renewed emphasis on the healing power of Christ. In addition, Dr. Simpson was noted for stressing the concept of "Advent Baptism"—the need for Christians to seek for an enduement of spiritual power. As the CMA movement expanded, reports of the Azusa Street revival started filtering eastward. The news was received with mixed emotions: joy and caution, because the Alliance, although vitally interested in a new Pentecost, was not willing to countenance fanaticism. A few individuals—John Coxe, William Cramer, J. T. Boddy—sought for and received the baptism of the Spirit and spoke in tongues somewhere in the Northeast, but they refrained from publicizing it in deference to their society's wish that members approach the matter of the *charismata* cautiously.

However, in May, 1907, at a service that was held on the campus of the Alliance-operated Nyack Missionary Training Institute,[46] a revival erupted. Some of the officials, fearing that the services would get out of control, called in Messrs. Cramer and Coxe (whom they knew to be "Pentecostally" inclined) to guide the proceedings. Sources indicate that when Cramer saw what was happening, he began to utter praise in another language.[47] Later Sally Botham, a student, commenced to speak in an unknown tongue that was recognized by two missionaries from the Belgian Congo as Kefonti.

Three months later, David McDowell, a student who had been present at the May meeting and who had subsequently been "filled with the Spirit" at an Alliance camp meeting at Rocky Springs Park in Pennsylvania, addressed the convention of about 1,000 people at Nyack in the following manner:

> I have received a wonderful experience. As yet I don't have a great

[46] A school which Simpson founded in 1882. It is located on the Hudson, twenty-five miles above New York City.

[47] Brumback, *Suddenly from Heaven*, p. 89.

deal of doctrine for it, but I know that it is from God and that it is for you. This is the Latter Rain for which we have been praying for years.[48]

The audience believed McDowell; they flocked to the altar, and about 100 received the Pentecostal blessing.

About this time, certain non-Alliance Pentecostals were emphasizing the principle that the evidence of a person's being filled with the Spirit is that he will speak in other tongues. Up to now the Alliance leaders had viewed with tolerance the charismatic outbursts that punctuated their Beulah Heights camp meeting near Cleveland, Ohio, and the Rocky Springs Park camp in Pennsylvania; however, they decided not to tolerate this emphasis. Therefore, they sponsored the drafting of a statement that has remained to this day the official Alliance position—speaking in tongues is but *one* of the evidences that a person has received a Holy Spirit baptism. Fission was inevitable.

A score of years before, many Alliance people had separated from the established denominations because they wished to pursue a "deeper religious experience" and because they desired to proclaim their belief that a supernatural visitation from God accompanied by signs and wonders was imminent. Now twenty years later, a contingent within the Alliance, feeling the growing opposition to their Pentecostal tendencies, decided to withdraw. The results of the separation, although unavoidable perhaps, were a legacy of ill feelings among brethren who had had so much in common: the loss of whole congregations to Pentecostalism, the loss of property, and the loss of missionary outposts in India and China, where some Alliance missionaries embraced Pentecostal views.

[48] Quoted in *ibid.*, p. 91.

CHAPTER 4

Pentecostalism Becomes an International Movement

Pentecostalism Crosses the Atlantic

The religious soil of nineteenth-century America was well-prepared to receive the implantation of Pentecostalism. The soil of Europe had been too. In England, between 1891 and 1907, a Holiness movement of rather large proportions had developed as a result of the Keswick conventions and The Pentecostal League.[1] Both organizations had stressed the need for a deeper spiritual experience than just conversion, namely, a cleansing from sin that was accomplished by the purifying work of a Holy Spirit baptism.[2]

To these English conclaves came many Continental clergymen like Pastor Stockmayer of Germany. Having been inspired and instructed in the matters of the so-called "deeper life," they returned to their pastorates to promulgate the same sort of pietism. Moreover, in the waning decades of the nineteenth century, an American evangelist, Dr. R. A. Torrey, while conducting a campaign in Berlin, popularized the view that an empowering baptism of the Holy Spirit is necessary for effective witness.

But perhaps the most influential single event in the British Isles which prepared the hearts and minds of the religious to accept a supernatural type of experience such as Pentecostalism was the Great

[1] Gee, *Pentecostal Movement,* p. 4.

[2] Unlike the later Pentecostal movement, however, these movements did not stress or even tolerate the charismatic.

Welsh Revival of 1904. In commenting on the awakening in Wales, Donald Gee says that its most significant contribution was the creation of a widespread spirit of expectation. Men justly asked, " 'Why just Wales only? Why not other lands? Why not a world-wide Revival?' Faith was rising to visualize a return to apostolic Christianity in all its pristine beauty and power."[3]

Scores of believers both in Great Britain (and the Empire too) as well as on the Continent were engaged in intercessory prayer, hoping for an outpouring of the Holy Spirit and eager to receive any news that seemed like an answer to their prayers. That is why the reports that reached them of what had transpired in Topeka, in Los Angeles, and in other parts of the States were treasured so. However, the flames of Pentecostal fire were to be ignited by the transoceanic voyage of Thomas Ball Barratt, a Cornishman who was pastoring a Methodist church in Kristiania (Oslo), Norway.

T. B. Barratt was born at Albaston, England, on June 22, 1862.[4] When he was four, his parents moved to Norway, where in time he was to become an accomplished musician (he studied under Edvard Grieg), poet, sculptor, and prominent Methodist pastor.[5] In 1902, he founded the Kristiania Bymission (City Mission) the expansion of which was so great that by 1905 Barratt decided to go to America to solicit funds for a larger structure. While in America there is a possibility that he visited the Azusa Street mission. In any case, it is definite that on November 15, 1906, just prior to returning to Norway he attended a Pentecostal meeting in New York City, where he experienced a Holy Spirit baptism and spoke in tongues. Here is his description of the occasion:

> I was filled with light and such power that I began to shout as loud as I could in a foreign language. I must have spoken seven or eight languages, to judge from the various sounds and forms of speech used. I stood erect at time, preaching in one foreign tongue after another, and I know from the strength of my voice that 10,000 might easily have heard

[3] Gee, *Pentecostal Movement,* p. 6.

[4] For a complete coverage of Barratt's efforts, see Bloch-Hoell's *The Pentecostal Movement,* a shorter English version of *Pinsebevegelsen* (Oslo: Universitets forlaget, 1956).

[5] Data taken from a tear sheet in my file entitled "Norway's Pentecostal Jubilee," which appeared in the *Pentecostal Evangel* (1957 [?]), p. 20.

all I said. The most wonderful moment was when I burst into a beautiful baritone solo, using one of the most pure and delightful languages I have ever heard. The tune and words were entirely new to me and the rhythm and cadence of the various choruses seemed to be perfect. . . . Oh, what praises to God arose from my soul for His mercy! I felt as strong as a lion. . . .[6]

Returning to Norway, Barratt went from place to place, preaching the Pentecostal truths. People thronged to his meetings, so that by early 1907 he was conducting them in a large gymnasium that accommodated crowds of from 1,500 to 2,000 people. "Folk from all denominations are rushing to the meetings," he wrote, and "a number have received their Pentecost and are speaking with tongues."[7] By 1916, Barratt was able to found the Filadelfia Church which had the distinction of having the largest dissenter (non-Lutheran) congregation in Norway.[8]

In January, 1907, a young Baptist minister in Sweden, Lewi Pethrus, was intrigued by a newspaper account of the revival that was sweeping Kristiania as a result of Barratt's ministry. He journeyed to Norway, was filled with the Holy Spirit, and spoke in tongues. In a short time after returning to Sweden, he too was instrumental in influencing thousands of his countrymen to accept the Pentecostal point of view. Prominent among those who did was Sven Lindholm, one of Sweden's best-known literary figures, who later became the first editor of the Pentecostal newspaper, *Dagen.* Needless to say, Barratt came to Sweden to conduct several revival campaigns during 1907–1908, doing much by way of personal influence to help the new movement get entrenched.

The ubiquitous Barratt also went to Denmark. In the summer of 1907, he conducted revivals which attracted the attention of the outstanding Danish actress, Anna Larssen. A year later, when Barratt was again in Denmark, she experienced the Pentecostal enduement of power,[9] and for some years afterward, having married Sigurd Bjorner,

[6] Quoted in Gee, *Pentecostal Movement,* p. 14.

[7] Frodsham, *Signs Following,* pp. 71 f.

[8] Today the Pentecostal Church in Norway, although only sixty years old, is second in size only to the State Church.

[9] Anna Larssen Bjorner, "From Stage to the Pulpit," *Pentecostal Evangel,* XXVI (July 2, 1938), 1, 11.

a former YMCA Secretary at Helsingör, she and her husband toured the Danish coast in a horse-drawn "Gospel Van," conducting revival meetings in huge tents.

Barratt's fame spread far and wide, and visitors and ministers came from various countries to see the happenings that had been featured in the secular press. One of these observers in 1907 was an Anglican vicar, Alexander A. Boddy, of All Saints' Church in Sunderland. In an article which he wrote to several English papers, he stated: "My four days in Christiania can never be forgotten. I stood with Evan Roberts in Tonypandy, but have never witnessed such scenes as those in Norway."[10] Boddy returned to his parish in Sunderland, determined to promote a similar Pentecostal awakening there that would hopefully affect all England.

First, at the 1907 Keswick convention, Boddy took thousands of copies of a pamphlet, *Pentecost for England,* which he had prepared and in which he bemoaned the fact that although some 20,000 people throughout the world reputedly had spoken or were now speaking in tongues, there were no more than a half-dozen Englishmen whom he knew to have had that experience.[11] Second, Boddy invited Barratt to All Saints' Church, assuring him that people from all over England were gathering, and that a volume of prayer was being offered in the hope that God would honor Barratt's ministry among them, and that there would be a mighty effusion of the Holy Spirit.

Barratt landed at Newcastle early in September, 1907, and proceeded to Sunderland. Soon after his arrival, Pentecostal phenomena became evident as, at the conclusion of his sermons, people gathered in the vestry for prayer. Services lasted all day, Tarrying ("Waiting Meetings" the British call them)[12] lasted far into the early morning. Visitors from all branches of Christendom flocked to All Saints' Church as they had a year earlier to Azusa Street. The newspapers publicized the events, sensing something unusual, and thus helped to broadcast the news of the revival all over the British Isles. Some

[10] Gee, *Pentecostal Movement,* p. 20.
[11] *Ibid.,* pp. 20 f.
[12] After the sermon, interested believers would engage in prayer, tarrying or waiting for the outpouring of the Holy Spirit upon them.

rather violent objections to the revival were raised by a few of Boddy's Anglican colleagues, but not one was forthcoming from his superior—Handley G. Moule, Bishop of Durham. In a few months a Pentecostal revival was in progress in the British Isles.

Just as the news of the supernatural occurrences in Norway had motivated both Lewi Pethrus and Alexander Boddy to go to the Norwegian capital in order that they might examine the happenings themselves, so likewise it was responsible for drawing Pastor Jonathan Paul of Berlin and Edward Meyer of the Hamburger Strandmission to Oslo.[13] They became convinced of the validity of the Pentecostal experience, even though they themselves did not experience any of the charismatic phenomena. Upon returning to Germany, however, Pastor Paul received the Spirit baptism in Friedrichstadt, and he commenced to preach about it throughout the land.[14]

Very soon thereafter, Dagmar Gregersen and Agnes Thelle—two Norwegian evangelists—joined Thomas Barratt in traversing Germany and Switzerland and proclaiming the message of Pentecost. Thus during 1907 and 1908, an intense interest developed in the possibility of forming a German Pentecostal movement. It culminated in December, 1908, when the first conference of Pentecostals convened in Hamburg.[15]

As one might expect, Barratt's indefatigable itinerating on behalf of Pentecostalism also accounts for its introduction into Finland. Right from the outset, when he left Methodism, Barratt commenced to publish *Korsets Seir* (*The Victory of the Cross*) not only in Norwegian but also in Finnish, Swedish, Russian, German, and Spanish. Therefore, although the earliest record we have of Barratt's presence in Finland is 1911,[16] it is reasonable to assume that his message had been popularized by means of his publications long before then. In any case, the Finnish work did not really take root until 1912 when intensive efforts were made by Pastor Gerhard Smidt, who arrived

[13] Bloch-Hoell, *Pinsebevegelsen,* p. 431.

[14] Gee, *Pentecostal Movement,* p. 42.

[15] Leonhard Steiner, *Mit folgenden Zeichen* (Basel: Verlag Mission für das volle Evangelium, 1954), p. 55.

[16] Inez Sturgeon, "Finnish Pentecostal Jubilee," *Pentecostal Evangel,* XLIX (Dec. 10, 1961), 28.

from St. Paul, Minnesota,[17] and William Pylkkanen, a Lutheran missionary recently returned from China by his board because he had espoused Pentecostalism while in the Orient.

Very few data exist about the origins of Pentecostalism in the other European countries during this period, 1901–1911. In *Religion in the Soviet Union,*[18] Walter Kolarz writes that the Pentecostal movement did not have a chance to spread in Russia until after the Communists had seized power. Frank Bartleman (one of the leaders in the Los Angeles revival) visited France in 1910 and made the comment that there was only one Pentecostal mission in the whole of France. It was located at Rosny-sous-Bois, about ten miles from Paris.[19] The news of a Pentecostal revival came to Holland via American periodicals. A few Dutch believers commenced to pray and search the Scriptures to see if there were a biblical basis for the awakening. The wife of the leader of a small mission in Amsterdam, Mrs. R. G. Polman, received her Spirit baptism on October 27, 1907. A year later so did her husband. From that time, their meeting place—Immanuel Haus—became the center from which the message of Pentecostalism radiated into all sectors of the Netherlands.[20] There was to be no major charismatic revival in the other European countries for another decade; for instance, Austria in 1923, and Poland and the Baltic States in 1925.[21]

Pentecostalism Penetrates the Orient, Africa, and Latin America

In the 1909 issue of the *American Journal of Theology,* Frederick Henke stated that the religious climate of opinion in the East had been conditioned to receive a spiritual movement like Pentecostalism by the following: (1) The great revival which Dr. Reuben A. Torrey

[17] Atter, *Third Force,* p. 48.

[18] London: Macmillan & Co., Ltd., 1961, p. 332.

[19] Frank Bartleman, *Two Years Mission Work in Europe* (Los Angeles: Privately Printed, n.d.), p. 12. Gee, *Pentecostal Movement,* p. 69, gives the additional note that a Madame Helene Biolley opened her Temperance Hotel, *Ruban Bleu,* at Le Havre for a Pentecostal center.

[20] See Steiner, *folgenden Zeichen,* pp. 60 f. and Gee, *Pentecostal Movement,* p. 27, for the sketchy information on Pentecostalism in Holland before 1912.

[21] Steiner, pp. 66, 73.

conducted in Australia in 1901. The success of this awakening, it was felt, resulted from the circles of prayer and prayer meetings; therefore, countless numbers of others sprang up all over the world. (2) The effects of the revival in Wales which were felt in such far-flung regions of the Empire as the Khasi Hills of India, where, said Henke, "the religious experiences of the natives were brought into closer conformity to those of the pristine church than had been the case in Australia or Wales."[22]

Up to this point, I have attempted to emphasize the historical continuity which appears to me to be evident as one studies the documents from the early decades of the Pentecostal revival. For instance, a connection of personalities and influences is apparent between the Topeka revival led by Charles Fox Parham and the Azusa Street awakening in 1906: it was Parham who financed the trip for one of his students—William J. Seymour—from Houston to Los Angeles. Furthermore, a direct line of influence can be traced between the New York mission which preached and practiced Pentecostal views—and more important for European Pentecostal history, where Thomas Ball Barratt received his Spirit baptism—and the Apostolic Faith Gospel Mission in Los Angeles. Finally, the introduction of Pentecostalism into the Scandinavian countries, Great Britain, Germany, and Switzerland is attributable to the widespread evangelistic efforts of Barratt. By way of contrast, however, the outburst of Pentecostal phenomena in India precedes the Los Angeles revival by one year and, furthermore, cannot be traced to the indoctrination by any one person, periodical, or organization.

In Mukti, India, a well-educated Christian lady named Pandita Ramabai[23] operated a home for 2,000 widows and orphans. In addition, she was concerned that her region experience a spiritual awakening; therefore, she asked for volunteers who would join her for daily prayers. From the original 70 who responded right from the start, the attendance grew to 500. Next she requested that some girls go into the nearby villages to conduct preaching missions. Thirty responded.

[22] "The Gift of Tongues and Related Phenomena of the Present Day," XIII (Apr., 1909), 193 f.

[23] For a comprehensive biography of this woman, see Helen S. Dyer's biography, *Pandita Ramabai* (New York: Fleming H. Revell Co., 1911).

They would meet with her each day to pray for an "enduement of power."

While there is no record of speaking in tongues at Mukti in 1905, there is ample testimony that the young women were experiencing what certain segments of the American Holiness movement called "the baptism of fire" which "burned away such negative qualities in the believer's life as pride, anger, worldliness, selfishness, and immoral tendencies."[24] Some of the girls responded to this "baptism" by shaking, dancing, seeing visions, and dreaming dreams. "The baptism of fire having been experienced," Henke remarked, "the desire for the 'gift of tongues' described in the New Testament was but natural."[25]

Glossolalia in India first occurred during a mission that was conducted by one of the Mukti evangelistic bands in Anrangabad in 1906.[26] At this meeting, a nine year old girl was deeply impressed with the need for a Holy Spirit baptism. After she returned to her boarding school in Bombay, she and four other girls began to pray daily for it. Before too long, one of them commenced to speak in a language which she did not understand. It is related that a Canon Haywood sought for a linguist who could interpret these tongues and that he determined that she was pleading with God "in an unknown tongue" for the salvation of Libya. The incident, says Gee, was published in a prayer circular, dated September, 1906—the month when the news of the Los Angeles revival first reached India.[27]

Through the incessant labors of the Mukti praying bands and the efforts of Pentecostal missionaries from the United States and Great Britain, by 1909[28] Pentecostalism had spread throughout India—Coonoor, Calcutta, Dhond, Allahabad, Gujerat, and even beyond, to Korea.[29]

That the embryonic Pentecostal revival was frequently criticized is evident from Pandita Ramabai's commentary on affairs in India.

[24] Minnie Abrams, "The Baptism of the Holy Spirit at Mukti," *The Missionary Review of the World,* XIX (Aug., 1906), 619 f.

[25] Henke, "Gift of Tongues," p. 194.

[26] Gee, *Pentecostal Movement,* p. 28.

[27] *Idem.*

[28] See Frodsham, *With Signs Following,* p. 113, and Donald Gee, *Upon All Flesh* (Springfield, Mo.: Gospel Publishing House, 1935), p. 47.

[29] Minnie Abrams, "Brief History of the Latter Rain Revival of 1910," *Word and Work,* XXXII (May, 1910), 139.

> Some features of this revival have stumbled [*sic*] not a few: the shaking of the body and other physical demonstrations, speaking in different tongues, simultaneous prayer, and such other things. Most of these were attributed to hysteria; alarming reports of people committing suicide, etc., have gone abroad and all such incidents have been attributed to the extraordinary condition prevalent among the people visited by the revival. Hence, friendly or bitter criticism on the part of some; and scornful silence and indifference to the revival on the part of others. All that I can say about the alarming reports is that in most cases mountains have been made of mole hills; things have been greatly exaggerated.[30]

Gee picks August, 1908, as the date when Pentecostal phenomena appeared in China, noting that it was then that the Christian and Missionary Alliance published an account of "a Pentecostal Revival in connection with their Wuchow Schools."[31] The gist of the report is that when a number of people began to speak in other tongues, the Alliance missionaries recognized the manifestation as being similar to that about which they had already heard. Their response to the outburst was cautiously temperate, for they realized the implicit danger in mere emotional extravagances. However, they also went on record as saying that they could not for a moment doubt that their fellow Christians had experienced a genuine and profound blessing. They noted, furthermore, that this was not merely a temporary joyous ecstasy, but a blessing which had had lasting fruit in the lives of believers, having given them a power and blessing in service such as they had never experienced before.

In the fall of 1908, Mr. and Mrs. A. G. Garr arrived in Hong Kong from Los Angeles. A rather caustic article in the *Independent* reports that they took quarters on Ladder Street, among the Chinese, and that soon their meetings were attracting great crowds.

> The meetings drew 300 people night after night. Hundreds went under

[30] Pandita Ramabai, "Showers of Blessing at Mukti, India, 39 Years Ago," *Pentecostal Evangel,* XXXIV (May 4, 1946), 1, 12–13.

[31] *Pentecostal Movement,* p. 44. In his recent history of the Pentecostal revival (*Third Force,* p. 250) Gordon Atter states that the first Pentecostal missionary to China was Miss Nettie Moomau who landed at Macao in October, 1907. One of her first acts was to address a gathering of missionaries who represented, among other groups, the Baptist denomination and the Christian and Missionary Alliance. Several of the missionaries and Chinese were baptized in the Holy Spirit, writes Atter, and thus Pentecostalism began in China.

the spell, shaking and shouting in "tongues," and in general conducting themselves like howling dervishes.[32]

The author continues his article by describing what he calls "these curious fanatics who had settled in Canton."[33] They were headed by a Mr. T. T. McIntosh and had succeeded in gaining the support of "a wealthy Chinaman of Canton, a much esteemed native church convert." It is strange, however, that none of these facts appear in any Pentecostal source material. Frank Bartleman, who visited Canton in 1910, mentions staying with a Brother and Sister Dixon, and Brother and Sister Bettex, and that he "had the privilege of preaching to a large, heathen congregation,"[34] but he makes no mention of a Mr. McIntosh.

The Pentecostal work among the Chinese was further enhanced during the early decade of this century by another of the Azusa Street "Graduates," so to speak. Miss Nettie Moomau,[35] a Presbyterian missionary in the late 1890's, had contracted tuberculosis and returned to America to die. While in Los Angeles, she received a Holy Spirit baptism and continued to live. Her former mission board dismissed her, so she returned to China, independent of any board, and established a mission in Shanghai. At first she worked in association with a Miss Phillips and Mr. and Mrs. A. M. Atter. Then when Miss Phillips died, and the Atters returned to Canada, she carried on alone. Gordon Atter, the son of the missionaries to China, describes her thus:

> Miss Moomau carried on the work for the rest of her life. Miracles were wrought, many churches were established on an extremely indigenous basis, manned by Chinese. Some of the leading Chinese intellectuals came into the Mission.[36]

[32] "The 'Tongue' Movement," LXVI (June 10, 1909), 1288.

[33] Tragically, the Garrs lost their three year old daughter and a Negro co-worker in a smallpox epidemic. The anonymous correspondent from Hong Kong indicts the Garrs thus: "Of course the enthusiasts would have no medical attendance." He states that the Garrs left for Japan, leaving their mission in the hands of a Mr. Mok [Lai Chai], "an intelligent former government employee." See *Ibid.*

[34] *Around the World by Faith* (Los Angeles: Privately Printed, n.d.), p. 73.

[35] See Frodsham, *With Signs Following,* pp. 121–124; and Atter, *Third Force,* pp. 252 f.

[36] Atter, *loc. cit.*

Early in 1910, the British-operated Pentecostal Missionary Union sent workers to China. Among the first was John C. Beruldsen, who was to labor for over thirty-five years in northern China (principally Kalgan). From 1911, the English missionary thrust was equally intensive in southwestern China (Province of Yunnan).[37]

Perhaps the most sizable accession of Chinese believers to Pentecostalism occurred in 1912. W. W. Simpson, a Christian and Missionary Alliance worker in Taochow, Kansu (three miles from the Tibetan border), experienced the gift of tongues while praying alone in his home.[38] Soon thereafter, his wife and whole family, together with about 100 people who were associated with the mission, received a similar "infilling" of the Spirit. As in the case of the other missionaries we have mentioned who were affiliated with denominational missionary boards, Mr. Simpson was asked to resign. This he did, eventually allying himself with the Assemblies of God, USA. What is important, though, is that in a relatively short period of time 50 churches and about 3,000 adherents were added to the Pentecostal movement in China.[39]

Finally, one cannot overlook the Pentecostal missionaries who came from Scandinavia, Holland, and Canada in those early years, and who worked tirelessly to spread their testimony, especially in northern China.[40]

American evangelists John G. Lake and Thomas Hezmalhalch are generally credited with introducing the Pentecostal message to the African continent.[41] These two men, reputed to be former adherents of John Alexander Dowie who abandoned the "prophet of Zion" for Pentecostalism, began their campaign in a native church in Johannesburg, Union of South Africa, sometime before 1910. Soon, out of curiosity, many whites came. Scores received the Pentecostal baptism. A larger tabernacle was obtained, one that accommodated over 1,000 people. It was filled every night. David J. duPlessis, Secretary of the Apostolic Faith Mission of South Africa, in a speech which he made in

[37] Gee, *Pentecostal Movement,* pp. 47 f.
[38] *Ibid.,* p. 85; and Atter, pp. 64 f.
[39] Gee, p. 85.
[40] *Idem.*
[41] Frodsham, *With Signs Following,* p. 155.

1938, said of that revival: "It stirred the city. Jews and Gentiles were saved."[42]

When Lake and Hezmalhalch left Johannesburg in 1913, the direction of the work was undertaken by Peter Louis leRoux, formerly a missionary in the Dutch Reformed Church. The church was registered with the government as the Apostolic Faith Mission of South Africa; however, there is no direct connection between the name of this work and that of the numerous Apostolic Faith Missions which sprang up in America.

Another North American, Charles Chawner, came to South Africa in 1908 from the Hebden Mission in Toronto. He evangelized both the Negroes and the whites throughout the province of Natal, but his primary ministry was among the Zulus.[43]

The vast Central African territory was not penetrated by Pentecostals until 1914–1915, when William F. P. Burton and James Salter arrived from Preston, England, to found the Congo Evangelistic Association.[44] However, it is necessary to cease speaking about these developments, since 1914 is a point beyond the chronological scope of this chapter. The same will have to be said for the phenomenal growth of Pentecostalism in areas like Kenya, Tanganyika, and Mozambique.

It is often said that in Latin America, eight out of ten evangelical Protestants are Pentecostal.[45] They thrive especially in Chile and Brazil, countries which were penetrated very early in this century with the Pentecostal ideology.

Unlike most of the other countries in Latin America, the rise of Pentecostalism in Chile was not due to the missionary efforts of Americans, Canadians, or Europeans. Charismatic phenomena first appeared in 1907 within a Methodist church in Valparaiso. The pastor, Willis C. Hoover, was an American, engaged in building a new sanctuary, which, he prayed, would be filled not only with people but also with the Holy Spirit. In 1907, Minnie Abrams, who had attended the

[42] David J. duPlessis, "Pentecost in South Africa," *Pentecostal Evangel,* XXVI (July 30, 1938), 2–4.

[43] Atter, *Third Force,* pp. 71 f.

[44] Gee, *Pentecostal Movement,* p. 99.

[45] Brumback, *Suddenly from Heaven,* p. 340.

Chicago Training School for Home and Foreign Missions with Mrs. Hoover, sent her a copy of an eighty-page book entitled *The Baptism of the Holy Ghost and Fire*. It described the outpouring of blessing upon the child widows at Mukti, India. The reading of this volume, together with the news of people in the States being "filled with the Spirit," awakened a desire in the hearts of the Rev. Mr. and Mrs. Hoover to see a similar revival in Chile.

> So we set ourselves, like Daniel, to seek the Lord with fasting and prayer. . . . Now with this new hunger awakened in us, as we came together in the new church, we purposed with our whole heart to have a revival.
>
> On the first night of the Evangelical Week of Prayer, on calling to prayer a most astonishing thing occurred—the whole congregation of perhaps one hundred and fifty burst forth as one man in audible prayer![46]

From this time on, remarkable phenomena are recorded as having occurred in Hoover's church. He alluded to them as "experiences . . . that are very adequately described in numerous particulars in Acts 2." Needless to say, multitudes came to see what was happening. Attendance at the Sunday night service exceeded 900.

> In the course of about three months, more than one hundred fell to the floor under the power of the Spirit, nearly half of them speaking in tongues. The city was moved, the church filled. . . . An accusation was lodged against me and I was cited to appear before the judge of the criminal court. My replies appeared satisfactory and there was no case. The sensational papers with flaming headlines, published in daily instalments for two weeks the story of "The Great Impostor." I was a "hypnotist," "suggestionist," I "gave them to drink a beverage which was called the blood of the Lord, which caused them to fall into a lethargy."[47]

The events in Valparaiso apparently offended the sense of propriety of Hoover's ministerial colleagues. At the Annual Conference that was held in February, 1910, charges were leveled against him for teaching anti-Methodist and anti-scriptural doctrines. It was decided to spare Hoover any local embarrassment by sending him back to the States. When the members of the pastor's official board learned of

[46] Willis C. Hoover, "Pentecost in Chile," *World Dominion*, X (Apr., 1932), 157.

[47] Hoover, "Work in Chile," *Word and Work*, XXXIII (July, 1911), 220 f.

these matters, they, together with about 400 others, resolved to separate from the Methodist Church and found the Methodist Pentecostal Church. This was in April, 1910. Subsequently, two other Methodist congregations in Santiago, which were sympathetic with the Pentecostal beliefs and practices of their brethren in Valparaiso, seceded. They asked Hoover to be their superintendent. He agreed, and from that point on the ranks of the Pentecostals in Chile continued to swell until at present they number 500,000.[48]

In Brazil, the Pentecostal revival has continued unabated since 1910, when Louis Francescon left the United States for São Paulo, Brazil.[49] Here, after rather inauspicious beginnings (for he knew no Portuguese), Pentecostalism took root and has grown so that São Paulo now has a church accommodating 5,000 worshipers. The larger endeavor which Francescon founded—Congregacioni Christiani—now numbers 1,400 congregations and nearly 500,000 communicants.

However, this was not the only work that the Pentecostals founded in Brazil. The Assembléias de Deus do Brasil, which numerically equals the organization founded by Louis Francescon, was begun in 1910 by two Swedish-American missionaries—Daniel Berg and Gunnar Vingren, who arrived in Pará, Brazil, from Chicago. In a short time, they were joined by Nels Nelson and Samuel Nystrom, Pentecostal missionaries from Scandinavia.[50] Together they organized a flourishing Brazilian work on a completely indigenous basis, a rather unique approach for that time.

From all that has been written thus far, one cannot deny that Pentecostalism rapidly extended its sphere of influence during the first decade of the twentieth century. However, now we must proceed to examine those factors that might have facilitated its early success as well as those features which were detrimental to its own well-being and objectionable to other religious groups.

[48] Theo Tschuy, "Shock Troops in Chile," *Christian Century,* LXXVII (Sept. 28, 1960), 1118.

[49] Atter, *Third Force,* p. 216.

[50] Samuel Nystrom, "Miracles Wrought in Brazil," *Pentecostal Evangel,* XXXII (Sept. 30, 1944), 6–7.

CHAPTER 5

Causes for the Initial Success of Pentecostalism

During the early decades of the twentieth century, the embryonic Pentecostal movement enjoyed a period of rather successful growth. North and South America, Europe, Africa, and Asia were honeycombed with Pentecostal Missions, Assemblies of God, Gospel Halls, Tabernacles, Glad Tidings Halls, Churches of God, or Full Gospel Assemblies. The Latter Rain, Apostolic Faith, or Pentecostal movement—as it was variously called—was well known in the English-speaking world, as was the *Pfingstbewegung* among the Germans, and the *Pinsebevegelsen* among the Scandinavians. Although statistics from that period are rather scanty, it would be safe to say that many thousands had received the novel religious experience of a Holy Spirit baptism accompanied by speaking in tongues. What were the important factors that enhanced the spread of Pentecostalism during these early years? Why did it appeal to so many?

For some decades before the turn of the century, thousands of Christians the world over had been conditioned to expect the supernatural. They were not repelled, therefore, by an emotionally oriented, experiential type of religious expression like Pentecostalism which preached the "full Gospel." They had been prepared to accept supernatural occurrences since the days of the divine healing campaigns of John Alexander Dowie and Dr. A. B. Simpson. As a matter of fact, many ex-Dowieites, who were disenchanted with the "Autocrat of

Zion," allied themselves with Pentecostalism.[1] And as mentioned earlier, scores of Pentecostal leaders had been nurtured in Simpson's Christian and Missionary Alliance society.

Furthermore, in the Holiness movement in America, The Pentecostal League in England, and the *Gemeinschaftsbewegung* in Germany, Christians had been prepared to expect manifestations of the Spirit. Outward evidences, they were told, would attend the person who was being "baptized in the Holy Spirit" (i.e., sanctified). It is no wonder, then, that former Holiness groups like the Church of God (Cleveland, Tennessee), the Fire-Baptized Holiness Church, and the Church of God in Christ associated themselves with Pentecostalism very early in the 1900's. To these bodies, the Pentecostals represented everything that the Holiness movement had projected for itself when it first evolved in the post-Civil War era: they were fundamentalistic; they honored the role of the Holy Spirit in the believer's life; they were revivalistic; and they were puritanical in their rejection of things worldly—tobacco, alcoholic beverages, the theater, cosmetics.

Moreover, the early Pentecostals emphasized an experience rather than a system of doctrine or church government. Thus Arminians and Calvinists, Holiness folk who believed in a "second work of grace" and Baptists who adhered to the theory of "the finished work at Calvary," Methodists, Brethren, and Anglicans—all of whom represented variant forms of church doctrine and polity—all met around the same altar to pray and to expect the impartation of the Holy Spirit and his charismatic gifts.

Like so many spiritual movements before them, the early Pentecostals did not consider themselves to be a separate entity. They thought of themselves as a movement within the Christian Church, used of God to revitalize it. "There was no intention of establishing a Pentecostal branch of the Church, but an insistence that the entire

[1] One of the founders of the Assemblies of God, USA had been a Dowieite—Daniel C. O. Opperman, head of Zion's educational system until he embraced Pentecostalism. (See Brumback, *Suddenly from Heaven,* p. 72.) William J. Mitchell, Pentecostal pioneer in Massachusetts, wrote: "We belonged to the Dowie movement in 1905" (*ibid.,* p. 82). The Pentecostal revival in South Africa was started by ex-Dowie followers among a Dowieite congregation. (Atter, *Third Force,* p. 54.)

tree was to be Pentecostal."[2] That the early Pentecostal leadership in England adhered to such a policy is clearly outlined in the following citation:

> The dominant leaders in the earliest years of the Pentecostal Movement in the British Isles never encouraged the formation of separate Pentecostal assemblies as such. . . . The counsel usually given was to "receive the baptism in the Holy Spirit, but remain in your church, whatever the denomination may be."[3]

The thrust of the Pentecostal message during the early years of the revival was directed at the nominal Christian, the lethargic believer, rather than to the unconverted. The view was that the Holy Spirit baptism was considered to be an enduement of power for more effective Christian service by those who were already followers of Jesus Christ. It was the culmination of a person's spiritual growth which had commenced with the experience of conversion. By adhering to this principle of "undenominationalism" the Pentecostals were able to infiltrate various segments of the Christian Church. That some denominations tolerated these "Spirituals" is evidenced by the fact that the Swedish Baptists in Stockholm accommodated those of their membership who manifested spiritual phenomena by establishing a "special Pentecostalist congregation in 1910"[4] whose pastor was the Spirit-filled Lewi Pethrus. Apparently it was not until the Pentecostals began to manifest certain eccentric tendencies, irritated their more quiescent brethren, or felt that their own spiritual growth was being stultified, that they decided (or were forced) to withdraw from having fellowship with some of the established churches. Meanwhile, their views had appealed to many people within these communions; therefore, when the Pentecostals separated themselves and opened their own missions and store-front churches, virtually a host of people from various denominations followed them, thus forming the nucleus of hundreds of Pentecostal churches.

Many church historians and sociologists of religion have observed that at the turn of the century some denominations neglected their

[2] Brumback, *Suddenly from Heaven,* p. 151.

[3] Gee, *Pentecostal Movement,* p. 88.

[4] Einar Molland, *Christendom* (London: A. R. Mowbray & Co., Ltd., 1961), pp. 302 f.

ministry which heretofore had been directed to the lower strata of American society.[5] These groups had accumulated wealth, built enormous churches, appointed them handsomely, eliminated the "prayer and praise" service from the program of worship, and in some instances even provided little or no room for the people of the laboring class in the sanctuary itself. The result was that multitudes severed their affiliation with the so-called "middle-class" denominations like the Methodist and the Baptist. Charles B. Braden commented on this reaction in an article for the *Christian Century* some years back: "Many in humbler circumstances do not feel at home in the comfortable middle class churches of the community."[6] Social standards had been set which the lower income groups had difficulty in maintaining, especially in matters of dress or in the ownership of the more expensively made automobiles.

It was from among these lower classes, who after all constitute the bulk of any nation's population, that Pentecostalism recruited its membership. To reach them, it relied on a variety of the following methods.

The Pentecostalists were like the Methodist circuit riders of a century before, *sans* horses. That is, they did not wait for the people to come to them; they went out to the people, meeting them singly or collectively—it mattered not. Books about the pioneer days of the Pentecostal revival are rare. In one that is available, Howard A. Goss describes his first evangelistic venture:

> A young German brother and I were sent out [from Texas], instructed only to go South toward the Gulf of Mexico and stop anywhere we could find a place to preach. For capital to launch our project, our leader [Parham(?)] gave us a silver dollar apiece—all that he had left. At least we were on our own as evangelists.
>
> We went to Alvin and received a little money, and thus reinforced, arrived in Angleton, Texas, on February 27, 1906.
>
> A room in the Angleton Hotel cost us fifty cents a day. The Court House Auditorium was free for a few meetings, and there we opened the first Gospel meeting of which I had ever had full charge.

[5] Smith, *American Christianity,* pp. 215–217; Olmstead, *History of Religion,* pp. 447 f.; and Sweet, *Story of Religion,* pp. 345–352.

[6] "Churches of the Dispossessed," *Christian Century,* LXI (Jan. 26, 1944), 108.

We soon found an old abandoned saloon building which we could use regularly. As we had received no more money, we borrowed planks of new lumber . . . for seats, and laid them across a few . . . empty up-ended kegs. . . . When the building was cleaned and ready for use, *we set out to get a crowd,* . . . [Italics mine.][7]

Later on in the same book, Mrs. Goss recalls her husband's observation: "We all strove to be great soul-winners, always attempting to pack 'just one more' fish into the usually full Gospel net. 'Action' was our watchword. Jesus 'went about' doing good."[8] One could narrate countless illustrations of this compulsion on the part of the Pentecostals to acquaint people with the gospel, but one more incident will suffice. It concerns a band of Pentecostals who arrived in Houston, Texas, in July, 1905.

We held two or three street meetings on different corners every night and *visited from house to house during the morning,* by twos, stopping to pray if the people would let us and we would tell them about the meetings. In the afternoon we would rest and pray for the meeting. If any requests came in to go and pray for the sick some were sent out for that.[9] [Italics mine.]

Very early in their development, the Pentecostals realized the salutary effect that mass meetings had on their followers. By meeting in larger groups than would perhaps be the case in their locale, Pentecostal believers could experience the sense of belonging to a community, a fellowship. Furthermore, these occasions could be times of united witness to the non-Pentecostals. Conventions or conferences of this sort seem to have originated among European Pentecostals; American Pentecostals preferred the tent-meeting or camp-meeting mode of evangelism.

In 1908, Alexander A. Boddy inaugurated the first Pentecostal convention in Europe—what was to become for nearly a decade the famous Whitsuntide conference at All Saints' Church in Sunderland, England. During the same year, the first German conference was held at Mülheim. It was a larger convention, because there had been a wider acceptance of the Pentecostal point of view in Germany than

[7] Ethel A. Goss, *The Winds of God* (New York: Comet Press Books, 1958), p. 41.

[8] *Ibid.*, p. 64.

[9] Brumback, *Suddenly from Heaven,* p. 32.

in England. Albert Weaver, a New Englander who visited Mülheim in 1910, reported in the *Word and Work,* a Pentecostal journal published in Massachusetts, that the meetings were held in a large hall, seating 1,600 people, "packed even to the doors, with every seat occupied, and many standing."[10]

As was already intimated, American Pentecostals used evangelistic and divine healing revivals as the means to attract the masses. From the outset, Pentecostal evangelists carried on the revival tradition that had been established by Finney, Moody, and Sunday. One of the outstanding personalities during the early years of the Pentecostal movement was Mrs. Mary B. Woodworth-Etter[11] who in 1912, although sixty-eight years old, was at the height of her evangelistic ministry. Thousands flocked to her meetings to be prayed for. In her book, *Marvels and Miracles,* she described a camp meeting which she conducted for two weeks near Alexandria, Indiana, to which an estimated 25,000 people came.[12] Further on in the book, she describes her meeting in the Coliseum on the Chautauqua Grounds in Montwait, Massachusetts:

> Thousands attended the meetings. The miracles were as great as in the days of Christ and the apostles. The fear of God came on the people as they saw the sick carried in, dying on beds, and then rise up and shout praises to God and walk and run. They saw them leap and dance.[13]

Interestingly enough, the other Pentecostal evangelist whose revival campaigns attracted tens of thousands was also a woman—Aimee Semple McPherson.[14] Carl Brumback, historian of the Assemblies of God, has evaluated her efforts thus:

> Aimee Semple McPherson was a member of the Assemblies of God for only three years (1919–1922), but it was her great campaigns (before, during, and after these years) which placed innumerable "Council" (i.e., Assemblies of God) Churches on the map. Before "Sister Aimee" came, many of the assemblies were but small, struggling missions in city after

[10] "Mulheim Conference," *Word and Work,* XXXII (Sept., 1910), 282 f.

[11] See her *Acts of the Holy Ghost* (Dallas: John F. Worley Publishing Co., [1904?]), for an account of her life and a record of her sermons.

[12] Indianapolis: Privately Printed, 1922, p. 45.

[13] *Ibid.,* p. 157.

[14] See *This Is That* (Los Angeles: Echo Park Evangelistic Association, 1923), for a collection of her personal experiences, sermons, and writings.

city: Washington, D.C., Baltimore, Philadelphia, Rochester, Akron, Dayton, Canton, Tampa, Miami, Jacksonville, St. Louis, Chicago, Wichita, Tulsa, Denver, Dallas, San Diego, Los Angeles, San Francisco, Montreal, and Toronto. Everywhere Mrs. McPherson preached mammoth crowds were attracted and the attention of churches and ministers was drawn to the Pentecostal message.[15]

In addition to mass meetings, tabloid-size newspapers were an effective means of disseminating the message of Pentecostalism to the far-flung corners of the globe. The intent of all thirty-four periodicals which came into existence between 1900 and 1908[16] is perhaps most lucidly presented in A. A. Boddy's lead editorial in the first issue of *Confidence* which appeared in England in 1908. As recorded by Donald Gee, Boddy affirmed that the paper of which he was editor was

> meant to be a means of grace and encouragement. Encouragement to lonely ones and scattered bands, to those who are attacked by doubt and difficulty, but longing to be loyal to the Almighty Deliverer. They will find from these columns that they are not alone, as regards even human fellowship, but there are many who have perfect "confidence" that this work is of God, and who will be rejoiced to know that His Pentecostal blessing is spreading all the time.[17]

The content of those early Pentecostal newspapers included sermonic material that dealt predominantly with the Pentecostal experience and attendant spiritual blessings,[18] information concerning Pentecostal activities—openings of new missions, announcements of tent meetings or camp meetings—and an extensive "testimony section" which contained accounts of people who had been healed or "saved, sanctified, and filled with the Holy Ghost" (a phrase which appears often in those early periodicals). In an anthology of articles which he selected from *The Church of God Evangel,* Charles W. Conn, a former editor, wrote: "These testimonies have consistently

[15] Brumback, *Suddenly from Heaven,* p. 272.

[16] This information was gleaned from the files of the Canadian Pentecostal paper, *Pentecostal Testimony* (Apr., 1936), pp. 8–9, which are available in broken series at the Missionary Research Library, Union Theological Seminary, New York.

[17] Gee, *Pentecostal Movement,* p. 41.

[18] The writer is indebted to *The Evangel Reader,* edited and compiled by Charles W. Conn (Cleveland, Tenn.: The Pathway Press, 1958), for data concerning the substance of these early Pentecostal papers.

been and remain today some of the most touching items within the covers of the paper."[19]

The pioneering effort in American Pentecostal journalism was Charles Fox Parham's *The Apostolic Faith,* which appeared just before the turn of the century.[20] It was published twice a month and distributed freely. In the next few years other papers with the same masthead appeared, originating from such places as Los Angeles, and Portland, Oregon. As mentioned earlier, by 1908 about thirty-four other journals had come into being, proclaiming the "Latter Rain," "Apostolic Faith," or "Pentecostal" point of view. (It is interesting to note that only in a few instances is the word "Pentecostal" used.) A partial list of the papers that appeared in America includes: *Word and Work* (Framingham, Massachusetts), *The Mid-Night Cry* (Seattle), *The Bridegroom's Messenger* (Atlanta), and *Pentecost in the Twin Cities* (Minneapolis). Canadian Pentecostals were publishing *The Apostolic Messenger* (ed. A. H. Argue), and *The Promise* (Toronto). As noted, Alexander A. Boddy was engaged in editing *Confidence,* and *Liberty and Gladness* was coming out of Edinburgh, Scotland. Thomas Ball Barratt involved himself in the herculean task of printing *Korsets Seir* not only in Norwegian but also in Swedish, Finnish, Russian, German, and Spanish. *Pfingstgrüsse* was the German Pentecostal publication which was edited by Jonathan Paul, and *Spade Regan* originated in Amsterdam.

After 1908, a host of other Pentecostal newspapers appeared. Those whose names are known to us include: *Latter Rain Evangel* (ed. William H. Piper of Chicago), *The Pentecostal Testimony* (ed. William H. Durham of Chicago), *The Word and Witness* (ed. Eudorus N. Bell), *Christian Evangel* (ed. J. Roswell Flower of Indiana), *A Call to Faith* (ed. D. W. Griffin of Wardensville, West Virginia), and *New Acts* (ed. Levi R. Lupton).[21]

The Pentecostal movement, writes Carl Brumback, "is at home

[19] *Ibid.,* p. 14.

[20] Kendrick, *Promise Fulfilled,* p. 46.

[21] Most of these journals were short-lived. There were too many of them to be absorbed by a rather small constituency. Most of the larger ones united under new mastheads to become denominational periodicals. For example, *The Word and Witness* and the *Christian Evangel* combined (*ca.* 1914) to become the *Pentecostal Evangel*—weekly "voice" of the Assemblies of God.

among the people of all languages, lands, and climes."[22] It was this democratic tendency more than anything else we have mentioned thus far which drew men and women of both high and low estate to the youthful movement. There was little or no discrimination among the early Pentecostals; it seemed to be eradicated by the profound religious experience through which they passed.

Ethel Goss tells about a camp meeting in Houston in August, 1906: "Fresh from the revival in Los Angeles, Sister Lucy Farrow returned to attend this Camp meeting. Although colored, she was received as a messenger of the Lord to us, even in the Deep South of Texas."[23] This more vivid account of an encounter between a Negro and a Southerner appears in Brumback's *Suddenly from Heaven:*

> G. B. Cashwell, a minister of the Holiness Association of North Carolina, went to Azusa in 1906. While waiting before the Lord, Cashwell was disturbed to notice that a young colored man was praying with him, and even more disturbed when he asked, "Do you want me to pray for you so that you will receive the Holy Ghost?" This was a little too much for this *Southern* Christian, and he was just at the point of telling the would-be helper to help someone else, when the Lord whispered to him, "This young man is deeply in earnest, and I have sent him. How badly do you want to be filled?" Cashwell wanted God to manifest His power more than he wanted to manifest his racial prejudice, so he meekly consented. The result of this desegregation at the throne of grace? A proud Southerner was filled by the "Holy Ghost sent down from heaven" where there are no racial distinctions at all.[24]

Perhaps this excerpt from Frank Bartleman's diary epitomizes the philosophy of the early Pentecostals regarding such things as color and status. In speaking of the Azusa Street revival, which was presided over by William J. Seymour, a Negro, and indicating that there was no platform or pulpit that would separate the pastor from the people, Bartleman said: "All were on a level. . . . We did not honor men for their advantage, in means or education, but rather for their God-given 'gifts.' "[25]

[22] *Suddenly from Heaven,* p. 118.
[23] *Winds of God,* p. 56.
[24] P. 84.
[25] Bartleman, *Pentecost,* p. 58.

Further evidence of their democratization is that very early in their history the Pentecostals recognized the vital role that women could play in a spiritual awakening. They utilized them as pastors, evangelists, and missionaries. Perhaps this accounts for the multitudes of women who were won to Pentecostalism in those early years.

Without a doubt, the emphasis on divine healing, one of the most distinctive Pentecostal tenets, was responsible for attracting great crowds in the early days. An editorial entitled "Marvelous Healings" which appeared in the 1914 issue of *The Church of God Evangel* perhaps illustrates this:

> There have been some remarkable cases of healings reported occasionally through the press for many years, but since the falling of the "latter rain" in Los Angeles eight years ago, these reports have grown more numerous.
>
> During this period of time a large number of Pentecostal papers have been circulated throughout the world. The contents of these papers have been principally reports of great meetings, healings, miracles, and wonders performed by the power of God. Almost everything that is recorded in the Book of Acts has been reported, from the slightest pain to the most stubborn disease of long standing. Broken bones, . . . burns have been instantly healed. . . . Many kinds of incurable ailments have yielded to the power of God in answer to the prayer of faith. . . .
>
> . . . .
>
> The names of a few people have become so noted that wherever they go great crowds are attracted to their meetings.[26]

We have already noted how successful Mrs. Mary B. Woodworth-Etter and Charles Fox Parham were in establishing flourishing centers for the new movement because vast crowds attended their meetings. For example Galena, Kansas, became a stronghold of Pentecostalism because of Parham's campaign there in 1903–1904; and, furthermore, he had been invited there initially because one of the townspeople, Mrs. Mary Arthur, had been healed in one of his meetings in El Dorado Springs, Missouri. The Cincinnati *Inquirer* reporter who was assigned to cover the Galena revival wrote:

> But of all the wonderful things which has [*sic*] transpired in connection with these meetings *nothing has attracted the attention of the people* as has

[26] James A. Cross (ed.), *Healing in the Church,* p. 42.

[*sic*] the "healings" [italics mine], which have not been confined to the ignorant, uneducated class of people. On the contrary, some of the most conservative, intelligent persons, not only here but within a radius of over 100 miles, have visited "the healer," with wonderful results.[27]

In a typically modest British manner, Donald Gee indicates a similar correlation between healings and the opening of new works: "In another part of Edinburgh, Mrs. MacPherson, who had received a miraculous healing, also commenced Pentecostal meetings in her home, where many were blessed."[28]

The Pentecostals received a fair hearing in southern Texas during one of their first revivals because the wife of a Houston attorney, Mrs. DeLaney, was healed after three years of untold suffering. She had been injured in a streetcar accident, and there had been considerable publicity in the papers as a result of her paralytic condition and the litigation proceedings against the transit company. One day as she was being wheeled down the street, she chanced to hear the Pentecostals who were conducting an outdoor meeting. She became interested and was brought to Bryan Hall, where they worshiped indoors. What happened at that service has been reported by Henry Tothill, one of the men who helped to carry her upstairs to the meeting:

> She said that the Lord had said for her to get up; they helped her to her feet, and she walked and was healed. This healing attracted the attention of the entire city.[29]

In addition to ministering to the physical needs of people, the Pentecostals also met their psychological requirements. Some years ago Charles B. Braden suggested that one of the reasons for the phenomenal growth of sects is that they provide members with an opportunity for emotional release which fulfills for them a genuine psychological function.[30] Pentecostal music provided ample opportunity for such emotional release. In commenting on congregational singing in the "early days," Howard A. Goss said: "It was generally not the con-

[27] Quoted in Kendrick, *Promise Fulfilled,* p. 59.

[28] Gee, *Pentecostal Movement,* p. 33.

[29] Quoted in Brumback, *Suddenly from Heaven,* p. 32.

[30] "Sectarianism Run Wild," *Protestantism* (a symposium edited by William K. Anderson, Nashville: Commission on Courses of Study, The Methodist Church, 1944), p. 115.

ventional church-hymn singing of that era. . . . It could have been most aptly described, I think, Scripturally as a 'joyful sound.' "[31] Further on in this delightful essay on "gospel singing" Goss recalls that when the young people got a chance to sing, "they exploded. Every particle of their being was poured into worship as they sang, nothing slowed them down, nor did their leaders attempt to curb them."[32] It is Goss's opinion that this crescendo of joyous, happy people "singing unto the Lord" was infectious, and he concludes by saying that "without it the Pentecostal movement could never have made the quick inroads into hearts that it did."[33]

Furthermore, if a person played a musical instrument—string, wind, or percussion, it mattered not—he felt free to bring it to church. Even the smallest missions had an orchestra. When French psychologist, Jules Bois, visited some Pentecostal missions in New York City during the early twenties, he wrote: "In an angle of the hall, the ministers have organized a little orchestra of three violins, two huge trombones, and a piano."[34]

At a Pentecostal meeting a person could, if he wished, clap his hands, tap his feet, cry, pray audibly, speak forth in tongues if he "felt the Spirit leading," dance, or exhort his brethren during the testimony meeting. While it may be true, as Braden intimates, that the masses who comprised the early Pentecostal constituency were those who did not have access to the usual avenues of emotional release utilized by the membership of the "regular" churches—the theater, sports, travel, literature, and art—one wonders if the Pentecostal revival meeting did not also compensate in some measure for the austere holiness code which the Pentecostals inherited from their progenitors, the Holiness movement. It was not so much that the Pentecostals could not afford amusements, athletics, or a cultured existence, as it was that they felt these things to be "sinful" or "worldly." Thus they "sanctified" activities which would under differing conditions be construed as "worldly" —dancing, shouting, clapping, "jazzy" singing and playing—with the explanation that they were now Spirit-directed.

[31] Goss, *Winds of God,* p. 128.
[32] *Ibid.,* p. 130.
[33] *Ibid.,* p. 132.
[34] "The New Religions of America," *The Forum,* LXXIII (Feb., 1925), 146.

The view of some psychologists of religion like Anton Boisen is that Pentecostalism provided many who were frustrated by the sorrows and injustices of the world in which they lived a hope—in a future world.[35] While attending a Pentecostal convention in Chattanooga, Boisen noted that nine of the eleven songs which he heard during an evening service had an other-worldly theme: "That Home of the Soul Over There," "When We Cross the Great Divide," "I'll Never Feel at Home in This World Anymore," to list just a few. Thus it might be said of the Pentecostals that they did not seek to save the world, but rather to save individuals out of a world which they felt was getting progressively worse, and that this approach gained them many adherents in the hard, lean years just prior to and following World War I.

In conclusion, as one reads the fragmentary source materials that remain from the early decades of the Pentecostal movement, one is impressed by the conviction of its early adherents. Assurance and confidence seem to exude from their meager biographies, memoirs, editorials, and sermons. A sentence which frequently appears in their writings is, "We want a fresh touch [or anointing] from God." When they received that "touch" (usually associated with an impartation of, or refilling by, the Holy Spirit), they seemed to acquire a poise and a boldness which prepared them to face any exigency. It was this certainty, the sense of reality that emanated from them, which undoubtedly attracted people. The Pentecostals were convincing, someone has said, because they themselves were convinced.

To put it another way, the Pentecostal preacher believed that he was proclaiming an "End Time" message. He was convinced that the experiences of Acts 2 were relevant not only to the past. He expected signs and wonders to accompany his ministry. He believed that miracles were not obsolete. He preached that there could be power and happiness in the life of a person who had been truly regenerated and filled with the Spirit. All of this ran counter to what Goss informs us was "a defeatist religion that was proclaimed and believed everywhere."[36]

[35] Anton Boisen, "Religion and Hard Times," *Social Action,* V (Mar., 1939), 16.

[36] Goss, *Winds of God,* pp. 11, 148 f.

The tremendous sacrifices which Pentecostal preachers and evangelists made in the early days also impressed the onlookers. Like Chaucer's "Povre Persoun" ("first he wroughte, and afterward he taughte"), there was nothing that would not be sacrificed—material possessions, fame, time—for God's work. Goss writes concerning his call to the ministry (1905):

I sold my horse, rig, and everything I had and bought a ticket to Houston [for on-the-job training in evangelism under the tutelage of Charles Parham]. I gave the remaining funds to the general treasury, since we were to have all things in common. Thus I started out with my pockets empty of money, but my heart brimful of zeal and courage for the Lord.[37]

Many of the early Pentecostals were lay preachers. One such was William J. Mitchell, who wrote about his efforts in Chelsea, Massachusetts. In the spring of 1907, a Brother and Sister Lee, evangelists from the South, arrived in Chelsea and stayed until late June. During that period of time and in the months immediately after, about forty seekers received the Holy Spirit baptism. The important point to this phase of the discussion is the sentences: "With the help of the brethren, I continued to carry on the meetings the rest of the year, besides working at my trade as a carpenter. The news spread that the Lord was blessing, so that people came from everywhere, making it necessary for us to move into a larger building."[38]

Men such as Mitchell obviously had to make a sacrifice of time. So too did the participants in the following incident.

A young woman was mentally ill and some Pentecostal people had been praying for her recovery. When she had fully regained control of her senses, and her benefactors reported her healing, they wrote: "It was not accomplished by a single prayer, but it took a regular campaign of united prayer, night and day for nearly five days. Relays of workers were kept at the home to watch and pray continuously, for it was a desperate fight. . . . But oh, how precious has been the deliverance and the testimony of the sister in our meetings."[39]

The sacrifice and devotion of Pentecostals in the area of foreign

[37] *Ibid.*, p. 29.

[38] Quoted in Brumback, *Suddenly from Heaven*, pp. 82 f.

[39] "The Early Days of Pentecost," *Pentecostal Evangel*, XXXIII (Aug. 11, 1945), 3.

missions also enabled them to gain adherents rapidly. Their missionary program in those early days, like Parham's school in Topeka, the publication of newspapers, and the services of evangelists and preachers, was a "faith" venture. This unique mode of financing is best described by Gee as he recounts the formation in 1909 of the British "Pentecostal Missionary Union."

> The principles of the Pentecostal Missionary Union were very largely formulated upon the model of the China Inland Mission. . . . It was therefore what is generally known as a "faith mission," and the Directors did not guarantee any fixed amount of support of workers, but sought faithfully to distribute the funds available.[40]

Back in 1910, the Church of God (Cleveland, Tennessee) did not even have a "faith" program for R. M. Evans, their first missionary. He sold his home in Durant, Florida, and his few cows, hogs, and chickens. With the proceeds, he bought a wagon and a team of mules. Accompanied by his wife, he drove to Miami, which was three hundred miles away, stored the wagon, and sold the mules for enough money to book passage to the Bahamas.[41]

Perhaps the one policy above all others that accounted for the warm reception which people in other lands accorded both Pentecostal missionaries and their message was the principle of establishing indigenous churches. It was not a consciously developed policy, but it proved to be successful, and it was to be imitated later by many of the larger denominations. Noel Perkin, an elder statesman among Pentecostal missions directors, summarized the indigenous policy thus:

> We do not go to Americanize the people, but to Christianize them and allow them to conduct their work, ministry, and worship in the way that conforms to their own interpretation of the Scriptures. We seek to establish national self-supporting churches in every land.[42]

The triumphant tone of these pages notwithstanding, the youthful Pentecostal movement, while experiencing phenomenal growth, was likewise forced to encounter several serious crises during its early history. Some of the personalities who had led it so successfully at first

[40] Gee, *Pentecostal Movement,* p. 47.
[41] Conn, *Like a Mighty Army,* p. 112.
[42] Cited in Brumback, *Suddenly from Heaven,* p. 343.

fell into error, and some of the *distinctive* features of the early revival which at the outset were attractive to many because of their novelty lost their appeal. Thus, Pentecostalism was rent by internal dissension and encountered severe opposition from other religious groups.

CHAPTER 6

Pentecostals Encounter Violent Opposition

ANTI-PENTECOSTAL SENTIMENT

That Pentecostalism was initially successful cannot be gainsaid. It seemed to be scripturally oriented and appeared to be the answer to the prayers of countless thousands as the revitalizing force needed to combat the spiritual lethargy which they felt had engulfed the religious world of the early twentieth century. Within a short time, however, the Pentecostal revival became the object of scurrilous attacks. It was denounced as "anti-Christian," as "sensual and devilish," and as "the last vomit of Satan." Its adherents were taunted and derided from the pulpit as well as in the religious and the secular press. Some leaders were actually subjected to violence. Those ministers and missionaries from the old-line denominations who embraced the doctrine of a Holy Spirit baptism were removed from their pulpits or dismissed by their mission boards. A few examples of the various expressions of anti-Pentecostal sentiment will obviously suffice.

Most of the established denominations rejected anyone who was a Pentecostal sympathizer, so to speak. Joseph Smale, pastor of the First Baptist Church in Los Angeles, feeling that a revival was desirable in his church, commenced to pray and instruct his people to expect a supernatural visitation from God. Frank Bartleman reports:

The meetings had run daily in the First Baptist Church for fifteen weeks.

It was now September [1905]. The officials of the church were tired of the innovation and wanted to return to the old order. He was told to either stop the revival or get out. He wisely chose the latter.[1]

In eastern Canada there flourished a group called the Mennonite Brethren in Christ, which was headed by an outstanding evangelist-pastor, Solomon Eby. About 1909, A. G. Ward, who had received his Pentecostal experience in the Chicago revival two years earlier, was invited to preach at the Mennonite Church in Berlin (now Kitchener), Ontario. A Pentecostal revival occurred; many were filled with the Holy Spirit and were speaking in tongues, among them Elder Solomon Eby. But there were also many who objected to the Pentecostal teaching, and "Solomon Eby was turned out of the church that he had served for forty years and of which he had been the founder."[2]

The Baptists in Sweden also banished those members who accepted the Pentecostal viewpoint. Lewi Pethrus, formerly a Baptist pastor and now a revered member of the Filadelfia Church (Pentecostal) in Sweden, recalls the event thus:

> In 1910, a Baptist chuch was organized in Stockholm which stood for Pentecost, and I was called to be their pastor. All the members were baptized in the Spirit and they said, "This assembly shall remain Pentecostal." The church began with 29 members but in 1913 it had grown to 500 members. Then something happened. The Baptist church excommunicated us from their denomination.[3]

In Chile, where Pentecostalism was rampant in 1909, Dr. Willis C. Hoover was encountering criticism from his colleagues and his bishop for his permissive attitude. Finally,

> in February, 1910, the conference met. They felt that they would settle the matter by sending Dr. Hoover home on furlough. . . . Knowing the disposition of the bishop, the pastor resigned from the pastorate of the Methodist Episcopal church.[4]

Although Donald Gee does not elaborate on his comment regarding the relations between Pentecostal believers and other English Protestants, he does state that "in Britain the Pentecostal Movement received

[1] Bartleman, *Pentecost,* pp. 28 f.
[2] Frodsham, *Signs Following,* pp. 54 f.
[3] *Ibid.,* p. 78.
[4] *Ibid.,* pp. 180 f.

the most determined, capable and prejudiced opposition that it encountered anywhere in the whole world."[5]

To summarize the reaction of the Presbyterian Church to Pentecostalism, here is the motion passed in a meeting of the session of the Los Angeles Presbyterian Church (date not given):

> The session declares most emphatically that our Confession of Faith gives no room for holding, teaching, or expressing sympathy for, participating in, or attending so-called "Pentecostal" or tongues meetings.
>
> . . . From this time onward, no man or woman will be allowed to hold membership in this church who is sympathetic with, has part in, or attempts to bring this teaching among our people, or attempts to send members or attendants of this church to places where this so-called Pentecostal movement holds sway.[6]

Perhaps the event which illustrates the anti-Pentecostal sentiment most dramatically occurred at the 1919 General Assembly of the Pentecostal Church of the Nazarene. The motion was made and adopted that the word "Pentecostal" be deleted from the official title of the denomination.

> in order that the Church of the Nazarene might not be confused with the modern Pentecost of "tongues" movement which advocates speaking in tongues as an evidence of holiness. This view is repudiated by the Church of the Nazarene.[7]

While many who espoused Pentecostalism were frequently rejected by various denominations, happily only a few were subjected to physical abuse. In North Carolina, however, for a period of six years, concluding in 1902, the people who preached and practiced the Holiness-Pentecostal way of life were terrorized in the most inhuman ways. It is well to recall that one of the very first outbursts of Pentecostalism in the United States occurred in Cherokee County, North Carolina. It was here that a nucleus of Pentecostal-Holiness believers was formed that became the precursor of the extensive Pentecostal group—the Church of God (Cleveland, Tennessee). At first, writes Charles W.

[5] Gee, *Pentecostal Movement,* p. 89.

[6] Cited in "Persecution of Pentecostals," in *Pentecostal Testimony* (May, 1938), p. 11.

[7] Harold W. Reed, "The Growth of a Contemporary Sect-Type Institution as Reflected in the Development of the Church of the Nazarene" (Unpublished Th.D. dissertation, University of So. California, 1943), p. 126.

Conn, the Methodists discounted the revivals as nothing more than an extreme manifestation of what had transpired earlier among themselves in the frontier revivals, and the Baptists shrugged off the revivals as being nothing more than an extreme form of Methodist fervor. However, when it became clear that these Pentecostal-Holiness people were engaged in speaking languages that could not be understood, that they were falling into trances under the power of God, and that they were praying for the healing of the sick and afflicted, toleration ceased.[8]

First, the doctrine of a Holy Spirit baptism was repudiated as being heretical. Those who claimed it or sought it were accused variously of lunacy or idiocy and disfellowshiped. The Liberty Baptist Church in Patrick, North Carolina, excluded 33 persons for having "Pentecostal" inclinations.[9]

Next, the officials of Cherokee County prohibited those early Pentecostals from using the Shearer School for worship. Heretofore, it had been available for use by all local religious groups. The locked-out believers were awarded a plot of land by a sympathetic onlooker. They hewed and trimmed logs, cleared the land, and erected a crude log church. For a year things remained quiet; then the Pentecostals began to be persecuted with ferocious intensity. The church was set on fire; homes were burned. Then came the culmination of the vandalism—since a downpour had doused the fire that had been set earlier, the attackers resorted to dynamite. A sizable section of the log structure was destroyed. Soon thereafter, in a brazen daylight raid, writes Conn, a mob, composed of "several ministers, stewards and deacons, one justice of the peace and one sheriff" tore down the structure log by log and then set fire to the logs.[10]

Finally, William F. Bryant, who had been the leader of the original Cherokee County revival as a co-laborer with R. G. Spurling, was struck down by buckshot. Homes were plundered, sources of water polluted, and crops destroyed. The persecution ceased and violence declined only after 106 men were prosecuted by Cherokee County.

[8] *Like a Mighty Army*, p. 29.
[9] *Ibid.*, p. 30.
[10] *Ibid.*, pp. 32 f.

Reasons for Mounting Opposition

Donald Gee reminds us that the more conservative elements of the Christian Church have always looked askance at revival movements.

Even the preceding "Holiness" movements had been either rejected or treated with cool caution. The Welsh Revival had come in for much criticism in many quarters on account of its emotional scenes. How much more, therefore, the new Pentecostal Movement.[11]

However, atypical scenes such as the following—which were read, or which were reported orally, or which were witnessed firsthand—were certain to arouse caustic criticism from a vast segment of Christendom,

In Portland, Oregon, . . . what we saw and heard beggars description. The excitement was nerve-wracking. As many as a dozen prayed—rather *screamed*—at one time. "Tongues" were much in evidence, and here there were interpreters too. . . . Almost at our feet a man fell over on his back, writhing and foaming as in an epileptic fit. I suggested getting him out of the close, hot room. . . . "Keep your hands off God's ark," someone shouted. "This is the Holy Ghost." For forty minutes by the clock he writhed there on the floor and at last fell back limp and lay as though dead. Then a "worker" jumped on his breast, put his mouth to the unconscious man's nose, and cried, "Receive ye the Holy Ghost!" and blew powerfully into the nostrils. This was repeated over and over again—a most disgusting spectacle. Finally the man opened his eyes, rose, sat quietly on a chair, weary, and with no apparent result. . . . I was told afterwards of seven persons sent to insane asylums from that mission; and I saw and conversed with a baldheaded girl of about seventeen, who had contracted brainfever through the unnatural excitement, and had lost her hair in her illness.[12]

Robert P. Richardson submitted an account of a Pentecostal meeting which used to be held in Victoria Hall on Spring Street in Los Angeles. Somewhat laconically he remarked that it was referred to as the "Free Vaudeville Show on Spring Street." After presenting what strikes this writer as being a rather flippant, nevertheless graphically picturesque, description of the preliminaries, he proceeds to inform us that the "meeting gets warmed up" and "the saints begin to speak in tongues."

[11] Gee, *Pentecostal Movement,* p. 17.
[12] Stolee, *Speaking in Tongues,* p. 66.

> Concurrently with the speaking in tongues, dancing is going on. . . . An elderly matron arises and holding her arms out horizontally, pirouttes [*sic*] majestically to and fro in front of the altar. A sturdy, bearded, son of the soil jumps up and down, rising each time an astonishing distance in the air. On the platform the pastor, while likewise leaping up and down, whirls around and around like a dancing dervish. A female saint takes it into her head to dance up one aisle and down the other, and proceeds to do this, keeping time to the music provided by a burly negro who follows her with a banjo. . . . All the saints proceed to stand on tip toe and groan and shriek at the top of their voices for several minutes.[13]

Modern Pentecostals do not deny that such extravagances did occur in the developmental stage of the movement. "Truth must honestly admit that there were scenes in the first rush of new spiritual enthusiasm and experience that no reputable Christian worker would now seek to defend or excuse."[14] The explanations which Pentecostals have offered for such intemperate indulgences include the following: (1) The emotional excesses were a reaction against the stiffness and formality of the churches from which they came.[15] (2) There were few leaders in those early days with enough experience in orgiastic behavior to be able to discern it; most of them were fearful lest they "quench the Spirit."[16] (3) The early Pentecostals attributed *everything* to the "leading of the Spirit," not realizing, as Carl Brumback points out, that what occurs is attributable

> both to the divine and the human: the divine responsible for the inward feeling [the warmth, the thrill of the presence of God], the human for the outward manner in which the divinely-kindled feeling is expressed.[17]

Some religious groups such as the Christian and Missionary Alliance, perhaps, would have tolerated someone who obviously was "under the inspiration of the Holy Spirit" to speak forth in tongues, provided that it was interpreted and brought edification to all; but they, together with the majority of other religious groups, frowned upon the superfluity of *glossolalia* which characterized so many of the

[13] Robert P. Richardson, "Pentecostal Prophets," *Open Court,* XLII (1928), 678 f.
[14] Gee, *Pentecostal Movement,* p. 18.
[15] *Idem.*
[16] *Idem.*
[17] Brumback, *Suddenly from Heaven,* p. 111.

Pentecostal meetings: the dozen or more messages in tongues which Brumback implies frequently occurred.[18]

Apparently the gift of prophecy was likewise prostituted. To the Pentecostal, prophecy is entirely supernatural. "As speaking with tongues is supernatural utterance in an unknown tongue, so prophecy is a supernatural utterance in a known tongue. It is a manifestation of the Spirit of God, and not of the human mind."[19] The gift has strong support for its congregational use in the writings of St. Paul (I Cor. 12); but what happened in the early days of the Pentecostal movement was that many preoccupied themselves with the acquisition and the demonstration of this gift, using it to correct, rebuke, foretell, and direct. Thus functioning as the voice of the Spirit, they placed greater emphasis upon themselves as prophets and upon their utterances than upon the leadership of the appointed pastor or in the instruction which the scriptures give. Needless to say, this misguided emphasis would be deplored by the established churches on the grounds that Pentecostals were prophesying out of their own spirit rather than *the* Spirit. Sad to say, there is ample evidence to prove that people who were completely unsuited for the mission field were directed by a prophetic utterance to go abroad.[20] Others were instructed "by the Spirit" as to whom they should marry, and the gullibility accorded such prophecies often led naïve couples to be mismatched.[21]

Many denominations were obviously disturbed by the fact that their members withdrew to join a tent meeting of a store-front mission and that before too long the tent would be folded up, the mission abandoned, and the itinerant Pentecostal preacher would move on. Apparently this was quite common, and Pentecostalism was justifiably denounced as a "fly-by-night" religion. Why the sudden departures? Brumback supposed that two factors were responsible: (1) The itinerant preacher-evangelist had probably run out of sermons. "Few

[18] *Ibid.*, p. 112.

[19] Horton, *Gifts of the Spirit,* p. 178.

[20] Brumback, *Suddenly from Heaven,* p. 112.

[21] For an interesting narrative about a Spirit-directed marriage see Goss, *Winds of God,* pp. 105 f. and 140–47. Consult Joseph Campbell, *The Pentecostal Holiness Church* (Franklin Springs, Ga.: The Publishing House of the Pentecostal Holiness Church, 1951), pp. 267 ff., for a description of the "Gift Movement" which flourished in Virginia around 1916.

Pentecostal preachers had enough sermons to last longer than a month of meetings."[22] (2) The evangelist firmly believed that he had been "called" to evangelize, not to pastor. His function was to ignite the fires of revival, and "to get a forest fire going on a grand scale; all that one need do is to run from place to place, apply the torch, and get out of the way! Never look back, just keep going."[23]

To the detriment of the Pentecostal movement, too many of its early leaders tenaciously held to the view "that those who were filled with the Spirit needed no one to instruct them."[24] Admittedly the following citation is extreme, for it represents the thinking of a radical group within Pentecostalism; however, the sentiment expressed does reflect the anti-intellectualism of many of the early Pentecostals. It concerns the Holy Rollers of Dayton, Tennessee, who worshiped in an "arbor church" because they had no church building. ("God frowns upon money!") Preacher Joe Leffew speaks:

> "I ain't got no learnin' an' never had none. . . . Glory be to the Lamb! Some folks work their hands off'n up 'n to the elbows to give their young-uns education, and all they do is send their young-uns to hell."
>
> "Glory to His name," shouted the huddled figures, mist-gray in the night damp.
>
> "I ain't let no newspaper in my cabin for nigh unto a year since the Lord bathed me in His blood." . . .
>
> "Glory to the Lamb," wailed the chorus of the saved.
>
> "I never sinned enough to look in one of these here almanacs."
>
> "Praise His name," wailed the chorus of the saved.[25]

A more temperate account reflecting the same attitude—the superiority of being divinely trained rather than book trained, as it were—is this commentary by Howard A. Goss:

> Scriptural preaching is entirely dependent for its power upon the Holy Spirit. . . . While we poured in the Holy Scriptures, heated on our part by prayer, by fasting, by self-denial, by consecrated zeal, . . . God was adroitly manipulating every heart and mind and every conscience that few people could ever be the same again after sitting through one service. . . .

[22] Brumback, *Suddenly from Heaven,* p. 108.
[23] *Idem.*
[24] Campbell, *Pentecostal Holiness Church,* p. 204.
[25] Allene M. Sumner, "The Holy Rollers on Shin Bone Ridge," *The Nation,* CXXI (July 29, 1925), 138.

Those who succumbed to being bookworms, . . . He gently steered toward quiet, shallow waters where we lost sight of them. They *could be satisfied with less,* so less they got! Why? Because books are in themselves only dead things. . . .[26]

This antipathy toward education, this premium that seemed to be placed on sanctified ignorance, was revulsive to a host of Protestants, even the fundamentalists, who had established Bible institutes in Chicago (Moody) and New York (Nyack) as junior-grade seminaries in which they attempted to fuse the spiritual and the scholarly pursuits.

Pentecostalism, not unlike most religious groups, was embarrassed rather early in its development by the immoral behavior of a few of its early leaders and adherents. Because of their status in the movement and because of the lofty claims which Pentecostals had laid on a superior type of spirituality, the disclosure of their promiscuity got widespread publicity, and the Pentecostal movement was again bitterly denounced—especially in denominational journals and religious publications.

As one searches through Pentecostal literature, one is able to recover little factual data as to the precise nature of the alleged indiscretions. Brumback offers the explanation for these lacunae:

We do not possess all the facts. In some cases, no actual proof of transgression was submitted. . . . Some of the offenders made a courageous comeback, and by their impeccable conduct regained the respect of the entire Movement. Relatives are the only ones left, in many instances, to bear the stigma and shame.[27]

In any case, most of the information that is obtainable is couched in generalized statements or allusions. Joseph Campbell, historian of the Pentecostal Holiness Church, states that "Mr. Cashwell [a prominent figure for a time in Pentecostal Holiness circles] did grievously fail God and bring reproach on the cause of the full gospel of Pentecostal Holiness."[28] Howard Goss informs us that while he was engaged in evangelistic work in McGregor, Texas, in 1907,

The greatest test of our lives came for Satan struck our movement a terrible blow from within. One of our leading ministers fell into an awful

[26] Goss, *Winds of God,* p. 65.
[27] Brumback, *Suddenly from Heaven,* pp. 113 f.
[28] Campbell, *Pentecostal Holiness Church,* p. 24.

sin, which turned out to be only a temporary affair, as he repented, confessed, was forgiven, and afterward lived an exemplary life so far as I ever heard.[29]

And Brumback offers the following equally vacuous statements:

> Some divinely called men were also guilty of grave misconduct. Some preachers who were but a step removed from profligacy took that step backward. A few prominent men, after meriting the respect of all for their godly, capable leadership, failed to walk worthy of their high calling.[30]

Finally, the Pentecostals antagonized most of the denomination contemporaneous with themselves by acting as though they were selected by God as a sort of spiritual aristocracy.[31] Had not the insights regarding a Holy Spirit baptism and the gifts of the Spirit been revealed to them? they boasted. These manifestations of spiritual pomposity were perhaps a reaction to the charges which had been leveled at Pentecostalism by the established churches. Pentecostals were referred to as "the scum of society."[32] No decent person would have anything to do with such a religion—nobody, that is, except poor whites and Negroes.[33] But whatever the reason, and regardless of who precipitated the battle of words, the Pentecostals were quite supercilious in their attitude toward their fellow Christians. And this approach hardly earned them or their movement a hearty endorsement.

In his article, "Pentecostal Prophets," Robert P. Richardson describes a meeting in southern California in which the assistant pastor led the congregation in singing over and over again

> Out of the rubbish heap the Lord lifted me!
> Out of the rubbish heap the Lord lifted me!

The rubbish heap, as it turned out, was the Baptist Church in Seattle from which he had been drawn into Pentecostalism.[34]

[29] Goss, *Winds of God,* p. 78.
[30] Brumback, *Suddenly from Heaven,* p. 113.
[31] Gee, *Pentecostal Movement,* pp. 18 f.
[32] Campbell, p. 222.
[33] *Idem.*
[34] Pp. 676 f.

Another journalist, Duncan Aikman, relates the vision of a Church of God seeress which likewise reflects a subtle denigration of the established denominations.

> The power to discern spirits came upon her and she saw two churches. One was a fashionable church of fallen Methodism, and in its doorway a single devil lay fast asleep. But across the road, in the vestibule of a Holy Roller chapel, a score of demons flitted about as busy as bees. The sanctified are in more danger of Hell-fire than their merely "saved" neighbors because they are giving Satan his worst scare since the Apostolic Age.[35]

Another image that frequently titillated the fancies of Pentecostals, but whose exposition did little to endear them to the other religions, concerned their use of chiliastic vocabulary like "Church" and "Bride." Many Pentecostals expounded the view that while all believers were considered to constitute the "Church" only those who have been Spirit-baptized would be the "Bride of Christ." In short, at the "marriage supper of the Lamb," all the other believers would be on hand—to serve the "Bride."[36]

Other Pentecostal practices which aroused the hostility of Protestants include their asceticism, their denunciation of doctors and medicine, their opposition to "worldly ornamentation"—neckties and jewelry—and their alleged proselyting tactics.[37] Moreover, since few notable personalities embraced Pentecostalism in those early years, its critics decided that it must *obviously* be radical, spurious, and ephemeral.[38] Therefore, they felt obliged to repudiate the embryonic charismatic movement.

While it was annoying for Pentecostalism to be discredited, vilified, or ignored by outsiders, it was even more vexing to be rent by internal dissension and controversy.

[35] Duncan Aikman, "The Holy Rollers," *American Mercury,* XV (Oct., 1928), 187.

[36] For this recollection, the writer is indebted to Brumback, *Suddenly from Heaven,* p. 114.

[37] For a detailed summary of these points, see Campbell, *Pentecostal Holiness Church,* p. 204; and Conn, *Like a Mighty Army,* pp. 41 f.

[38] This seems to have been true especially in England, for Gee refers to it in his *Pentecostal Movement,* p. 17.

CHAPTER 7

Pentecostalism Menaced by Dissension

In retrospect, it appears that the most important causes for the factious attitude which developed rather early among Pentecostals centered around two matters: (1) leadership and authority, and (2) acceptable principles of organization and practice.

Discord Regarding Leadership and Authority

From the very beginning Pentecostals associated their introduction to the charismatic experience with the ministry of a certain outstanding personage in their area. In the deeply rural confines of the Tennessee-North Carolina-Georgia area, a modest group of Spirit-baptized believers which had organized originally in 1886 as the Christian Union, and which reorganized themselves on May 15, 1902, as The Holiness Church, and in 1907 finally adopted the name, Church of God, esteemed most highly A. J. Tomlinson.

Charles Fox Parham was the recognized leader in Kansas and Texas, for it was he who coined the distinctive name that was widely used by early Pentecostals—the Apostolic Faith. It was he who published the first Pentecostal periodical, *The Apostolic Faith;* it was he who organized the first large gatherings of Pentecostal believers on an interstate level; and it was he who first issued ministerial credentials to those who allied themselves with him.

The Pentecostals in the Los Angeles area revered William J. Seymour. Those in the Portland-Seattle area looked to Florence Louise

Crawford for guidance. William H. Durham, forceful pastor of the North Avenue Mission in Chicago and editor of *The Pentecostal Testimony,* became titular head of the Pentecostals in the Midwest and the East. As a matter of fact, Bartleman, a contemporary of Durham's, observes that "his word was coming to be almost law in the Pentecostal missions even as far as the Atlantic Coast."[1]

In Europe too each coterie of Pentecostal believers considered the person who had been responsible for spearheading the revival in their country to be their leader. Thus the British venerated Alexander A. Boddy; the Swedes, Lewi Pethrus; the Norwegians, Thomas Ball Barratt; and the Germans, Jonathan Paul. Around these dynamic individuals—"charismatic leaders," the sociologists of religion call them—developed deep allegiances. Their followers breathlessly awaited each new pronouncement, imitated every action.

> Each group, unconsciously, even copied its own leaders' mannerisms, even as they copied his life. Looking over a Camp Meeting or Convention audience, you could soon spot the followers of various leaders. Some might yell a quick "Amen" in a happy falsetto like Brother Pinson. Another might jerk his head a little to one side as Brother Durham did when the touch of God came upon him. Or some might have still more noticeable manifestations, if their leader happened to be of the spectacular type.[2]

The inevitable result was an invidious partisanship. Goss, with a tinge of sadness, picturesquely compares these tragic developments to the early days of the open West:

> It was obvious that we were almost following the primitive pattern of the wild Western mustangs which had once roamed the prairies. These creatures grouped themselves into many small bands, each following their own leader, but fighting every other leader and his band as well.
>
> This primeval state of things had never served the best interests of civilization; neither was our system now serving the best interests of the Kingdom of God.
>
> The cohesiveness which God had given us in the Baptism of the Holy Ghost through love was rapidly being lost through our lack of co-operation, and the spirit then abroad in the land which was endeavoring to separate us.[3]

[1] Bartleman, *How Pentecost Came,* p. 150.
[2] Goss, *Winds of God,* p. 166.
[3] *Idem.*

Not a single one of the early Pentecostal leaders could ever speak for the entire movement. Charles Fox Parham, for instance, had announced himself as "The Founder and Projector of the Apostolic Movement."[4] It was under this title that he issued ministerial credentials to those workers who labored with him in the Southwest. It was he, of course, who subsidized the trip of one of his students—William J. Seymour—to Los Angeles. And Seymour respected his mentor; he invited him to the Azusa Street Mission for a revival campaign in order that Parham could correct certain fanaticisms which were manifesting themselves. And yet when Parham arrived and attempted to instruct the people, he was denied access, and he was forced to conduct the rest of his services in the YMCA.[5] The animosity between the Pentecostals in Los Angeles and the Apostolic Faith movement represented by Parham and Seymour is perhaps best illustrated by this somewhat caustic comment:

> Why should they claim authority over us? We prayed down our own revival. The revival in California was unique and separate as to origin. It came from Heaven, even Brother Seymour not receiving the "baptism" until many others had entered in here. He did not arrive in Los Angeles until the "eleventh hour."[6]

William H. Durham was revered by a host of Pentecostal believers; nevertheless, when he returned to the Apostolic Faith Mission on Azusa Street—the place where he had received the Spirit baptism in 1907—and because he was instructing the people in a manner which contradicted a theory of sanctification that Seymour held, Frank Bartleman reports that "Brother Seymour . . . hastened back from the east and with his trustees decided to lock Brother Durham out."[7] Somewhat later in his narrative Bartleman adds that "the opposition against Brother Durham was tremendous and he was finally tempted to strike back."[8] How intense the opposition was to this outstanding Pentecostal leader is contained in Brumback's account of these events.[9] One of the members of the congregation, who is only identi-

[4] Brumback, *Suddenly from Heaven,* p. 58.
[5] *Ibid.,* p. 59.
[6] Bartleman, *How Pentecost Came,* p. 69.
[7] *Ibid.,* p. 146.
[8] *Ibid.,* p. 150.
[9] Brumback, *Suddenly from Heaven,* pp. 103 f.

fied by the name "Bridgitt"—a converted prostitute from the infamous Barbary Coast—resented Durham's teaching so intensely that she attacked him with her hat pin.

The situation was no different in Europe. In England, Alexander A. Boddy, the godly vicar of All Saints' Church in Sunderland, was generally acknowledged to be the leader of British Pentecostalism. It was in his parish that the charismatic revival had erupted; he was the editor of the Pentecostal journal, *Confidence;* and it was he who inaugurated the Whitsuntide conventions which were attended by many Pentecostals in the British Isles as well as those from the Continent. But Boddy was first and foremost an Anglican. He practiced "infant sprinkling"; he discouraged the formation of separate Pentecostal assemblies, saying "receive the Holy Spirit, but remain in your church, whatever the denomination may be."[10] Thus, regardless of how pious or astute Boddy was, he could never assert his views authoritatively and expect them to be endorsed by the entire Pentecostal constituency.[11] Under these conditions, one would expect to find divisions appearing, and one does. In the south of England, in 1908, W. O. Hutchinson and his followers set up headquarters of the Apostolic Faith Church at Winton, Bournemouth. They wished to set themselves off as a distinctive "Pentecostal" organization; they were unwilling to heed Boddy's advice to remain as a sort of spiritual leaven within the established communions. They desired to stress speaking in tongues, the interpretation of these unknown tongues, and inspired utterance in English (prophecy—another of the gifts of the Spirit) as a method for conducting the affairs of the Church.[12]

Many Pentecostals were often not amenable to human leadership and authority because of their preoccupation with, and misunderstanding of, what they called "the leading of the Spirit." In brief, unless the impulse to act or to obey ("the leading") came either from within

[10] Gee, *Pentecostal Movement,* p. 88.

[11] *Ibid.,* pp. 76 f. Gee presents the candid observation: "All visitors to the Conventions [Whitsuntide Conventions for Pentecostals at Sunderland] did not accept the beloved Chairman's Anglican views concerning baptism in water, and so England awoke one morning to find the entire front page of the *Daily Mirror* taken up with a picture of Smith Wigglesworth [a Pentecostal from Bradford, England] baptising a company in the North Sea. . . ."

[12] *Ibid.,* pp. 73, 106.

or by charismatic announcement, they tended to ignore direction. Perhaps these excerpts from sources dealing with the early days of the Pentecostal revival will illustrate what I mean.

> Brother Seymour was recognized as the nominal leader in charge. But we had no pope or hierarchy. We were "brethren." We had no human programme. The Lord Himself was leading. We had no priest class, nor priest craft. *These things have come in later, with the apostatizing of the movement.*[13] [Italics mine.]
>
> . . . .
>
> No one knew what might be coming, what God would do. All was spontaneous, ordered of the Spirit.[14]
>
> We did not have to get our cue from some leader. . . . The meetings were controlled by the Spirit, from the throne.[15]
>
> . . . .
>
> There was a little raise of about a foot, for a platform, when we moved into the church. On this I generally lay, while God ran the meetings.[16]

Needless to say, this highly intuitional, subjective basis for determining one's authority could have some unfortunate repercussions—and did, when it was discovered that many people *thought* that they were under the administration of the Holy Spirit when they espoused certain causes.

Disputes Regarding Organization and Practice

The variety of denominations from which the early leaders of the Pentecostal movement came was a factor that undoubtedly influenced the diversity of opinion that existed with regard to polity, ordinances, and modes of worship. To recapitulate briefly: Charles Fox Parham, as a seventeen year old lad, had been licensed to preach by the Methodist Church, but he later affiliated with the Holiness movement. Alexander A. Boddy was an Anglican. Jonathan Paul had been a successful Lutheran pastor. Lewi Pethrus had ministered for nearly a decade in the Swedish Baptist Church, and Thomas Ball Barratt had capably administered a diversified program for the Methodists in

[13] Bartleman, *How Pentecost Came,* p. 58.
[14] *Idem.*
[15] *Ibid.,* p. 59.
[16] *Ibid.,* p. 69.

Norway. Just because they embraced Pentecostalism was no reason to renounce their views and preferences relative to baptism, liturgy, church government, and so forth. Barratt refers to this in an article which he wrote in 1911:

> Many who formerly were Lutherans, Methodists, Baptists, Quakers, and so on, *still retain their old views* regarding various important questions. The *object, value, time,* and *method* of observing *water baptism* is still a matter of discussion, likewise the *necessity, meaning,* and *importance* of the *Lord's Supper,* and the proper method for conducting it. Besides this, there are other questions on which many do not agree. Even in the matter that interests us all so greatly—*the tongues,* there is some difference in the way in which their value and importance has been stated by teachers within the Revival.[17]

One of the first principles over which Pentecostals quarreled was that of organization *vs.* independency. The Apostolic Faith movement which Charles Fox Parham established was only minimally organized. Because of earlier unpleasant conflicts with authoritarian officials in the Methodist Church, Parham deplored any kind of hierarchical control. This statement which he made in 1907 is ample evidence of that.

> In resigning my position as Projector of the Apostolic Faith Movement, I simply followed a well-considered plan of mine, made years ago, never to receive honor of men, or to establish a new church. I was called a Pope, a Dowie, etc., and everywhere looked upon as a leader or a would-be leader and proselyter.
>
> These designations have always been an abomination to me and since God has given almost universal light to the world on Pentecost there is no further need of my holding the official leadership of the Apostolic Faith Movement. Now that they are generally accepted, I simply take my place among my brethren to push this gospel of the Kingdom as a witness to all nations.[18]

Of the early Pentecostals, perhaps nobody was more antagonistic to organization than Frank Bartleman of California. It was his belief that God could not use a sectarian party as a channel "through whom He

[17] T. B. Barratt, "An Urgent Plea for Charity and Unity," *Word and Work,* XXX (Apr., 1911), 105 f.

[18] Brumback, *Suddenly from Heaven,* p. 61.

could evangelize the world, blessing all people and believers."[19] He states at one place in his diary that God showed him that they (Azusa Street Mission) were going to organize, so he arose in one of their services, admonishing them that "the 'baptized' saints were to remain 'one body,' even as they had been called, and to be free as His Spirit was free, not 'entangled again in a yoke of (ecclesiastical) bondage.' "[20] A little later on, he makes this entry somewhat sadly: "Sure enough the very next day after I dropped this warning in the meeting I found a sign outside 'Azusa' reading 'Apostolic Faith Mission.' . . . They had done it [i.e., organized]."[21]

On the other hand, many other Pentecostals who had been nurtured in the Apostolic Faith movement realized the necessity of organizing in order to remedy the evils of independency—doctrinal instability, variable standards of ethical behavior, vulnerability of local assemblies to unscrupulous clerical poseurs, and financial inefficiency. They, like the independents, claimed a biblical basis for their action, quoting from passages such as Acts 6 (where there is mention of nominations, voting, officials, records) and Acts 8 (where there is an account of the Jerusalem congregation exercising the function of overseer).[22]

Around 1910, a rather bitter quarrel developed between two segments of the Pentecostal movement over the matter of Sanctification. This controversy pitted those Pentecostals who had formerly been in the Holiness movement against those who had emerged from the Baptist wing of the Church. On the one hand, there were a host of Pentecostal believers in the Church of God, the Pentecostal Holiness Church, and the various Apostolic Faith Associations, who stressed what is known as the "second work of grace" theory. Briefly, it means that there is an experience subsequent to salvation whereby the believer is "entirely sanctified"; that is, one's inner nature "becomes dead to sin," the soul becomes clean, and man is freed from sinful inclinations.[23] On the other hand, there is the view which was broad-

[19] Bartleman, *How Pentecost Came,* p. 68.
[20] *Idem.*
[21] *Idem.*
[22] Brumback, *Suddenly from Heaven,* pp. 159 f.
[23] Atter, *Third Force,* p. 134 f.

cast by William H. Durham that a second work of grace is superfluous since salvation, which is an inward work, changes both a man's heart as well as his nature. Thus "the old man" or "the old nature"—to use the theological jargon that was employed during the controversy—which was sinful and depraved is "crucified, i.e. dead with Christ."[24] There is, therefore, no need for a *"second* work of grace."

The debate hinged on chronology. The Holiness contingent, because of their heritage, was used to thinking that the Holy Spirit baptism was imparted only after a period of cleansing (which occurred when a person was sanctified), for, they reasoned, the Holy Spirit "will not take up his abode in an unclean vessel." Durham turned this argument in his favor by referring to the hundreds of non-Holiness people throughout the world who had been "filled with the Spirit." Since they had not experienced "sanctification" subsequent to the crisis experience, salvation; and since according to the "second work" proponents the Holy Spirit does not indwell an unclean (unsanctified) vessel, *ergo* sanctification is not distinct from, but rather somehow related to, their conversion experience.

In England, Pentecostals were rent by a controversy which developed naturally enough, it seems, from the great emphasis which they placed upon an inner, highly emotional experience such as the Holy Spirit baptism. Because of a desire to give greater prominence to the manifestation of spiritual gifts such as prophecy, *glossolalia,* and the interpretation of tongues, in 1910 some British Pentecostals severed their connections with the original organization, The Pentecostal Missionary Union. They proceeded to institute an elaborate system of church government and ministry, based exclusively on the charismatic gifts. Some British Pentecostals repudiated the newly formed Apostolic Faith Church for equating a revelation of truth through the media of prophecy or tongues and their interpretation with the objective revelation of God's truth—Holy Scripture. Nonetheless, the Apostolic Faith folk, claiming a "fuller vision" from God, practicing a form of inspirationalism that smacked of Montanism, and

24 Brumback has an entire chapter devoted to this controversy. See his *Suddenly from Heaven,* pp. 98–106.

endowing themselves with such New Testament titles as "Apostles" and "Prophets," proselyted successfully and caused "great pain in several centres of Pentecostalism—especially Wales and Scotland."[25]

Pentecostal literature that was published around the time of World War I contains intimations that a similar preoccupation with revelations, visions, and prophetic utterances characterized the German wing of the Pentecostal movement. This tendency was, however, promptly renounced by the Pentecostals from Sweden. At an International Pentecostal Convention that was held in Amsterdam in 1921, "the Scandinavian leaders would not allow prophetic utterances to settle matters of doctrine."[26] A remarkable illustration of overruling the prophetic element occurred on the last day of the conference.

> All were startled when the leading German "prophet" suddenly said that he saw as in a vision one of the most outstanding leaders present "smoking five pipes at once." This, he declared, represented uncleanness in his soul. By that time the Conference was getting rather tired of these personal visions, and upon the interpretation being submitted to the judgement of all present they unanimously rejected it, even though given through a prophet held in high esteem in the churches.[27]

This proclivity for utilizing *glossolalia* or prophesying as a basis for guiding and governing the Church never achieved any widespread popularity in North America. However, that does not mean that Pentecostal leaders in the United States were not susceptible to spiritual subjectivism. As a matter of fact, Howard A. Goss notes that "a preacher who did not dig up some new slant on a Scripture, or get some new revelation to his own heart ever so often . . . was considered slow, stupid, unspiritual."[28] This being the case, it was unavoidable that Pentecostalism was besieged by various and sundry Spirit-prompted insights. One such revelation, observes Brumback, almost tore the movement apart.[29]

This crisis occurred at a Worldwide Pentecostal Camp Meeting

[25] Gee, *Pentecostal Movement,* pp. 72–74, 106–8.
[26] *Ibid.,* pp. 122 f.
[27] *Ibid.,* p. 123.
[28] Goss, *Winds of God,* p. 155.
[29] Brumback, *Suddenly from Heaven,* p. 191.

held at Arroyo Seco, California, in 1913. Mary B. Woodworth-Etter was conducting services and experiencing phenomenal success, especially in her ministry to those who were ill. It must be remembered that most Pentecostals when praying for the sick preface their rebuke of the illness with the phrase, "In the name of Jesus. . . ." Brumback, in recounting the events which transpired in California, says:

> Many miracles were wrought through the wonderful name of Jesus. One man, John G. Scheppe, was so inspired that he spent a night in prayer. Along toward morning he was given a glimpse of the power of that blessed name. Leaping to his feet, he ran through the camp, shouting to all the early risers what the Lord had shown him.[30]

To be sure, the "revelation" impressed many, and they hastened to examine the Bible for what teaching it contained regarding the "name of Jesus." Their research produced a revolution within Pentecostalism, for they fastened upon two texts—Acts 2:38 and John 3:5—and asserted that *true* baptism *must* be only "in the name of Jesus" rather than "in the name of the Father, and of the Son, and of the Holy Ghost." The result? Many of the early Pentecostal leaders, like Eudorus N. Bell and Howard A. Goss in the United States and Robert E. McAlister and George A. Chambers in Canada, accepted the new "revelation" and were rebaptized.[31] This created numerous divisions among Pentecostals as some supported the view and others denounced it as rank heresy.

The next development in this controversy, which received the title "The New Issue" or the "Jesus Only" heresy, was a denial of the Trinity. Men like Frank Ewart and Glenn A. Cook, spokesmen for the new teaching, denied the trinity of persons in the Godhead, maintaining that while God is a threefold Being, Father, Son, and Holy Spirit, there is but one Person and that one is Jesus. This teaching spread like wildfire, leaping "from mission to mission, assembly to assembly, until it became *the* issue of the day."[32] Its emphasis on the name of Jesus, the seemingly supernatural method of its being revealed, and its promise of additional power to all who accepted it,

[30] *Idem.*
[31] Atter, *Third Force,* p. 132.
[32] Brumback, *Suddenly from Heaven,* p. 193.

advises Brumback, accounts for the rapid spread of the theory among Pentecostals.[33]

Especially affected by this new viewpoint was the recently organized Assemblies of God. Some of its outstanding leaders—Goss, Bell, Opperman—defected. In the state of Louisiana where the organization had but twelve ministers, all twelve embraced the "Oneness" principle.[34] Nonetheless, others like J. Roswell Flower and John W. Welch remained stanchly Trinitarian, criticizing the new "revelation" on the ground that it was too dependent upon the subjective feelings of the individual and not enough on traditional historico-theological principles. In any case, dissension rent the young movement. One hundred fifty-six ministers withdrew from the Assemblies of God,[35] and a new Pentecostal body was organized—the Pentecostal Assemblies of the World.[36]

Since so many early Pentecostals came from the Holiness movement they naturally held some rigid views regarding dress, entertainment, eating habits, physicians, divorce, and so forth. Furthermore, they were resolute and often obstinate when they discussed these matters with their fellow Pentecostals, who often were equally implacable. The result: acrimonious dispute.

For example, among some Southern Pentecostals in the early days, one was forbidden to wear all jewelry, even wedding rings. The practice of wearing ties by men and colored dresses by women was likewise frowned on. That these practices were not universally endorsed, however, is attested to by this passage from Goss:

> The lady workers [in the Apostolic Faith Bands] dressed in the current fashions of the day . . . silks . . . satins . . . jewels or whatever they happened to possess. They were very smartly turned out, so that they made an impressive appearance on the streets where a large part of our work was conducted in the early years.
>
> It was not until long after, when former Holiness preachers had become part of us, that strict plainness of dress began to be taught.[37]

[33] *Idem.*
[34] Brumback, *Suddenly from Heaven,* p. 197.
[35] *Ibid.,* p. 210.
[36] Kendrick, *Promise Fulfilled,* p. 172.
[37] Goss, *Winds of God,* p. 38.

Mary B. Woodworth-Etter was outspokenly intolerant of the medical profession as well as the use of medicine. In her book, *Questions and Answers on Divine Healing,* are contained derogatory statements such as this one:

Q. Is not the ministry of physicians for the body designed of God, the same as the ministry of the gospel for the soul?

A. No. The greater portion of the physicians of the land are ungodly people, many of them professed infidels, and were never designed of God to administer drugs and poisons to any one; much less to the people of God, whose bodies are the sacred temples of the Holy Spirit.[38]

Such calumnious remarks must have been common in Pentecostal circles during the early years, for it was finally necessary for the 1929 General Assembly of the Church of God (Cleveland, Tennessee) to pass the following resolution: "We recommend that our people in testifying to divine healing refrain from using expressions making thrusts at physicians or the use of medicine. Preach and testify to divine healing as a privilege, giving God the glory."[39]

As is to be expected, on no topic have Pentecostals been more vigorously legalistic than on the one concerning speaking in tongues. They are almost rabid in their assertion that *glossolalia always* accompany an "infilling with the Holy Spirit." Through the years only a few Pentecostal leaders—Americans such as A. G. Canada and F. F. Bosworth, for example—have advocated a more lenient attitude. They contended that any one of the gifts of the Spirit could be the immediate, outward manifestation of a Holy Spirit baptism. In England, however, one of the largest Pentecostal bodies—the Elim Pentecostal Alliance—endorsed the view that there may be other signs of a Spirit baptism than just "tongues." Thomas Ball Barratt from Norway, while supporting the view that speaking in tongues was the *normal* evidence, allowed that there could be exceptions. "The tongues may have been kept back by will-force, from fear, distrust, unwillingness, ignorance or unbelief."[40]

[38] Indianapolis: Printed by the author, n.d., pp. 12 f.

[39] *Church of God Minutes* (Cleveland, Tenn.: Church of God Publishing House, 1962), p. 239.

[40] Atter, *Third Force,* p. 149.

In addition to these matters of faith and practice about which Pentecostals[41] quarreled, one might add the dispute within the Assemblies of God which led to the elimination of fermented wine from the communion service.[42] Or the discussion which developed over the article in the Church of God's statement of faith that feet washing was a legitimate ordinance and that together with communion it ought to be observed at least once a year.[43] Then, too, while most Pentecostals believe in water baptism by immersion, in 1909 the Pentecostal Holiness Church adopted a latitudinarian approach to the sacrament, permitting the candidate to choose the mode he preferred.[44] And whereas those who were affiliated with the Crawford wing of the Apostolic Faith movement held to the principle forbidding divorce and remarriage under any circumstances,[45] the adherents of the Church of God of Prophecy advocated that there was a cause to justify divorce and remarriage—fornication.[46] Thus one could continue to enumerate topics which Pentecostals have disputed: the eating of pork, the use of tobacco, the drinking of coffee and soda pop, participation in the military, labor unions, and so on.

It is rather clear by now that all of this diversity of opinion regarding matters both of faith and order and life and work, to use ecumenical phrases, and the obvious fragmentation of Pentecostals into groups which favored either ardor or order, spontaneity or ritual, legalism or tolerance, and independency or hierarchical control, would preclude the development of a unitive Pentecostalism. Not even a common religious experience—the Holy Spirit baptism—would be a sufficiently strong cohesive force, for the taproots of the movement reached back into too many differing personalities, cultures, and religious heritages. Proliferation, then, would be inevitable.

[41] Barratt, "An Urgent Plea," p. 106.

[42] Brumback, *Suddenly from Heaven,* p. 202.

[43] Conn, *Like a Mighty Army,* p. 65.

[44] Campbell, *Pentecostal Holiness Church,* p. 251.

[45] Tract No. 83 entitled "Divorce" published by The Apostolic Faith (N. W. Sixth & Burnside, Portland 9, Ore.).

[46] Tract No. D0–01 entitled "The Divorce and Remarriage Question" published by the Church of God of Prophecy (Cleveland, Tenn.).

CHAPTER 8

Varieties of Pentecostalism in America (I): The Oldest and the Most Prominent Branches

During the first decade of the Pentecostal revival, few of its leaders thought of forming a separate denomination. True, they had embraced the teaching concerning a Holy Spirit baptism, speaking in tongues, and the possession of Spiritual gifts; nevertheless, they thought of themselves first and foremost as Baptists, Methodists, Lutherans—different only in the fact that they had received "the Promise of the Father," the empowering blessing of the Holy Spirit.[1]

Therefore, there was no Pentecostal organization which people were asked to join; rather all were coaxed to seek a charismatic experience. And as we have seen, many of those who did were assailed or rejected by their denominations; they were offered the choice of either compromising their beliefs or else withdrawing. Many selected the latter alternative, and Pastor Barratt was able to write in 1911 that

[1] When Dr. Willis C. Hoover resigned from the Methodist Episcopal Church in Chile, after he had been reprimanded by his superiors for countenancing a Pentecostal revival in his church in Valparaiso, he became head of the *Methodist* Pentecostal Church. Alexander A. Boddy, early leader of Pentecostals in England and editor of a Pentecostal publication, *Confidence,* never rescinded any of his Anglicanism. He remained vicar of All Saints' Church in Sunderland, England, yet chaired Pentecostal conventions both in his parish as well as in London.

Pentecostal Centers are springing up in every country *outside the churches,* and in some lands will soon be found in every town and in every rural district. This is mainly due to the *opposition* the Revival has met from the churches generally. The same was the case *in Wales,* after the Revival there under Evan Roberts; the converts have extensively been obliged to band together and are called *"the children of the Revival,"* the older Christian communities having in such cases *shut out* the fresh glorious flow of Revival grace and power, that God in his mercy sent them. *It is just so with this Pentecostal Revival!*[2]

Even when forced to withdraw, few Pentecostal Christians were remotely interested in establishing any type of organization. Almost to a man they deplored anything that smacked of ecclesiasticism and denominationalism, mostly because of the abuse that they had experienced as members of the older, organized religious bodies. As Brumback put it: "After giving years of service they had been 'cast out of the synagogue,' charged with 'departing from the faith.' "[3] Therefore in a chorus many exclaimed, "God has brought us out of old, dead ecclesiasticism and denominationalism. He has made us a free people, and we are not going back to 'Babylon' any more."[4]

What many Pentecostals failed to realize, however, was that from the very outset they had had rudimentary forms of organization. Years later Howard A. Goss made this observation:

Everyman, of necessity, had his own unwritten organization, his own unwritten manual, but a manual and an organization nevertheless.

Younger ministers . . . naturally grouped themselves around the more fatherly type of minister looking to him for counsel, example, and fellowship. These groups grew in ever-widening circles, until we really had an unwritten organization, with each group functioning separately, however much we had tried to avoid it.[5]

Charles W. Conn's impression is that organization was unavoidable. His group, the Church of God, was growing, and "a loosely organized body of unwieldy proportions was singularly susceptible to false

[2] Barratt, "An Urgent Plea," pp. 103 f.

[3] Brumback, *Suddenly from Heaven,* p. 156. They also feared that a reliance upon an organization—with all the legislative machinery that unavoidably develops—would replace the reliance upon the Spirit.

[4] Ernest S. Williams, "Forty-five Years of Pentecostal Revival," *Pentecostal Evangel,* XXXIX (Aug. 19, 1951), 3 f.

[5] Goss, *Winds of God,* pp. 164 f.

teaching and fanaticism."[6] Finally, others merely explained that it was not organization but the abuse of it that was bad.

Above all else as the first decade of the twentieth century drew to a close, it became quite obvious that the evils of independency far surpassed those that organization might create: there were no uniform regulations to deal with those who proclaimed spurious doctrines; there was no discipline for the emotionally unstable or the personally erratic; there was no legislation to prevent unscrupulous opportunists from preying on unsuspecting congregations, for they could claim that they were Apostolic Faith preachers who had been directed by the Spirit to minister to a particular congregation;[7] there were no efficient fiscal policies which would provide monies for the expenses of those missionaries under appointment, many of whom had been released by the large denominations as soon as it became noised abroad that they had become tainted with "Pentecostalism"; there was no provision for replacing the sense of national and international fellowship which people had had as members of the established communions; and there was no adequate educational system for the training of ministers.

It was imperative that the Pentecostals organize. And they did, but not into one massive body. Unfortunately, most interpreters of Pentecostalism have overlooked this fact—that it is not a singular movement. Since a normative Pentecostalism is virtually nonexistent, I have found it necessary to establish the following divisions as a means of classifying the numerous Pentecostal organizations in America: in this chapter the earliest Pentecostal associations and the most prominent denominations will be described; in Chapter 9 the innumerable small, regional, ethnic, and somewhat bizarre groups will be depicted.

Earliest Pentecostal Associations

Apostolic Faith Movement. Charles Fox Parham, although an outspoken critic of any kind of ecclesiasticism, was nevertheless responsi-

[6] Conn, *Like a Mighty Army,* p. 39.

[7] For an account of how some missions were victimized, see Goss, *Winds of God,* pp. 167–169; and Brumback, *Suddenly from Heaven,* p. 159.

ble for initiating the trend toward organization during the first decade of the Pentecostal revival.[8]

He "advocated a simple congregationalism in which individual churches were administered by local elders amenable to no central authority,"[9] apparently not even his. This is perhaps best illustrated in a letter which he wrote from Los Angeles where he had been summoned by his friend William J. Seymour to stamp out the " 'hypnotic forces and fleshly contortions as known in the Colored Camp Meetings in the South.' "[10] which had erupted in the Azusa Street Mission.

> I have no desire to assert my authority (For I have none to assert over the people of God), but to help and strengthen and forever make plain to all people that extremes . . . fanaticism and everything that is beyond the bounds of common sense and reason do not now and never have had any part or lot in Apostolic Faith work and teachings.[11]

After his death on January 29, 1929, the task of publishing *The Apostolic Faith* was assumed by his wife Sarah (Thistlewaite). She was assisted by two sons—Robert and Claude, and the latter's wife, Lula. When "Mother" Parham died in 1937, Robert continued as editor until his death in 1944; then his widow, Pauline, and Claude's widow, Lula, took over respectively as editor and associate editor.

For many years, in addition to its publishing activities, the group also continued its founder's policy of conducting short-term Bible school programs on a "faith basis." As many as 134 students at a time enroll for these sessions, which generally last for three months. No charge is made for board or tuition, and even members of the administration and teaching staff serve without any guarantee that they will be paid; however, they have "faith" that "God will provide." Seemingly, He does.

The Apostolic Faith, a modest tribute to the evangelistic efforts of Parham, differs little from other Pentecostal groups.[12] Because it does

[8] See above p. 81.

[9] Kendrick, *Promise Fulfilled,* p. 64.

[10] Quoted by Brumback, *Suddenly from Heaven,* p. 60.

[11] *Idem.*

[12] Except, perhaps, for adhering to the Holiness view of sanctification as being a "second work of grace," for accepting feet washing as an ordinance to be observed together with communion and baptism, and for practicing a policy of "faith" in financial matters.

not report to any local or national religious agencies, there are few data concerning it. The only available statistics, now obsolete, indicate that in 1951, 136 ministers were affiliated with the Baxter Springs (Kansas) branch of the Apostolic Faith movement, and that 83 churches were scattered throughout a thirteen-state region.[13]

The Apostolic Faith. Another organization with a title similar to that of Parham's group, but having no connection with it whatsoever, is *The* Apostolic Faith. It was founded in Portland, Oregon, in 1907 by Florence Louise Crawford, who only a year before had experienced sanctification and the baptism of the Holy Spirit at the Azusa Street revival. Before settling in Portland, Mrs. Crawford had conducted evangelistic campaigns in Salem (Oregon), Seattle, Minneapolis-St. Paul, and Winnipeg. It was in Minneapolis that she felt divinely compelled to return to Portland and to establish her headquarters there.

Through her efforts, two huge churches were built. One, located at Northwest Sixth Avenue and Burnside Street, seats more than 1,000 persons; the other, at Southeast 52nd Avenue and Duke Street, a domed tabernacle situated on an eleven-acre park site, seats 2,400 people.

The chief concern of The Apostolic Faith, states its literature, has never been that of "swelling its numbers."

> Rather, its concern is with members who have "prayed through" to that born-again experience which enables them to live a life of victory over sin and to keep themselves "unspotted from the world."[14]

Recent membership figures are, consequently, not too impressive. They reveal that The Apostolic Faith has 42 churches, presided over by a similar number of ordained clergy, and that the inclusive membership is 4,764.[15]

Statistics are no true measure of the elaborate evangelistic program which The Apostolic Faith conducts. During its existence, the group has utilized cross-country buses in its home missions work, motor

[13] *The Apostolic Faith,* XXVIII (Apr., 1951), pp. 10 f.
[14] *A Historical Account of The Apostolic Faith,* p. 21.
[15] Landis, *Yearbook,* p. 14.

boats for carrying its witness to seamen in local ports, an airplane for transporting ministers and missionaries to various outposts, and above all—the printing press. During its nearly sixty-year history, The Apostolic Faith has stressed printed literature. Today it produces religious materials in more than seventy languages and dialects and mails it postage prepaid and subscription free to many points around the world.

Like Parham's group, The Apostolic Faith believes in sanctification, the sacrament of feet washing, and a policy of not soliciting church funds. In addition, it advocates a rather stern code in matters of conduct and dress:

> Worldly amusements and sinful pleasures, such as dancing, card-playing, theatre going, smoking and drinking, have no part in the life of its members; and they also refrain from unequally yoking "together with unbelievers" (II Corinthians 6:14 and Ephesians 5:7).
>
> The standard of dress upheld for the Christians is that the women attire themselves "in modest apparel," no extreme fads, no facial makeup or bobbed hair. . . .[16]

The governing body of the movement is a duly appointed and elected board of five trustees, of which the General Overseer is the chairman.[17] In addition, there is a board of elders and a secretary-treasurer. The polity of The Apostolic Faith is presbyterian in form; however, all branches of the organization are under the leadership and direction of the headquarters' office in Portland.

Most Prominent Pentecostal Denominations

Church of God. In 1896, ten years before either the appearance of the Pentecostal phenomena at Topeka, Kansas, or the massive outburst at Los Angeles, at least one hundred people, who at the time were worshiping in the Shearer schoolhouse in Murphy County, North Carolina, received the baptism of the Holy Spirit and spoke in tongues. They were members of an organization called the Christian Union whose name was changed to the Holiness Church in 1902 and finally

[16] *A Historical Account of The Apostolic Faith,* p. 21.

[17] It is not at all clear in any of the available sources how the "duly appointed and elected board of five trustees" gets appointed and elected.

to its present Church of God in 1907.[18] At that time, there existed but five churches in North Carolina, Georgia, and Tennessee, with a total membership of less than two hundred.

Until 1908, the Church of God was confronted with a dilemma: its most capable leader was a former colporteur of the American Bible Society and American Tract Society—A. J. Tomlinson, who, although an ordained minister in the denomination since 1903, had not experienced a Holy Spirit baptism. At the Third Assembly which convened at Cleveland, Tennessee, in 1908, however, he finally "came through," as the Pentecostals say.[19] At the very next Assembly (1909), Tomlinson was elected general moderator (now called general overseer). He was selected over two older influential leaders —R. G. Spurling and William F. Bryant—probably because he was "a fluent and powerful speaker, poised and dynamic, and well educated in comparison with the two older preachers."[20] Whatever the reason, the man selected to guide the Church of God would rule for a period of fourteen years.

During that fourteen-year period, Tomlinson handled almost all of the administrative matters personally: he managed and distributed funds among the clergy; he had oversight of all publications as well as of the educational program. Finally in 1923, the General Assembly placed some restrictions upon his authority and set up a committee to investigate his fiscal policies. After conducting an audit, the committee submitted an unfavorable report to the Council of Twelve Elders.[21] Impeachment proceedings were filed against Tomlinson, and on July 26, 1923, he was relieved of his office.

Needless to say, these proceedings affected the growth of the denomination, and the public-relations damage was incalculable. Nonetheless, the Church of God was able to recover and has made sig-

[18] The definitive work on the Church of God is Charles W. Conn's well-documented, scholarly history, *Like a Mighty Army.* A shorter summary, also by Conn, appeared in the *Pentecostal Evangel,* XLV (Aug. 25, 1957), 20 f. See also Kendrick, *Promise Fulfilled,* pp. 188–97.

[19] For a vivid description of this event, see Conn, *Like a Mighty Army,* pp. 84 f.

[20] *Ibid.,* p. 94.

[21] This Council had been established in 1916 to assist the General Overseer in the administration of the church.

nificant strides forward in the last four decades. A mammoth million-dollar printing plant has been constructed in Cleveland, Tennessee. Orphanages are maintained at Sevierville, Tennessee; Kannapolis, North Carolina; and Gaffney, South Carolina. The denomination has provided its youth with both junior college and Bible college facilities at Lee College in Cleveland, Tennessee, West Coast Bible College at Fresno, California, Northwest Bible College in Minot, North Dakota, and International Bible College at Moose Jaw, Saskatchewan. In 1951, the Church of God effected an amalgamation with the Full Gospel Church in South Africa, thus increasing its membership by 30,000 and its churches by 175.

The Church of God is administered by a General Assembly, the highest governing body. It meets biennially, and is attended by at least 10,000 members.[22] Before each Assembly, a General Council of all the ordained ministers gathers to prepare recommendations relative to polity or doctrine. An Executive Committee (general overseer, first, second, and third assistant general overseers, a general secretary-treasurer, and a director of world missions) is elected by the Assembly for a period of four years. These men are joined by twelve counselors, who are also elected biennially, to form what the Church of God calls the Executive Council. It is the highest administrative body to function between General Assemblies.

The doctrinal position of the Church of God is similar to that of the other Pentecostal groups that emerged from the Holiness revival. Stress is placed on sanctification[23] and personal holiness. While a doctoral candidate at Yale, John Bernard Oliver made an intensive study[24] of this area of personal holiness. He observed that the Church of God is extremely puritanical in matters relative to recreation, luxury, and sex. Members, he found, are required to abstain from

[22] This body is composed of ministers and laymen from recognized local churches who wish to attend the biennial conference "to search the Scriptures and to put them into practice." All local churches are subject to the government, teaching, and practices promulgated by the General Assembly.

[23] According to a Church of God representative, sanctification is the God-given power to aid the convert in carrying out God's standards of holiness. See Paulk, *Your Pentecostal Neighbor,* p. 98.

[24] "Some Newer Religion Groups" (unpublished Ph.D. dissertation, Yale University, 1946), *passim.*

practices like drinking alcoholic beverages, using tobacco, wearing ornamental jewelry, joining lodges, swearing, bobbing hair, attending and/or operating motion pictures, and speculating in the stock market. Indulgence in any of these practices is a sign of "worldliness," which, according to one Church of God writer, is any illegitimate activity or desire that controls the flesh, or anything that is in contrast to the spiritual.[25]

The Church of God is perhaps the only large Pentecostal body which observes feet washing as an ordinance.[26] It endorsed the practice at its Assembly in 1906, basing it on an interpretation of John 13:4–17 and the belief that it had once been common among the revivalistic churches of the nation. From its inception, feet washing has been considered a manifestation of subservience and brotherhood, and thus an integral part of Pentecostal worship.[27]

Despite what some observers may consider to be an inflexibility in matters of faith and practice, the Church of God has grown from the five-church denomination of 150 members that convened at Union Grove, Tennessee, in 1907 to a rather respectable size: 3,411 ordained ministers; 3,575 churches; and an inclusive membership of 205,465.[28]

Church of God in Christ. Similar to other Pentecostal bodies which were founded by and featured a dynamic personality, the Church of God in Christ—the largest body of Negro Pentecostals in the world—is a tribute to the leadership of one man, Charles H. Mason.[29]

Founder-organizer, Mason received his early ministerial training in the Missionary Baptist Church in Tennessee, but he joined the Holiness movement during the 1890's and established the Church of God in Christ in Memphis.

In 1906, Mason heard about the outstanding Azusa Street revival.

25 Paulk, *Your Pentecostal Neighbor,* p. 191.

26 For a fuller explanation consult *ibid.,* pp. 165 f.

27 Conn, *Like a Mighty Army,* p. 65.

28 Landis, *Yearbook,* p. 33.

29 A very rare biography of his life is Mary Mason's *The History and Life Work of Bishop C. H. Mason, Chief Apostle, and His Co-Laborers* (Memphis: n.p., 1934).

Accompanied by J. O. Jeter and D. J. Young, he journeyed to Los Angeles, spending five weeks there. During that period of time he received the Spirit baptism and spoke in tongues.[30] Meanwhile back in Memphis, Mason's Holiness congregation was being exposed to Pentecostalism through the preaching of Glen A. Cook, himself recently returned from Los Angeles. Tensions developed over the question of the Pentecostal experience. Then when Mason returned and commenced to stress the need for a Holy Spirit baptism and speaking in tongues, it became clear that division was imminent. At the 1907 General Assembly that convened in Jackson, Mississippi, the non-Pentecostal faction headed by C. P. Jones withdrew.[31] Subsequently, Mason called for an Assembly to be held in Memphis, at which time it was declared that the Church of God in Christ was henceforth Pentecostal. At this first General Assembly, Mason was elected general overseer of the dozen or so churches that were located at that time in Tennessee, Arkansas, Mississippi, and Oklahoma.

From the beginning, the entire administration of the denomination was carried on by Mason, who bore the title "Chief Apostle" (Bishop) as well as "Elder." In 1933, however, four assistant bishops were appointed to help administer what had become a complex, large organization. In time, each state had its own bishop and the states were then divided into districts over which superintendents presided. This episcopal type of polity differed radically from the loose congregational-presbyterian forms of government practiced by most contemporaneous Pentecostal groups.

The doctrinal stance of the Church of God in Christ differs little from that of other perfectionistic Pentecostal denominations like the Church of God (Cleveland, Tennessee) and the Pentecostal Holiness Church.

The Church supports missionary efforts in South Africa, Thailand, Jamaica, Haiti, Liberia, and West Coast Africa. The denomination has not developed its educational program, owing, perhaps, to the

[30] Kendrick, *Promise Fulfilled,* p. 198.

[31] United States Bureau of the Census, *Religious Bodies: 1936,* Vol. II, Part 1 (Washington: Government Printing Office, 1941), p. 448.

lower economic status of its predominantly southern Negro constituency. It does, however, maintain a junior college in Lexington, Mississippi.

The development of the Church of God in Christ has been remarkable. In 1963, it claimed to have 4,100 churches, an inclusive membership of 413,000, 3,850 ordained ministers, and more than two million adherents around the world.[32] When one compares these statistics with those reported in 1926—1,444 churches and 63,558 members—one realizes that the denomination has experienced phenomenal growth.

Pentecostal Holiness Church. This denomination is the result of a merger of three separate Holiness bodies that had embraced Pentecostalism during the early years of the twentieth century: The Fire-Baptized Holiness Church, the Holiness Church, and the Tabernacle Presbyterian Church.

The Fire-Baptized Holiness Church was formed in the 1890's through the efforts of Benjamin H. Irwin, a lawyer turned Holiness preacher,[33] who popularized the teaching that there was a religious experience beyond salvation and sanctification, namely, a "baptism of fire." This "Third Blessing Heresy," as it was called by the mainline Holiness groups, spread throughout Iowa, Nebraska, Kansas, Oklahoma, Texas, North and South Carolina, Georgia, and Florida. Then growth ceased, largely because of Irwin's defection. "It looked as though the little church would evanesce completely."[34]

The group was revitalized, however, by the Pentecostal revival that was penetrating the Holiness movement during the early 1900's. Miss Agnes Ozman, the first person to receive the Pentecostal baptism at Parham's school in Topeka, joined the Association of Fire-Baptized Holiness Churches as pastor and evangelist. J. H. King, who succeeded Irwin as general overseer, experienced a Holy Spirit baptism at Toccoa, Georgia, during meetings that were conducted by G. B. Cashwell—a recent arrival from the Azusa Street Mission. The Pente-

[32] Cf. Landis, *Yearbook,* pp. 36 f.; Atter, *Third Force,* p. 91.

[33] A comprehensive history of this group may be found in Campbell's *Pentecostal Holiness Church,* pp. 193–215.

[34] *Ibid.,* p. 205.

costal revival, according to Campbell, rejuvenated the Fire-Baptized Holiness work in Oklahoma where for a time it had almost disappeared.[35] Elsewhere, it was largely responsible for the expansion which the church experienced in states like Kansas, Nebraska, Texas, Arkansas, Iowa, and Arizona.

The second religious organization, which subsequently joined the Fire-Baptized Holiness Church to form the Pentecostal Holiness Church, was the handiwork of Rev. A. B. Crumpler. In 1899, because of his vigorous endorsement of the doctrine of sanctification, Crumpler was forced to withdraw from the Methodist Church. He proceeded to organize the Holiness Church, and from 1900 to 1906 the work prospered, principally in North Carolina. Then a controversy developed: it concerned the fast-spreading Pentecostal revival which G. B. Cashwell conducted in a Dunn, North Carolina, warehouse.

> A considerable portion of the preachers and many of the laymen of the Holiness Church were there. Many also were in attendance from the Fire Baptized Holiness Church. Nothing like this meeting has ever struck that town or country before or since. Great and marvelous manifestations of God's presence filled the warehouse and all the town. The best and most spiritual people of all the churches came and many of them received the baptism of the Spirit and spoke in tongues.[36]

Not too long thereafter, most of those who had been associated with the Holiness Church in North Carolina became convinced Pentecostals. However, Crumpler denounced the charismatic experience, and at the 1908 convention in Dunn announced his withdrawal from the Holiness Church. Saddened, but not despairing, the delegates elected A. H. Butler to be their new leader; and they amended the *Discipline* to include the following article:

> We . . . need to receive the filling of the Spirit, the baptism with the Holy Ghost, the abiding Comforter, that which was promised by John the Baptist (Matt. 3:11) and corroborated by Jesus Christ (John 14: 15–17) that on receiving the baptism with the Holy Ghost we have the same evidence that followed Acts 2nd, 10th, and 19th Chapters to wit: The speaking in other tongues as the Spirit gave utterance.[37]

[35] *Ibid.*, pp. 210 f.
[36] *Ibid.*, p. 241.
[37] *Ibid.*, p. 246.

The idea of consolidating the two former Holiness bodies which were now Pentecostal—the Fire-Baptized Holiness Church and the Holiness Church—was quickly raised, but it took three years to consummate the merger. Finally in 1911, about three dozen representatives gathered in a small octagon-shaped tabernacle in Falcon, North Carolina, to effect a consolidation which brought into being the Pentecostal Holiness Church.

The last faction to affiliate itself with the Pentecostal Holiness Church was the numerically small Tabernacle Presbyterian Church. Its leader, Rev. Nickels John Holmes, had withdrawn from the South Carolina Synod of the Presbyterian Church because it had questioned the emphasis which he placed on the doctrines of sanctification and divine healing. In time, Holmes, together with many within his independent Presbyterian organization, espoused the concept of a Pentecostal blessing and in 1915 joined the Pentecostal Holiness Church.

In his very brief survey of this group,[38] Elmer T. Clark observes that the Pentecostal Holiness Church is different from most other Pentecostal bodies in these two respects: (1) it is somewhat more tolerant, and (2) its polity is less democratic than that of other Pentecostals.

Its toleration is manifested, perhaps, in its attitude toward medicine and physicians, both of which were reviled unmercifully by many Pentecostals who were rabid adherents of the divine healing principle. Not so the Pentecostal Holiness Church. While never relinquishing their belief in divine healing as "a more excellent way" than resorting to doctors, they never engaged in denunciations either:

> It [Pentecostal Holiness Church] believes that the provision was made in Christ's atonement for the healing of the body, but it does not antagonize the practice of medicine as something essentially evil.[39]

The church is equally tolerant on the matter of baptism. While almost all other Pentecostals practice immersion, candidates for baptism in the Pentecostal Holiness Church "have the right of choice between the various modes as practiced by the several evangelical

[38] *The Small Sects,* pp. 107 f.
[39] *Religious Bodies: 1936,* II:2, p. 1321.

denominations."[40] The church also allows parents of infants to select either dedication or baptism—an option that is not given by any other Pentecostal body.

Like all of the Pentecostal churches that evolved from the Holiness revival, the Pentecostal Holiness Church endorses a doctrine of sanctification: "We believe in Sanctification as preached by John Wesley. . . . We do not teach 'absolute perfection' but that sanctification is a progressive work of grace as well as an instantaneous second work of grace."[41] Unlike the other churches the history of which we have already described, the Pentecostal Holiness Church does not practice the ordinance of feet washing.

In matters of polity the Pentecostal Holiness Church is decidedly more rigid than most other Pentecostal groups. The church, reflecting its Methodist Episcopal heritage, is divided into conferences: general, annual, district, and missionary.[42] The General Conference, a representative body of the entire organization, meets quadrennially. It is composed of the General Board of Administration—an executive committee which meets annually—which is made up of a general superintendent (holding the honorary title of bishop), four assistant superintendents, a general secretary, a general treasurer, the superintendents of each Annual Conference, and four members at large—two of whom must be laymen. In addition, the General Conference includes at least one clerical delegate from each Annual Conference (but not more than one for every twenty-five ministers) and at least one lay delegate from each Annual Conference; however, the lay representation must never be larger than the clerical.

The Annual Conference is also a representative body. The superintendent of the conference together with all the ordained and licensed ministers, as well as at least one lay delegate from each local church

[40] Kendrick, *Promise Fulfilled,* p. 185, citing the *Discipline of the Pentecostal Holiness Church* (Franklin Springs, Ga.: Pentecostal Holiness Church, 1953), p. 43.

[41] *Ibid.,* p. 184, quoting an article in *The Pentecostal Advocate,* XXVI (Jan. 29, 1953), p. 4.

[42] Kendrick, *Promise Fulfilled,* p. 184 quoting an article in *The Pentecostal Advocate,* XXVI (Jan. 29, 1953), p. 4. Kendrick gives a comprehensive account of Pentecostal Holiness Church polity, based on an examination of their *Discipline* as well as on correspondence he had with the Bishop, J. A. Synan.

(but not more than one for every fifty members) meets each year in order to assign pastorates and to examine and approve all ministerial candidates. The administrative business of the conference is handled by an official board: a superintendent, an assistant superintendent, a secretary-treasurer, and two other elected members.

District Conferences are geographical entities and meet every three months. The composition of this body is as follows: the superintendent of the Annual Conference, the pastors and their assistants, evangelists, mission workers, and delegates (not more than one for every fifty members).

The Pentecostal Holiness Church is smaller than some of the other Pentecostal denominations, yet it has a vigorous educational program. It maintains Emmanuel College—a fully accredited Academy and Junior College, located at the church's headquarters in Franklin Springs, Georgia. It likewise operates Holmes Theological Seminary in Greenville, South Carolina, where students can take undergraduate work in theology, and Southwestern Pentecostal Holiness College in Oklahoma City.

The denomination cares for about eighty boys and girls at its Falcon Children's Home in North Carolina. The elderly are looked after at the Carmen Home in Carmen, Oklahoma. It operates a modern printing establishment, The Advocate Press, which publishes the denominational weekly, *The Pentecostal Holiness Advocate,* as well as church school literature for its 200,000 members. Its 70 missionaries are serving in the following conferences: Union of South Africa, Nigeria, Northern Rhodesia, India, Hong Kong, Argentina, Costa Rica, Mexico, and Latin America.

Although the growth of the Pentecostal Holiness Church has not been spectacular, it has been consistently steady. In 1916, the church's statistics read thus: 192 churches, and 8,096 members;[43] they now read as follows: 1,331 churches, and 60,665 members.[44]

Assemblies of God. Until this organization came into existence, Pentecostals in America were governed either by a small association

[43] *Religious Bodies: 1926,* II, p. 1092.
[44] Landis, *Yearbook,* p. 77.

with a dynamic leader at its head—like Charles Fox Parham or Florence Louise Crawford of the Apostolic Faith—or they were governed by bodies like the Church of God and the Pentecostal Holiness Church, which were largely regional. No national organization existed to serve the thousands of Pentecostals who were either not from the South, or, if they were, who were not from the Holiness wing. A few men were aware of this, however, and it was they who provided the impetus for establishing the Assemblies of God, a denomination which would fuse the heterogeneous Pentecostal assemblies, missions, and tabernacles which were scattered from New England to the Pacific Coast and from the Great Lakes to the Gulf Coast.[45]

As far back as 1909, a handful of ministers in the Southwest had become disenchanted with the leadership of Charles Fox Parham and had banded together for fellowship. In the group were Howard A. Goss, W. F. Carothers, Arch P. Collins, Eudorus N. Bell, and Daniel C. O. Opperman. Bell—a pastor in the Southern Baptist Convention for seventeen years, educated at Stetson University, the Baptist Seminary at Louisville, and the University of Chicago—was selected to edit still another publication called *Apostolic Faith.* Opperman, formerly the principal in the Zion, Illinois, school system, was chosen to conduct scores of six-week-long Bible schools in Houston, Fort Worth, Hattiesburg (Mississippi), Joplin (Missouri), Des Moines and Ottumwa (Iowa), Anniston (Alabama), and Hot Springs (Arkansas).[46] These schools were operated on the traditionally Pentecostal "faith" policy. Studies consisted chiefly of a "verse-by-verse exposition of a 'Pentecostal' Passage of Scripture,"[47] and since most of the student's time was spent in evangelistic work, there was little time "to establish the prospective ministers in sound doctrine."[48]

Meanwhile, in the southeastern section of the United States, the nucleus of another Pentecostal group was forming under the leadership

[45] The definitive history of the Assemblies of God is Carl Brumback's *Suddenly from Heaven.* Another lengthy history appears in Kendrick's *The Promise Fulfilled,* pp. 73–144. A popular treatment is Irwin Winehouse's *The Assemblies of God: A Popular Survey.*

[46] Brumback, *Suddenly from Heaven,* p. 110.

[47] *Idem.*

[48] *Idem.*

of H. G. Rodgers of Alabama. In 1909, he invited all ministers who were uncommitted to any other Pentecostal organization to attend a three-day session at Dothan, Alabama. Those who attended referred to themselves as Church of God, completely unaware that a group of Pentecostals in Tennessee had prior claim to the name. Two years later they met at Slocomb, Alabama. Twenty preachers were on hand to rejoice in the ordination of four new clerics and the licensing of seven others, as well as to discuss the need to change the name of the organization.

The men in the Southwest were equally dissatisfied with their appellation, Apostolic Faith, so Howard A. Goss called on Elder Charles H. Mason of the Church of God in Christ and received permission from that Negro body to borrow its title. Armed with a new name, the southwestern contingent communicated with Rodgers and his followers and plans were laid to effect a merger. It became an actuality in 1913. The name of the periodical which Bell had been editing was changed to *Word and Witness,* and over three hundred ministers united in a common effort. However, the organization was most frail, most inadequate.[49] To remedy the situation, it was decided to issue a call for a "general council" in the pages of the *Word and Witness*. The December 20, 1913, issue summoned all "Pentecostal saints and Churches of God in Christ" to meet next April in Hot Springs. It stressed five reasons for calling such a conference: (1) to achieve better understanding and unity of doctrine,[50] (2) to know how to conserve God's work at home and abroad, (3) to consult on protection of funds for missionary endeavors, (4) to explore the possibilities of chartering churches under a legal name, and (5) to consider the establishment of a Bible training school with a literary division.[51]

[49] This was simply a loosely organized association of ministers, writes Goss, one of the members. "We had no organization beyond a 'gentleman's agreement,' with the understanding for withdrawing of fellowship from the untrustworthy." See *Winds of God,* pp. 163, 174 f.

[50] Disputes on doctrinal issues such as the sanctification controversy between the Pentecostals who had emerged from a Holiness tradition and those whose heritage had been Baptistic confused many Pentecostals. They sought some sort of central authority to define such issues.

[51] These are summarized in a public relations' document *In the Last Days*

From the time that the announcement appeared in December until the time when the interested Pentecostals arrived at Hot Springs, the plan was attacked in scores of editorials and sermons as "anti-Pentecostal" and "anti-Scriptural." In spite of such intense opposition, about 120 pastors and evangelists from 20 states and several foreign countries arrived in Hot Springs and registered as delegates. When the time for adjournment arrived, they had made the following constitutional declaration:

We recognize ourselves as a GENERAL COUNCIL of Pentecostal (Spirit Baptized) saints from local Churches of God in Christ, Assemblies of God and various Apostolic Faith Missions and Churches, and Full Gospel Pentecostal Missions, and Assemblies of like faith in the United States of America, Canada, and Foreign lands, whose purpose is neither to legislate laws of government, nor usurp authority over said various Assemblies of God, nor deprive them to their Scriptural and local rights and privileges, but to recognize Scriptural methods and order for worship, unity, fellowship, work, and business for God, and to disapprove of all unscriptural methods, doctrine and conduct, and approve all Scriptural truth and conduct, endeavoring to keep the unity of the Spirit in the bonds of peace, until we all come into the unity of the faith, and of the knowledge of the Son of God, unto a perfect man, unto the measure of the stature of the fulness of Christ, and to walk accordingly, as recorded in Eph. 4:17–32. . . .[52]

Furthermore, the convention attacked two very difficult matters that confronted it from the outset: the establishment of an accepable system of organization, and the formulation of a doctrinal statement to which the delegates, coming from such diverse religious traditions, could subscribe. The first problem was resolved by adopting a very simple kind of polity. The relationship of the local churches to the national body, as the aforementioned declaration asserts, would be one of equality, unity, and cooperation; the rights of sovereignty of each local affiliated church would not be violated. The central administering body, the Executive Presbytery, would be elected by the General Council, and its function would be to expedite the denomina-

(p. 11), published by the Assemblies of God and obtainable at 1445 Boonville Avenue, Springfield, Mo.

[52] The complete text of the "Preamble and Resolution on Constitution" appears in Kendrick, *Promise Fulfilled,* pp. 84–86.

tion's program of missions and evangelism. The second problem was not resolved. Action was postponed on the matter of a doctrinal statement. Perhaps there were just too many different doctrinal persuasions represented by the delegates for a newly created organization to tackle such a thorny problem. In any case, the convention seemed satisfied to state that "the holy inspired Scriptures are the all-sufficient rule for faith and practice and we shall not add to or take from them."[53]

Two years later (1916) at St. Louis, the fourth General Council[54] adopted a "Statement of Fundamental Truths," admitting its selective nature but declaring it to be sufficient for a "sound full-gospel ministry." A hasty perusal of these Truths reveals the Assemblies of God to be Trinitarian and Arminian; to practice two ordinances—water baptism by immersion, and the Lord's Supper; to hold to a view of sanctification that may be described as "progressive" rather than "instantaneous"; and, finally, to be strongly premillennial.

In the fall of 1918, four years after the meeting in Hot Springs, the Assemblies of God relocated its executive offices in Springfield, Missouri, where it has continued to maintain its headquarters. It listed 91 missionaries and slightly more than 500 ministers as being affiliated with it.

The polity of the Assemblies of God is an admixture of congregational[55] and presbyterian elements. The General Council is the legislative and policy-making body, having the highest constitutional authority. It meets biennially, and is composed of all ordained ministers and one delegate from each recognized church. The General Presbytery is chief administrative body, subordinate in its authority only to the the General Council. The district superintendents and two other persons elected by each district comprise the Presbytery, an important executive and judicial branch. The General Council elects eight resi-

[53] Brumback, *Suddenly from Heaven*, p. 174.

[54] Two Councils were held in 1914, one at Hot Springs in April, another in Chicago in November. This accounts for four Councils in three years.

[55] Its congregationalism is most evident on the local church level, where each church is an autonomous unit. It selects its own pastor, decides if it wants to support the national policies, and so forth. The purpose of the General Council is "not to use up authority over the various local assemblies, nor to deprive them of their scriptural and local rights and privileges. . . ." Winehouse, *Assemblies of God*, pp. 200, 217.

dent Executive Presbyters—a general superintendent, five assistant superintendents, a general secretary, and a treasurer—as well as eight nonresident executive presbyters, who represent eight geographical divisions. These sixteen men execute the mandates given at the General Council, and they serve as trustees of the Council. They are empowered to supervise and have oversight of all departments, acting for the corporation in all matters that affect its interests while the General Council is not in session. Finally, a District Council exists to supervise the religious activities of Assemblies of God churches within a prescribed geographical area, but under no conditions can it violate principles set forth in the General Council constitution or bylaws. A District Council elects its own officers and arranges for its own annual conventions.

From the outset, the Assemblies of God has been intensely missions-conscious.[56] It has more than 800 missionaries under appointment, serving in 71 countries. On its roster are listed 12,657 national workers who minister in 12,459 foreign churches and "preaching points." It operates 72 foreign Bible schools and claims a foreign membership (based on a record of converts) of 985,241.[57]

The denomination also conducts a diversified program of Home Missions: it has an extensive work among the foreign language groups in America; it has 100 workers on 30 Indian reservations in 14 states;[58] it has Jewish converts conducting missions in cities like New York and Chicago;[59] its prison work is also quite elaborate, as is the ministry to the deaf and the blind.

Publishing is another important phase of the work which the Assemblies of God does. (Gross sales in 1965–1966 fiscal year totaled $4,888,418.) It owns and operates an ultamodern printing plant, The Gospel Publishing House, which prints more than ten tons of religious literature each day. Here the *Pentecostal Evangel,* the denominational weekly, is published.

[56] In 1960, Assemblies of God Churches contributed $6,620,857.00 toward missions.

[57] These figures were supplied by Rev. Carl Conner, until recently Director of Public Relations for the Assemblies of God.

[58] Winehouse, *Assemblies of God,* p. 141.

[59] *Ibid.,* pp. 142–44.

As is true in many Pentecostal groups, educational facilities within the Assemblies of God have been slow in developing. However, as the denomination has grown so has its interest in education. Today, the Assemblies of God has two fully accredited colleges of arts and science. One is in Costa Mesa, California (Southern California College); another is in Springfield, Missouri (Evangel College). It likewise operates a variety of Bible colleges and junior colleges: Southwestern Assemblies of God College in Waxahachie, Texas; Central Bible College in Springfield, Missouri; Bethany Bible College in Santa Cruz, California; Northwest College of the Assemblies of God in Kirkland, Washington; North Central Bible College in Minneapolis, Minnesota; Northeast Bible Institute in Green Lane, Pennsylvania; and South-Eastern Bible College in Lakeland, Florida.[60]

The Assemblies of God is the largest Pentecostal denomination in America. It reports having 8,159 ordained ministers, 8,452 churches, and a membership of 555,992.[61]

Pentecostal Church of God of America. When editor of the *Word and Witness,* Eudorus N. Bell, used his paper to summon all interested Pentecostals to a "general council" at Hot Springs in April, 1914, there were many ministers who could not understand how a local church could possibly unite with a national organization and not lose its sovereignty and spiritual liberty. Therefore they refrained from attending and from joining the newly formed General Council of the Assemblies of God. They remained independent. Then when the fourth Council formulated a "Statement of Fundamental Truths," in order to combat an insurgent heretical faction within the denomination, many of these self-styled independents construed the act as a trend toward conventional ecclesiasticism.

By 1919, however, this former antiorganization party organized itself as the Pentecostal Assemblies of the USA.[62] Led by John C. Sinclair of Chicago who had attended the initial meeting of the Assemblies of God at Hot Springs, this group united, content to be bound

60 Brumback, *Suddenly from Heaven,* p. 364.

61 Landis, *Yearbook,* pp. 15 f.

62 See Kendrick, *Promise Fulfilled,* pp. 145–52, for a competent survey of this denomination.

by the principle that had been enunciated at Hot Springs in 1914, namely, that the Scriptures would be the all-sufficient rule for faith and practice. In a short time it also proclaimed the following rather liberal policy regarding membership and ordination:

> We deem it advisable, in order to avoid creating unscriptural lines of fellowship and disfellowship, to affiliate on the basic principles of love, righteousness and truth, with due recognition of each other, allowing liberty of conscience in matters of personal conviction.
>
> . . . .
>
> Two or more regularly ordained ministers in good standing shall have authority to ordain by imposition of hands and prayer such as have a call to the ministry and have proven their gifts and callings by actual success rather than the hopes of what they may be: This ordination shall be in conjunction with the pastor and local assembly.[63]

In 1922, the title Pentecostal Church of God replaced Pentecostal Assemblies of the USA. When the General Convention of 1933 authorized the relocation of its headquarters from Ottumwa, Iowa, to Kansas City, Missouri, in order to avoid confusing their church with a local independent church which bore the same title, the denomination added the phrase "of America." In 1950, the headquarters of the Pentecostal Church of God of America were moved to Joplin, Missouri, where it had built new facilities.

The General Convention which meets biennially and which is made up of denominational officers, ordained and licensed ministers, missionaries, plus one lay delegate for each hundred members of a chartered congregation, is the highest ruling body in the church. Next in authority is the Executive Board, composed of all the officials of the denomination together with the district superintendents, and one presbyter from each district. The officers of the church include a general superintendent, three assistant superintendents—chosen by the three geographical sections of the church (western, central, and eastern) and then confirmed by the General Convention—a general secretary-treasurer, and a director of world missions. Kendrick informs us that "the program of the General Convention is conveyed

[63] *Ibid.*, p. 146, citing Pentecostal Church of God, *Minutes* (Chicago: Pentecostal Church of God, 1922), pp. 3, 7.

to the local congregations through district organizations"[64] which are a miniature of the national pattern.

The Pentecostal Church of God of America has not been as active in the area of foreign missions as some of the other Pentecostal bodies. In 1960, it had but 36 missionaries in 13 fields; however, its work among the American Indians has been so extensive and fruitful that a separate division with a director for Indian missions was established in 1949. The church maintains but one degree-granting institution[65]—Pentecostal Bible College in Sacramento, California.

The practices of the Pentecostal Church of God of America coincide rather closely with those of most other Pentecostal groups. One commentator, however, feels that the church takes "a much more lenient attitude toward divorce and remarriage than does [*sic*] most of the other Pentecostal denominations," for it allows "those who have been divorced for the cause of fornication to be admitted to the ministry."[66]

In recent years the denomination has shown rapid growth. In 1936 it reported having 81 congregations and 4,296 members; the latest *Yearbook of American Churches* contained this entry: churches, 1,150; inclusive membership, 115,000; ordained clergy having charges, 1,200.[67]

Pentecostal Assemblies of the World. About the time of World War I, when Pentecostal organizations like the Assemblies of God were being organized, a doctrinal controversy that had originated on the West Coast swept through the heartland of the United States, especially around St. Louis and Indianapolis. The "New Issue," "Oneness," or "Jesus Only," as the doctrine has been called, contended that *true* baptism must be "in the name of Jesus" only, rather than in employing the traditional Trinitarian formula.[68] Furthermore, the

[64] *Ibid.*, p. 149.

[65] Approved only by the California State Department of Education, not by a regional accrediting agency.

[66] Everett LeRoy Moore, "Handbook of Pentecostal Denominations in the United States" (unpublished Master's thesis, Pasadena College, 1954), p. 99.

[67] *Religious Bodies: 1936,* II: 2, p. 1349; Landis, *Yearbook,* p. 76.

[68] Consult Brumback, *Suddenly from Heaven,* pp. 191–210, for a definitive study of this "New Issue" teaching and its effects. Also his *God in Three Persons* for a doctrinal refutation of what he calls a "heresy."

proponents of this view denied that there are three Persons in the Godhead, asserting instead that there are three manifestations of one Person, namely, Jesus.[69]

For a time, this teaching threatened to topple the newly formed Assemblies of God, because many of its leaders—men like H. G. Rodgers, Eudorus N. Bell, Howard A. Goss, and Daniel C. O. Opperman—submitted themselves for rebaptism in "Jesus' name." The ministerial roster of the Assemblies of God was decreased by more than 150, and the missionary giving shrank to less than $5,000. Despite these losses, however, the denomination withstood the "unitarian" onslaught within its ranks and at its fourth General Council in St. Louis (1916) prepared a "Statement of Fundamental Truths." The right to draft such a statement was challenged by the "Oneness" contingent on the grounds that the formative Council at Hot Springs had declared that the Scriptures *alone* were to be the "all-sufficient rule for faith and practice," and here was a man-made creed being proposed. They argued that this was a departure from the liberty which had characterized earlier Pentecostalism. The Assemblies of God withstood the challenge, and articulated a position that was stanchly Trinitarian. The "Oneness" faction withdrew and formed the Pentecostal Assemblies of the World, locating their headquarters in Indianapolis, where G. T. Haywood, one of the leading Negro evangelists, had a powerful "Jesus Only" congregation.

In matters of polity the Pentecostal Assemblies of the World resembles Methodism. The highest deliberative body is the General Convention which meets annually. It is presided over by a board of bishops, a general secretary, and a treasurer. In its practices the group differs from other Pentecostal bodies in the following ways: (1) its view of baptism "in the name of Jesus" and (2) its use of wine in the commemoration of the Lord's Supper. On the other hand, it is similar to many of the smaller charismatic groups in its opposition to secret societies, church bazaars, the wearing of jewelry, attractive hosiery, bobbed hair, bright ties, and short, low-neck dresses.[70]

[69] Winehouse, *Assemblies of God,* p. 46.

[70] Frank Mead, *Handbook of Denominations* (4th rev. ed., Nashville: Abingdon Press, 1965), p. 172.

In 1926, the Pentecostal Assemblies of the World reported having 126 churches and 7,850 members.[71] The 1960 figures reveal a substantial growth: 550 churches and 45,000 members, and 450 ordained clergy having charges.[72]

United Pentecostal Church. Originaly all "unitarian" Pentecostals were united in this one interracial body, the Pentecostal Assemblies of the World. Then in 1924, the white constituents, believing that integration hindered their efforts to evangelize the world, withdrew to form the Pentecostal Church, Inc. By 1936, it reported having 168 churches and 9,681 members, mostly in Illinois, Missouri, Tennessee, Louisiana, and Texas.[73]

In 1931, a number of churches in the Middle Atlantic, South Atlantic, and North Central States which had not affiliated with the Pentecostal Church, Inc., united to form another still larger denomination—the Pentecostal Assemblies of Jesus Christ. From a doctrinal and polity standpoint, however, there were so many similarities between the two groups that an eventual merger was inevitable.

At its annual conference in 1944, the Pentecostal Assemblies of Jesus Christ resolved to approach the Pentecostal Church, Inc. concerning a merger. The latter group accepted the invitation and plans for a quick amalgamation were initiated. One year later, in St. Louis, a merger was effected, and the United Pentecostal Church came into being.

Despite the fact that the new denomination was organized in accord with a congregational form of church government and fully recognized the sovereignty of the local church, a strong central administration developed. The General Conference, which meets annually and which is composed of all ministers and one delegate from each local congregation, became the highest legislative body. It was directed by an executive committee, the General Board, composed of a superintendent, two assistant superintendents, a secretary-treasurer, home and foreign missions secretaries, the editor of *The*

[71] *Religious Bodies: 1926,* p. 1088.
[72] Landis, *Yearbook,* p. 76.
[73] Information furnished by W. E. Kidson, General Secretary of The Pentecostal Church, Inc. in *Religious Bodies, 1936,* II:2, pp. 1330 f.

Pentecostal Herald, and one presbyter from each district. All of the major activities of the church—missions, Christian education, publications, and so forth—were placed under the jurisdiction of the General Board.

The United Pentecostal Church is unquestionably the largest "unitarian" or "Oneness" group of Pentecostals. In 1965, it numbered 1,800 churches, 1,800 pastors,[74] and more than 200,000 members. It maintains Bible training institutes at St. Paul, Minnesota; Portland, Oregon; Tupelo, Mississippi; Stockton, California, and East Massillon, Ohio; it sponsors "Harvestime," a radio program that is broadcast over 230 stations, and supports 78 missionaries and over 500 native workers.[75]

In addition to deviating from the so-called "normative" Pentecostal denominations by maintaining that "water baptism . . . must be administered in the name of the LORD JESUS CHRIST, as consistently taught in the Bible,"[76] and that there is only one person in the Godhead—Jesus Christ,[77] the United Pentecostal Church also seems to endorse a more rigorous code of social behavior for its constituents. For example, they are admonished to refrain from "indulging in any activities which are not conducive to good Christian and Godly living," namely, attendance at theaters or dances, wearing make-up or "apparel that immodestly exposes the body," listening to "unwholesome radio programs and music," possessing a television set, or women allowing their hair to be cut.[78] As a matter of fact, writes Kendrick, "The matter of cutting hair is considered so important that the central office distributed a special booklet on the subject giving fifteen reasons why women should have long hair."[79]

[74] Landis, *Yearbook,* pp. 77 f.

[75] Information supplied by the Foreign Missionary Department of the United Pentecostal Church.

[76] A tract entitled "Your Special Invitation" (St. Louis: Pentecostal Publishing House, n.d.).

[77] Oscar Vouga, *Our Gospel Message* (St. Louis: Pentecostal Publishing House, n.d.), p. 29.

[78] *What We Believe and Teach* (St. Louis: United Pentecostal Church, n.d.), p. 10.

[79] *Promise Fulfilled,* p. 175. The sixteen-page booklet is entitled *The Hair Question* and is written by Murray E. Burr (St. Louis: Home Missionary Department, United Pentecostal Church, n.d.).

International Church of The Foursquare Gospel. Like many other Pentecostal groups, the International Church of The Foursquare Gospel illustrates a tendency peculiar to many sects—the propensity of the masses to rally behind an outstanding personality.[80] Without a doubt, Aimee Semple McPherson, the founder of The Foursquare Church, epitomizes the leader in whom were blended physical attractiveness, personal charm, fluency, a sense of the dramatic, and simple orthodoxy. Furthermore, "Sister Aimee" was concerned for the "have nots" within our society; she was able to win their devotion. They remained faithful to her even during the times when she was allegedly involved in family quarrels, lawsuits, and kidnaping incidents.[81]

For several years during her early evangelistic career, Mrs. McPherson's name was carried on the ministerial rolls of the Assemblies of God.[82] In 1917, following brief missionary service in China, where Robert Semple (her first husband) died, and climaxing six years of religious activity, "Sister Aimee" commenced a long evangelistic crusade that was to carry her to the largest auditoriums around the world.

In 1921, while conducting a revival campaign in Oakland, California, Mrs. McPherson became fascinated by the prophetic vision of four faces (those of a lion, man, ox, and eagle) recounted in Ezekiel 1:4–10, and she immediately associated them with the four points which she incessantly emphasized in her gospel preaching: salvation, Holy Spirit baptism, healing, and the second coming of Christ. In her soul "was born a harmony that was struck and sustained upon four full, quivering strings, and from it were plucked words that leaped into being—THE FOURSQUARE GOSPEL."[83] The

[80] Parham was the individual around whom the multitudes gathered to form the Apostolic Faith movement; Florence Crawford, Homer Tomlinson, and "Sweet Daddy" Grace provided charismatic leadership for The Apostolic Faith, Church of God, World Headquarters, and the United House of Prayer for All People, respectively.

[81] Clark, *Small Sects,* p. 115.

[82] Kendrick, *Promise Fulfilled,* p. 154.

[83] McPherson, *The Foursquare Gospel,* pp. 22 f., quoted in Kendrick, *Promise Fulfilled,* p. 155. Until now she had been interdenominational, "without any concerted support, moral or financial, from organized groups or de-

phrase, writes Raymond Becker, editor of *The Foursquare Magazine,* instantly struck the fancy of her audience, as she declared to them that such a perfect (foursquare) gospel is the only answer to man's every need, "complete for body, soul, spirit, and for eternity."[84]

During the days that followed, a ministerial conference was held for the purpose of assembling those to whom such a foursquare gospel appealed. "Over one thousand names were signed to a statement of doctrine and purpose the first day,"[85] and The Foursquare Gospel Association was born. Not too long thereafter, on January 1, 1923, Aimee Semple McPherson dedicated the first church of The Foursquare Gospel—Angelus Temple, opposite Echo Park on Glendale Boulevard in Los Angeles. What had started out to be a modest frame structure evolved into a one-and-a-half-million-dollar sanctuary seating 5,300. Its strikingly impressive dome, stained-glass windows which depict the entire life of Christ, great proscenium arch, choir lofts, and red-carpeted aisles[86] made Angelus Temple an impressive center for religious activities. It was inevitable that Foursquaredom would develop from merely a local organization to one of national and international prominence, and that still another separate Pentecostal denomination would be born.

One Pentecostal historian, Klaude Kendrick, is convinced that Mrs. McPherson had no intention of starting another religious body when she was conducting her earlier revival campaigns or even while Angelus Temple was being constructed. It was simply that a host of people who had been attracted to her brand of Pentecostalism would never be content to return to any church that functioned differently.[87]

The International Church of The Foursquare Gospel expanded after 1923,[88] when an Evangelistic and Missionary Training Institute

---

nominations." From "Historical Data on the International Church of the Foursquare Gospel," a mimeographed document supplied by the headquarters office in Los Angeles.

[84] Becker, "The Church of the Foursquare Gospel," *The Foursquare Magazine,* XXVII (May, 1954), 15.

[85] *Idem.*

[86] Kendrick, *Promise Fulfilled,* p. 156.

[87] *Ibid.,* p. 157.

[88] For an interesting account just recently published, see Chap. VIII ("Sister

was started as an auxiliary of Angelus Temple. Soon many graduating students launched into the work of establishing home and foreign missions. Branch churches sprang up in the environs of Los Angeles. By 1925, thirty-two churches had been established in southern California and fifty others were appealing to Angelus Temple for permission to affiliate. Today, nearly forty years later, The Foursquare Church is one of the largest Pentecostal denominations. It has 741 churches, staffed by an equal number of ordained ministers, and an inclusive membership of 89,215.[89] The churches support 104 missionaries, who serve in 26 countries.[90] In 1957, the total valuation of Foursquare churches was in excess of 20 million dollars.[91]

As Frank Mead observes, "Mrs. McPherson was president of the church during her lifetime and was the ruling power and voice of the organization."[92] Thus she presided over all conventions, boards, cabinets, councils, and committees; she held the power of veto over the actions of the board of directors; she appointed all officers, including the five members of the board of directors—the highest administrative body—and chairmen of committees; she also hired all personnel, and set their salaries. Her successor, son Rolf K. McPherson, carries on this tradition. Otherwise, central legislative authority is vested in the Annual Convention, the voting constituency of which includes the officers and directors of the church, all ordained and licensed ministers, and one lay delegate from each 100 members of every chartered church.

Aimee Semple McPherson") in Gordon L. Hall, *The Sawdust Trail* (Philadelphia: Macrae Smith Co., 1964).

[89] Landis, *Yearbook,* p. 52.

[90] Howard P. Courtney, "International Church of The Foursquare Gospel," *Pentecostal Evangel,* XLV (Aug. 11, 1957), 22.

[91] *Ibid.,* p. 23.

[92] *Handbook,* p. 117.

CHAPTER 9

Varieties of Pentecostalism in America (II): The Regional, Ethnic, Small, Cultic Groups

The seven Pentecostal organizations that we have just described have expanded both nationally and internationally and represent the majority of Pentecostals in the United States. However, there are about two dozen other groups—many rather obscure—that have had an impact only upon certain sections of the United States, that are racially or ethnically oriented, that have never become numerically impressive, or that remain on the outer fringes because of a preoccupation with some bizarre practice. Since most of these groups are frequently ignored in popular summaries of American Pentecostalism, I shall survey the more typical ones in this chapter.

Regional Pentecostal Bodies

Among the many small charismatic groups the ministry of which is primarily to those residing in the Southeast are the Church of God of the Mountain Assembly, Pentecostal Fire-Baptized Holiness Church, Congregational Holiness Church, Emmanuel Holiness Church, and the Pentecostal Free-Will Baptist Church.

The Church of God of the Mountain Assembly. Although this group did not formally organize until 1906, it was really created in 1895 when "a number of ministers who were affiliated with the United Baptist Church of the South Union Association in Kentucky began to preach a closer communion with God and the danger of apostasy."[1] In 1903, they were disfellowshiped by the Association for "preaching the possibility of being lost after regeneration."[2] Three years later these ministers, together with a half dozen churches, met in council at Ryan's Creek, Whitely County, in eastern Kentucky, to form a new organization.[3] The name Church of God was adopted; however, when it became known that another group had already been using the same title, the qualifying phrase "of the Mountain Assembly" was added in 1911. One year after its incorporation in 1917, the church established permanent headquarters at Jellico, Tennessee. Its growth has not been as spectacular as that of some other Pentecostal groups. It numbers about 175 ministers, 100 churches and missions, and approximately 3,200 members.

Pentecostal Fire-Baptized Holiness Church. This small Pentecostal denomination thrives in North and South Carolina, Georgia, and Alabama. It came into being at Nicholson, Georgia, on August 9, 1918, when a group of people who had formerly been affiliated with the Pentecostal Holiness Church withdrew because of a controversy "over the wearing of adornments and elaborate dress."[4] Unlike the body from which it separated, the Fire-Baptized Church advocates a sterner discipline in "matters of dress, amusements, association between the sexes, the use of tobacco, and various other practices": filthiness of speech, foolish talking, jesting, slang; attendance at fairs, swimming pools, shows; jewelry, gold, feathers, flowers, costly apparel, and neckties. Young women are admonished to wear their dresses at least halfway from knee to floor; the older ones, to wear theirs longer; all are forbidden to have their hair bobbed or waved.[5] According to its former general secretary, A. O. Hood, spontaneity in worship is

[1] J. E. Hatfield, "The Church of God of the Mountain Assembly," *Pentecostal Evangel,* XLV (Sept. 8, 1957), 23.

[2] *Idem.*

[3] Moore, "Handbook," pp. 172 f.

[4] Clark, *Small Sects,* p. 110.

[5] *Idem.*

sanctioned; joyous demonstrations (shouting, crying, hand clapping) frequently punctuate the service.[6] Doctrinally, the Fire-Baptized Church stresses sanctification as a second definite work of grace, subsequent to regeneration and the baptism of the Holy Spirit, evidenced by speaking in other tongues, subsequent to sanctification. It is one of the smallest Pentecostal bodies, having 34 ministers, 36 churches, and only 574 members.[7]

Congregational Holiness Church. In 1920, a major portion of the Georgia Annual Conference of the Pentecostal Holiness Church withdrew to form the Congregational Holiness Church. The separation resulted from a controversy regarding the doctrine of divine healing.

> One faction contended that the provision in the atonement for the healing of the body was all-sufficient, and that it was unnecessary to supplement any human means to assist God in effecting a healing. This faction admitted the therapeutic value of any effective remedy, but it did not deem such as necessary for God to perform a healing in the body. The other side, which finally withdrew to form the Congregational Holiness Church, insisted that since God had placed remedies here He intended that these remedies should be used if a person expected to be healed.[8]

While little or no mention is made of this matter in most of the official publications of the Congregational Holiness Church, its disaffection with the episcopal type of polity by which the Pentecostal Holiness Churches are governed is rather pronounced. This too might have caused the separation. One senses this antipathy in the Preface to the *Discipline* of the Congregational body.

> Our purpose is to follow the techniques of the Bible. So in form of government we believe in a Congregational Government, . . . We observe how both State and Church have suffered when a few held the reins of government. So knowing by experience or observation, the injustice and suffering that is brought on individuals when the whole assembly is not allowed a voice, we do with a feeling of duty we owe to God and His followers, also with courage, organize the Congregational Holiness Church.[9]

[6] In an article which the Rev. Mr. Hood wrote for *Religious Bodies: 1936,* II:2, p. 1356.

[7] Landis, *Yearbook,* p. 77.

[8] Campbell, *Pentecostal Holiness,* p. 277.

[9] Greenwood, South Carolina: Congregational Publishing House, 1962, p. 2.

Conditions for membership in the Congregational Holiness Church are rather rigid, not so much in the areas of faith as in those of practice. For instance, one must abstain from the use of tobacco in every form, slang language, membership in "Oath Bound Secret Societies," wearing shorts and bathing suits, alcoholic beverages, and worldly entertainments like the theater, ballrooms, circuses, public swimming pools, ball games, lotteries, and games of chance.[10]

The work of the Congregational Holiness Church is concentrated in Alabama, the Carolinas, Georgia, and Virginia, although in recent years the group had begun to sponsor missionary projects in Cuba and Nigeria. In 1962, it is reported that 139 ministers were affiliated with it, and that 151 churches in the denomination served a constituency of 5,212.[11]

Emmanuel Holiness Church. One of the more recent entries into the catalogue of American Pentecostal groups, this denomination was organized on March 19, 1953, at the Columbus County Camp Ground in Whiteville, North Carolina, by a group of preachers from the Pentecostal Fire-Baptized Holiness Church. These men allegedly left the "mother church" because they had been forbidden to wear neckties.[12] During the past decade, the original dissidents have been joined by others, so that today this small denomination numbers 56 churches, having an inclusive membership of 1,200.[13]

Pentecostal Free-Will Baptist Church. The newest Pentecostal body was formed in 1959 by the merger of three Free-Will Baptist Conferences in North Carolina.[14] Their roots stretch back into the eighteenth century, to the time when the Free-Will Baptists, having emigrated from Wales, were organized in the South by Paul Palmer.[15]

When Pentecostalism manifested itself in the South at the turn of this century, some Free-Will Baptist churches embraced it; however, they remained autonomous and loosely organized until fifteen or

[10] *Ibid.,* pp. 3 f.
[11] Landis, *Yearbook,* p. 40.
[12] Moore, "Handbook," p. 217.
[13] Landis, pp. 75 f.
[14] *Ibid.,* p. 77.
[15] Mead, *Handbook,* p. 43.

twenty years ago.[16] Since the merger of the three North Carolina Conferences in 1959, the embryonic movement has grown to include 135 churches, 175 ordained clergy, and 10,000 members.[17]

For the sake of completeness, it is necessary to mention two other Pentecostal groups whose influence has likewise been primarily regional: the Pentecostal Church of Christ, and the Elim Missionary Assemblies.

Pentecostal Church of Christ. John Stroup is the founder of this rather small Pentecostal body, consisting of 45 churches and 1,243 members.[18] Prior to World War I, the Rev. Mr. Stroup, then an evangelist in South Solon, Ohio, having experienced the Holy Spirit baptism, "began zealously to preach his faith and experience" to those who lived in the area where the states of Ohio, Kentucky, and West Virginia meet.[19]

In a short time, several ministers embraced Stroup's faith, and on May 10, 1917, at Advance, Kentucky,[20] a number of them met with Stroup in order to organize a conference "for the purpose of drawing various like-minded persons together for fellowship and service to God." It was called the Pentecostal Church of Christ, and Stroup was chosen as its first bishop. At this time the organization was simply one which included ministers, but later the need to organize the churches was recognized.

In response to an item on a questionnaire which asked: "Although you may be affiliated with the Pentecostal Fellowship, are you in any way distinctly different from other Pentecostal groups?" Chester I. Miller, General Overseer of the denomination, wrote:

We are not different. Every point of doctrine, standard, and mode of

[16] Carl Conner, "Pentecostal Free-Will Baptist Churches," *Pentecost,* No. 50 (Dec., 1951), p. 4.

[17] Landis, *Yearbook,* p. 77. Conner points out that of the churches reported, only one small one is in Virginia; the remainder are all in North Carolina. He adds that there are an additional fifty churches in South Carolina holding similar beliefs that have not yet affiliated with the Pentecostal wing of the Free-Will Baptists.

[18] *Ibid.,* p. 76.

[19] "Cornerstone Laid in Memory of John Stroup," *The Witness and Messenger,* VI (Sept., 1964), 3.

[20] Mead, *Handbook,* p. 173, identifies the locale as Flatwoods, Ky.

operation is identical with some other group. . . . We are not like any one of them in all particulars but in the total sum we are very much like the "Holiness" Pentecostal groups.[21]

It is understandable, therefore, why recent issues of the denominational periodical have reported that steps have been taken to strengthen the bonds of fellowship between the Pentecostal Church of Christ, the Emmanuel Holiness Church, and the Pentecostal Holiness Church.

Among the proposals . . . suggested for further fellowship were joint participation in youth camps, joint Bible conferences and camp meetings, an offer to our churches to use the architectural drawings and blueprints which the Pentecostal Holiness Churches had drawn up for their own churches, increased fellowship in the exchange of evangelists and even pastors, etc.[22]

Elim Missionary Assemblies. This rather recent addition to the already sizable number of Pentecostal denominations was established in 1947, the outgrowth of a ministerial fellowship which had been formed in 1933, composed primarily of graduates of an independent Pentecostal school—Elim Bible Institute.[23]

The Institute had been established in 1924 at Hornell, New York, by Ivan Q. Spencer, for he desired to fill the void that had been created by the earlier closing of Elim Faith Home and Bible Training School in nearby Rochester. These institutions had had profoundly lasting influences on the embryonic Pentecostal movement,[24] and when they were forced to close, Spencer, an alumnus, felt compelled to establish a similar school.

Since its founding, the Elim group has experienced modest growth. Its 1961 reports listed 75 churches and approximately 4,000 members who are served by 80 ministers.[25] The churches, observed Everett

[21] Information in response to the author's questionnaire, Apr., 1962.

[22] "Pentecostal Holiness Church Promotes Fellowship," *The Witness and Messenger,* VI (Sept., 1964), 3.

[23] Carlton Spencer, "Elim Missionary Assemblies," *The Pentecostal Evangel,* XLV (Oct. 27, 1957), 20.

[24] See Brumback, *Suddenly from Heaven,* pp. 228–29.

[25] Atter, *Third Force,* p. 228; Landis, *Yearbook,* p. 75.

Moore in his study of Pentecostal groups, "are confined almost entirely to N.Y. and Pennsylvania."[26]

Although the fellowship is small, it sponsors forty missionaries in ten foreign countries—an enviable ratio of one missionary for every hundred members. In addition to its missionary activities, the denomination publishes *The Elim Herald* and operates the aforementioned Elim Bible Institute at Lima, New York.

Racial and Ethnic Groups

From the very beginning, Pentecostalism achieved great success among various racial and ethnic groups. While it may be possible to explain the popularity of Pentecostalism among the Negroes, who, according to Elmer Clark, "are given to emotional exercises, . . . shouting, . . . and bodily movement," it is more difficult to account for its appeal among other ethnic groups. And yet Pentecostalism has been widely accepted by the Italian- and the Spanish-speaking people as well as by the Negroes.

Fire Baptized Holiness Church of God of the Americas. At Anderson, South Carolina, in 1908, this Negro Pentecostal body separated from the predominantly white Fire Baptized Holiness Association of America.[27] W. E. Fuller, who subsequently became the General Overseer of the new group, gives the following somewhat obscure explanation for the separation:

> We were connected with the white people for 10 years and at the expiration of 10 years we met again at Anderson, S.C., 1908, and owing to the growing prejudice that began to arise . . . , it was mutually agreed that we have separate incorporations.[28]

In 1922, most of what is its present name was adopted; then four years later, following a meeting with the Mt. Moriah Fire Baptized Holiness Church at Knoxville, Kentucky, the phrase "of the Americas" was added.[29]

[26] Moore, "Handbook," p. 112.
[27] Mead, *Handbook,* p. 107.
[28] *Religious Bodies: 1936,* II:1, p. 695.
[29] Clark, *Small Sects,* p. 11.

As stated in its booklet of doctrine, "The Basis of Union," this Pentecostal body emphasizes the following teachings: repentance, regeneration, justification, sanctification, Pentecostal baptism, speaking in other tongues as the spirit gives utterance, divine healing, the premillennial second coming of Christ, and the sanctity of marriage. There is also an unequivocal statement to the effect that the Fire Baptized Holiness Church of God of the Americas "opposes the teachings of the so-called Christian Scientists, Spiritualists, Unitarians, Universalists, and Mormons."[30]

When the separation from the white group was effected in 1908, the membership of this group was a scant 925.[31] In 1936, it reported 1,973 as being members of 59 churches in 11 states and the District of Columbia.[32] The most recent statistics, already more than a decade old, reveal that the First Baptized Holiness Church of God of the Americas claimed to have 300 churches serving a constituency of 6,000.[33]

Apostolic Overcoming Holy Church of God. Like the Church of God in Christ, this Negro Pentecostal association, consisting of 300 churches and ministers and a membership totaling 75,000,[34] is largely the result of one man's leadership, that of W. T. Phillips.

The church was incorporated in Alabama in 1916 as the Ethiopian Overcoming Holy Church of God. Earlier, Bishop Phillips had withdrawn both from the Methodist Episcopal Church and the Negro branch of the Apostolic Faith Mission (for which he had abandoned Methodism). According to the few extant reports, Phillips had "failed to find the faith and liberty which he sought"[35] in both of the aforementioned organizations; therefore, following a quarrel with his superiors, he left to organize his own sect. The word "Ethiopian" re-

[30] *Religious Bodies: 1936,* II:1, p. 696.

[31] *Idem.*

[32] *Idem.* Most of the churches were in the South Atlantic States: N.C. had seven; S.C., twenty-one; Ga. and Fla., seven each.

[33] Landis, *Yearbook,* p. 49.

[34] *Ibid.,* p. 14.

[35] Moore, "Handbook," p. 277. Clark (*Small Sects,* p. 122) observes that Phillips, while a minister in the Methodist Episcopal Church, had received "certain supernatural revelations and enduements," but that he was restrained by the denomination when he attempted to preach about them.

mained as part of the official title until June, 1927, when it was replaced by "Apostolic."

Phillips, as founder and senior officer of his church, is in supreme control, and his term in office is unlimited: He has power to appoint overseers and junior bishops. All pastors to congregations are appointed by him or by the oversees acting in his stead.

Expenses of local churches are paid by "free will offerings"; ministers are compensated by tithes which members are obligated to contribute. But, writes Oliver, the clergy almost without exception have to do outside work besides their parish duties in order to make an adequate income.[36] The pastors pay their tithes to Bishop Phillips, who in turn contributes 10 per cent of such income to the poor fund, which is administered by him.[37]

The religious services in the Apostolic Overcoming Holy Church of God, writes Frank Mead, "are free emotional affairs bordering on the bizarre, with the participants speaking in tongues and engaging in ecstatic dances."[38] Oliver corroborates this observation in his dissertation. He writes that no hymnals are used; the songs are spirituals; rhythm is important; therefore drums, tambourines, the stamping of feet and the clapping of hands individually accompany the singing portion of the worship service.[39]

United Holy Church of America, Inc. At Oxford, North Carolina, on September 25, 1918, this association of Negro Pentecostals was incorporated. By 1936 it was able to report that it had 162 churches (91 of them in North Carolina) and 7,535 members.[40] By 1966, the *Yearbook of American Churches* recorded the group as having 470 churches, 379 ordained clergy, and 28,980 members.[41]

Elmer T. Clark contends that "there is nothing distinctive about this sect," except perhaps for the confusing practice whereby individual congregations often select names that resemble the title em-

[36] Oliver, "Some Newer Religious Groups," p. 24.
[37] Clark, *Small Sects,* p. 122.
[38] *Handbook,* p. 28.
[39] Oliver, p. 24.
[40] *Religious Bodies: 1936,* II: 2, pp. 1646 f.
[41] Pp. 96 f.

ployed by other Pentecostal groups, such as Union Pentecostal, Church of God, Holy Temple, Holy Tried Stone, House of Prayer, House of God, and Pentecostal Tabernacle, to mention but a few.[42]

National David Spiritual Temple of Christ Church Union (Inc.), U.S.A. Rev. David William Short was ordained by the Missionary Baptist Church, but he was convinced that "generally all denominational churches are founded on the theories, philosophies, and doctrines of men"[43] who completely disregard the examples of the saints of the primitive church, who are opposed to the doctrines of holiness, healing, prophecy, divers kinds of tongues, and who are burdened by all forms of race prejudice. Such views did nothing to endear Short with the Baptists. Soon, together with seven other pastors and delegates, he left the Baptist Church to organize the National David Spiritual Temple—a church which he declared to be "the true spiritual church of Christ" that honored the "gifts of the Holy Ghost which originated on the Day of Pentecost."[44]

In his study of the National David Spiritual Temple of nearly a decade ago, Everett Moore suggested that Archbishop Short's followers believe him to be a divinely sanctified and appointed Church Overseer. Thus he is subject only to the leadership of the Holy Spirit and not to the desires of his followers.[45]

In 1965, this group, whose national headquarters are in Los Angeles, reported having 66 churches, 63 ordained clergy, and 40,815 members.[46]

Christian Church of North America. This progressive body of Italian Pentecostals is an outgrowth of the efforts of three Chicagoans—Louis Francescon, Giacomo Lombardi, and P. Ottolini—who became advocates of Pentecostalism during the charismatic revival which swept their city in 1907. Having received their Spirit baptism accompanied by glossolalic utterances at William H. Durham's North Avenue

[42] Clark, *Small Sects,* p. 119.

[43] From information furnished by Bishop Short in *Religious Bodies: 1936,* II: 2, pp. 1259 f.

[44] Moore, "Handbook," p. 122.

[45] *Ibid.,* p. 126.

[46] Landis, *Yearbook,* p. 77.

Mission, these men proceeded to witness among their countrymen in some of the great metropolitan areas of the United States. Louis Francescon and Giacomo Lombardi went to California and Pennsylvania while P. Ottolini evangelized Buffalo, New York City, and St. Louis.[47]

Largely because of their labors, Pentecostalism spread rapidly among the Italo-Americans along the East Coast. From New York it penetrated the Middle Atlantic States and New England. Sixty-seven churches were established in New York, New Jersey, and Pennsylvania alone.[48] By 1936, another forty had sprung up in Ohio, Michigan, Illinois, West Virginia, and California, to mention only the states that had more than one church.

All of these churches were incorporated locally under state law as separate congregations, each one a distinct entity with its authority vested in elders, deacons, and trustees. Finally in April, 1927, several of these congregations convened at Niagara Falls, New York, in order to discuss the adoption of common articles of faith. This was the first step toward unity on anything more than the local level.

Because of their abhorrence of all forms of centralized authority, and their stress upon local autonomy, these congregations became known as the Unorganized Italian Churches of North America. In 1939, the word "Unorganized" was dropped, and as the use of English increased, the word "Italian" was deleted in 1942. The group was incorporated under its present name at Pittsburgh, in 1948. At the present time, the Christian Church of North America reports having 151 churches with a membership of 20,000.[49] It conducts a vigorous missionary program, supporting fifteen missionaries in Belgium, Italy, the Philippines, Puerto Rico, Mexico, and Canada. In addition, the organization publishes two monthly religious journals: *The Lighthouse* for the English-speaking constituents, and *Il Faro,* for its Italian readers. It also maintains a rest home in Miami, Florida.

Spanish-Speaking Pentecostals. The Spanish Eastern District, The

[47] Joseph Fiorentino, "A Summary of the Italian Pentecostal Movement in the USA and Abroad," *The Lighthouse,* V (July, 1961), 7.

[48] *Religious Bodies: 1936,* II:1, p. 753.

[49] Landis, *Yearbook,* pp. 52 f.

Latin American Council, Church of God—Spanish District Council for the East, Assembly of Christian Churches, Damascus Christian Church, and Defenders of the Faith are the six major Spanish Pentecostal groups in New York. It is said that they represent "one of the most important developments in evangelical religion in New York."[50] While in 1937 there were only twenty-five Spanish Pentecostal churches in the city, by 1960 the number had increased to 240, with a total membership of 18,500.

Most of the six groups originated in Puerto Rico, the result of organizations initiated by English-speaking missionaries who had been sent there by the Assemblies of God, the Church of God (Cleveland, Tennessee), and other religious bodies.

The Spanish Eastern District, the largest Pentecostal group, has 57 churches in New York City and an estimated membership of 6,000. It is affiliated with the Assemblies of God but is almost completely autonomous. It administers churches in the states east of the Mississippi and in Puerto Rico through executive and general presbyters. A superintendent, vice-superintendent, secretary-treasurer, and three additional members constitute the executive presbytery of the so-called "Eastern District" which includes New York, New Jersey, Pennsylvania, Ohio, Florida, Connecticut, Delaware, Massachusetts, and Puerto Rico.[51] There are 161 churches in the branch with a total Sunday school attendance of 11,450.

Concilio Latino-Americano de la Iglesia de Dios Pentecostal de New York, Inc., the second largest group of Spanish Pentecostals, began its work around 1925 while part of the Council of the Pentecostal Church of God of Puerto Rico. Recently, the New York Council "broke away and became an autonomous group, retaining only a tenuous connection with the Puerto Rican body."[52] It oversees the work of 31 churches having an estimated membership of 2,355. The administrative structure of the Council consists of a seven-member

[50] Frederick L. Whitam, "New York's Spanish Protestants," *Christian Century,* LXXIX (Feb. 7, 1962), 163.

[51] Frederick L. Whitam, "A Report on the Protestant Spanish Community in New York City" (Department of Church Planning and Research; The Protestant Council of the City of New York, July, 1960), p. 36.

[52] Whitam, "New York's Spanish Protestants," p. 163.

Executive Committee of a permanent character, and the business of the organization is conducted by the annual assembly, which consists of ministers and lay delegates who convene each September. For the training of its ministers, the Council operates the three-year Latin American Biblical Institute. Although most churches are financed locally, there is a central budget which provides subsidies to congregations just commencing as well as to the parent body in Puerto Rico.

According to Whitam, the Spanish churches that are associated with the Church of God have an organizational structure similar to that of the Assemblies of God; that is, the Spanish District Council for the East, although affiliated with the Church of God whose headquarters are in Cleveland, Tennessee, functions autonomously.[53] The Spanish District Council is smaller than either of the previously described bodies of Pentecostals. There are but 10 churches affiliated with it, having an estimated membership of 750. Since it was founded in 1950, it is likewise the most recent organization. In addition to supervising the work in New York, the Spanish District Council maintains churches in Chicago, Lansing, and Toledo.

In New York City, the Assembly of Christian Churches has 26 congregations with 1,600 members.[54] It is an independent group incorporated in Washington, D.C., New York, Illinois, California, and otherwise legally constituted in Puerto Rico and the Dominican Republic. The Assembly has churches in these areas as well as missions in Mexico and Cuba. It also operates the Arca Evangelical Bible Institute, and, unlike many Pentecostal groups, is concerned with civic and social work.

> It has purchased a former nursing home in Manhattan for use as an orphanage . . . encourages the assimilation of Puerto Ricans into the culture of the mainland and has made some efforts to train Puerto Ricans in knowledge of city, state, and federal laws, in elements of citizenship, and in the use of the English language.[55]

The other Spanish Pentecostal groups—Damascus Christian Church

[53] Whitam, "A Report," p. 38.

[54] In the Metropolitan area there are 64 churches (including the 26) and an estimated baptized membership of 4,000.

[55] Whitam, "New York's Spanish Protestants," p. 164.

and Defenders of the Faith—"have fewer that 10 churches with about 1,000 members each."[56]

Individual Spanish Pentecostal churches vary from tiny storefronts to impressive edifices, from having only a handful of members and a part-time minister to a membership of nearly a thousand served by several full-time staff members.[57] The weekly program of all of these churches tends to be crowded, as prayer services are scheduled for Monday, a meeting of the women for Tuesday, Sunday School lesson preparation for Wednesday, men's meeting for Thursday, young people's service for Friday, choir rehearsal for Saturday, and two long services for Sunday morning and evening. In spite of, or perhaps because of, this activity, the Spanish Pentecostal groups thrive, for

> the individual member has opportunities to direct the service, to tell his troubles, to recount his religious experiences, to ask for prayers, and to give thanks for prayers said, or to ask for help.[58]

The sense of isolation which so often buffets the foreigner, and the accompanying loss of orientation in life—anomie, the sociologists call it—is counteracted by the warmth, welcome, and participation which he finds in a Pentecostal meeting. This is reflected in the following comments, gleaned from interviews with twenty-five Spanish-speaking ex-Catholics: "I used to go to the Catholic Church, there nobody knew me . . . now in my church they call me sister." "Me senti como en mi casa (I felt at home)." "I was lost here in New York, a friend invited me and I liked the way they sang and that we all could sing."[59]

Smaller Organizations

One of the many problems that beset the historian of Pentecostalism is the existence of a veritable spate of small groups which keep

[56] *Ibid.*, p. 163.

[57] While the average membership is small—around 50, with a Sunday School enrollment of 80—the Juan 3:16 Church in the Morrisania section of the Bronx has a membership of 700, a Sunday School enrollment of 900, and property (a renovated movie theater) valued around $145,000.

[58] Renato Poblete and Thomas O'Dea, "Secretarianism as a Response to Anomie," in Robert Lee, *Cities and Churches* (Philadelphia: The Westminster Press, 1962), p. 204.

[59] *Ibid.*, p. 203.

appearing and disappearing, uniting and separating. Of those that have survived, perhaps the best known are the various Churches of God, the strongly pacific International Pentecostal Assemblies, and the progressive Open Bible Standard Churches.

Churches of God. The first schism to rend the Church of God (Cleveland, Tennessee) occurred in 1919 and resulted in the formation of a new organization, the Original Church of God. From the rather sketchy evidence that is available, one gathers that the division resulted from a disagreement regarding the practice of tithing. Those who withdrew detested the rigid tithing policy of the Cleveland group; they wanted the right to contribute to the support of their church of their own free will.[60]

The Original Church of God is a small denomination, consisting of 35 churches, 34 ordained clergy, and 6,000 members.[61]

It publishes a monthly religious periodical, *The Messenger,* and conducts a Correspondence Bible School, which, one is rather amazed to discover, offers courses leading to the Doctor of Divinity degree.[62]

The second schism, conceded by some Pentecostals to be one of the tragically scandalous divisions during their brief history, resulted from A. J. Tomlinson's attempt to gain autonomous control of the Church of God.

From 1909 to 1919, Tomlinson served his church with distinction. An able administrator, although somewhat egotistical and autocratic, he personally managed almost every important denominational department: he issued credentials to ministers, kept records, filled vacancies, and acted as moderator-clerk of the annual assemblies.[63]

All went well until 1920. Then some dissatisfaction was expressed with the way Tomlinson distributed the tithes which local congregations had been sending to headquarters. Suspicion mounted, and two years later the General Assembly restricted Tomlinson by appointing

[60] Cf. Conn, *Like a Mighty Army,* note 20 on p. 180; Moore, "Handbook," pp. 169 ff.

[61] Landis, *Yearbook,* p. 34.

[62] Mead, *Handbook,* p. 74.

[63] Cf. Kendrick, *Promise Fulfilled,* p. 191; Conn, *Like a Mighty Army,* p. 169.

two new officials: an editor-publisher and a superintendent of education. "Such restraint of his former almost unlimited authority," reports Kendrick, "was a severe blow to Tomlinson. He tendered his resignation."[64] At the insistence of friends, he reconsidered but remained in office for only a short time. A year later (June, 1923) a committee charged with the task of investigating Tomlinson's financial administration submitted an unsatisfactory report to the Council of Elders.[65] Impeachment proceedings were filed against him, and on July 26, 1923, he was relieved of his office. Tomlinson wrote of those events thus:

> The opposition forces were in possession of all the property and almost all of my twenty years of labor was swept away. Only a few of the ministers stuck to me. . . . I walked out on a street corner in Cleveland, Tennessee, under the starry sky with the Church of God banner and started building again. . . . By November, 1923, we had purchased a lot on Central Avenue at a cost of $900 and erected a tabernacle and held our Eighteenth Annual Assembly.[66]

"From the time A. J. Tomlinson was impeached . . . and expelled from the Church, matters grew worse," writes Charles W. Conn,[67] for the former General Overseer contended that he and his supporters constituted *the* Church of God. Furthermore, it was alleged, mail intended for the group which had expelled Tomlinson was delivered to and accepted by him. Court action was inevitable. On February 26, 1924, the Chancery Court of Bradley County, Tennessee, served Tomlinson with an injunction to

> desist and refrain from claiming or representing themselves to be connected in any way with the Church of God . . . from keeping and retaining any remittance or contribution sent to the Church of God; and from receiving any members . . . upon the claim or representation that the same is the original Church of God. . . .[68]

[64] Kendrick, p. 193.

[65] The shortage of funds was only a small part of Tomlinson's dereliction and malfeasance. Ten of the twelve elders who heard the case filed a total of fifteen charges against him. They ranged from disloyalty and conspiracy against the church to usurpation of authority. See Conn, *Like a Mighty Army*, pp. 177 ff.

[66] A. J. Tomlinson, *Answering the Call of God* (Cleveland, Tenn.: White Wing Publishing House, n.d.), p. 23.

[67] *Like a Mighty Army*, p. 188.

[68] *Ibid.*, p. 189.

Tomlinson promptly filed a cross bill, thus initiating an extensive struggle through the Tennessee Court of Appeals and, finally, to the Supreme Court of Tennessee which sustained the original decree of the Chancery Court.

The Tomlinson Church of God, as it was known during the thirties, claimed two thousand congregations in 1943, the year that its leader died. In the period following Bishop Tomlinson's passing, misunderstandings concerning leadership erupted between his sons, Homer and Milton.[69] The latter remained in Cleveland, succeeding his father as General Overseer. A decade later (March, 1953), the name of the church was changed to The Church of God of Prophecy, although it is difficult to say precisely why.[70]

According to its most recent published statistics (1963), The Church of God of Prophecy claims to have 1,383 churches, 39,154 members, 3,813 bishops, deacons, and male and female evangelists.[71] The missionary activity of the church includes the support of 810 native ministers and missionaries in "India, Haiti, Jamaica, Australia, Germany, Egypt and 44 other countries."[72] *The White Wing Messenger,* a religious periodical that is published weekly; the Sunday School Orphanage, Inc. which cares for about one hundred children; the Tomlinson Memorial School, which enrolls about one hundred students in its elementary and high school divisions; "The Voice of Salvation," broadcast over 150 stations; and a shrine—Fields of the Woods—commemorating the birth of the church on June 13, 1903, in Cherokee County, North Carolina, are the primary institutional concerns of The Church of God of Prophecy.

The doctrinal tenets of the church coincide rather closely with

[69] Homer's version appears in Vol. II of the *Diary of A. J. Tomlinson* which he has been editing (New York: The Church of God, World Headquarters, 1953), pp. 98–112; Milton's views are perhaps those expressed in the *Cyclopedic Index of Assembly Minutes,* 1906–1949 (Cleveland, Tenn.: White Wing Publishing House, 1950), pp. 370–75.

[70] One gathers, in reading tracts published by the church (No. IF–01), that its evolution from a modest fifteen-person assembly to one of worldwide proportions is a fulfillment of prophecies such as those appearing in Isa. 54:7, 8.

[71] *Assembly Minutes* (Cleveland, Tenn.: White Wing Publishing House, 1963), pp. 32, 50.

[72] *Introducing the Church of God* (Cleveland, Tenn.: White Wing Publishing House, n.d.).

those of other groups which comprise the so-called Holiness wing of the Pentecostal movement. Its practices, however, differ radically in some instances. In church business meetings, for example, women are advised "to take no open part in discussing or deciding questions." They should always be present, and they should "silently pray God to give wisdom and direct the men and show forth God's glory in being the glory of the men."[73] Furthermore, members are told to dress with moderation. This includes "paying moderate prices for clothing, wearing dresses of high-enough necklines, low-enough hemlines, sleeves of reasonable length."[74] Finally, the constituency is informed that

> dabbling with worldly amusements like professional ball games, horse races, stock car races, wrestling arenas, skating rinks, motion picture houses or drive-in theatres, bowling alleys and going swimming where men and women both use the same bathing area would give the devil a foothold or place in your life.[75]

Whatever the reasons were, and the issues are admittedly obscured both by time and emotion, Homer A. Tomlinson was bypassed when the State Overseers of the Tomlinson Church of God gathered to select his father's successor.[76] It is Homer's contention that Bishop A. J. Tomlinson had designated him, his "son and long-time associate . . . as his successor and General Overseer," but that this selection had been opposed by certain state overseers, including his sister and her husband.[77] In a magnanimous action, Homer placed the younger Milton in charge and resigned from all headquarters' activities in which he had participated for forty years, including the overseership of New York State.[78]

According to Elmer Clark, "the state overseers and the nonminis-

[73] *Assembly Minutes, 1963,* p. 152.

[74] *Ibid.,* p. 153.

[75] *Idem.*

[76] The New York *Times,* Dec. 9, 1943, p. 13, intimates that "policy differences of long standing between the *urban* and *rural* wings of the Church of God" were responsible for the confusion regarding the selection of a successor to Bishop A. J. Tomlinson.

[77] *Assembly Minutes, 1963,* p. 153.

[78] Cf. Clark, *Small Sects,* p. 103, and *Diary of A. J. Tomlinson,* II, pp. 100–109.

terial general overseer [Milton] then combined and expelled Homer A. Tomlinson from the church." It is possible that following Milton's election to the bishopric, Homer raised the question of the propriety of Milton's ordination. The older brother seemed to take an almost peculiar delight in his public statements to demean Milton. Homer emphasized the fact that Milton had merely been a printer and a deacon prior to his becoming General Overseer.[79] In addition, Homer seems to have advocated that the office remain vacant until a General Assembly could be convened, thus questioning the legislative function of the state overseers and particularly the legality of their selecting Milton.[80]

Having been cast out of the Tomlinson Church of God, and having observed a mourning period of thirty days, Homer, still convinced that he was General Overseer of the *true* Church of God, "summoned the whole church to New York, December 7th and 8th, 1943, and in mighty anointings was confirmed in his position."[81]

A center for the activities of the Church of God, World Headquarters, as Bishop Homer A. Tomlinson's group became known, was established at Queens Village, New York. Elmer Clark reports that Homer "reorganized his father's followers and renewed his evangelistic activities."[82] The denomination has grown; however, just how large it has become is conjectural, for the data that are avaliable seem to be somewhat exaggerated. *The Yearbook of American Churches for 1966* listed these figures: members, 74,511; ministers, 1,812; churches (in the United States alone), 1,903.[83]

On doctrinal matters, the Church of God, World Headquarters, differs little from the positions held by the other Churches of God. There is the belief in justification by faith, sanctification, baptism of the Holy Spirit with glossolalic manifestations, and the premillennial second coming.

As far as church government is concerned, the Queens Village group appoints its officials, whereas the Cleveland (Tennessee) body

[79] See The New York *Times,* Nov. 27, 1943, p. 14.
[80] *Diary,* II, pp. 109 f.
[81] *Ibid.,* p. 110.
[82] Clark, *Small Sects,* p. 104.
[83] Landis, *Yearbook,* p. 34.

elects its officers. The function and influence of the office of General Overseer is without any question greater in the Church of God, World Headquarters, than in the other branches. This is obviously the result of the vigorous if often unorthodox programs of Bishop-General Overseer Homer A. Tomlinson. In 1952, for instance, he visited sixty-nine foreign countries, "going boldly for Peace on Earth" and lifting high "the All-Nations Banner of love given him by his father." During the following year he proclaimed three great new goals for his church: (1) peace on earth; an end to the scourge of war; (2) the elimination of poverty; (3) greater efforts to evolve a holy church, one "without blemish." Many have claimed Homer A. Tomlinson to be an eccentric; few have questioned his sincerity, especially when they hear him preach as follows:

> We preach healing and people are healed. We preach Salvation, and people get saved. We preach sanctification, and people get sanctified. We preach the Baptism of the Holy Ghost and people get the blessing. We preach the Church of God, and people press into Her. Now let us preach peace, the gospel of peace. Don't be a war preacher any more. God is the God of Peace, the Gospel is the Gospel of peace (Acts 10:36; 2 Cor. 13:11; I Thess. 5:23).[84]

In the fall of 1964, students at the University of Kansas heard the seventy-two-year-old churchman describe why he was making another bid for United States President on the Theocratic Party ticket. His political platform advocated the adoption of (1) a new criminal code: forgive criminals 490 times if they are repentant (Matt. 6:14; 18:21–22), and use prisons for refuge cities wherein the wrongdoer may repent (II Pet. 3:9); (2) a new civil code: the covetous will be sentenced to lose all (Rom. 7:7; I Kings 21:19); (3) the practice of tithing to replace the present modes of taxation, the union of church and state, the policy of unlimited production and free enterprise, the endeavor to see that all nations attain to America's 1964 wage scale, and the abolition of divorce, gambling, tobacco, liquor, racial inequality.[85]

The efforts of Bishop Tomlinson, their abortiveness and naïveté

[84] *Diary,* II, p. 120.

[85] "Bishop Tomlinson at University of Kansas," *The Church of God,* XXI (Oct. 15, 1964), 1, 3–4.

notwithstanding, should do something to silence those who criticize the Pentecostal movement for its lack of social consciousness.

International Pentecostal Assemblies. In 1936, the amalgamation of two older Pentecostal associations—The Association of Pentecostal Assemblies[86] and the National and International Pentecostal Missionary Union[87]—resulted in the formation of the I. P. A., as it is known in Pentecostal circles.[88] The purpose of the reorganized group has been "cooperative fellowship, dedicated to the task of carrying the full gospel to the ends of the earth."[89]

The International Pentecostal Assemblies is one of the smaller Pentecostal denominations. In the 1936 census it reported having 98 churches and 6,333 members.[90] Most of the churches were located in the Middle Atlantic States and in the East North Central area—18 in New York, 10 in Ohio, 9 in Illinois, and 15 in Michigan. The churches which had been established in other states reported pathetically small memberships.[91] Unlike most other Pentecostal bodies which have been experiencing postwar gains, the I. P. A. has sustained some losses: in 1960, for example, it reported having only 50 churches and ministers, and 5,000 members in 23 states.[92]

Despite its small size, the International Pentecostal Assemblies has conducted a vigorous missionary program in Kenya, East Africa, where they claim to have twenty-two churches, staffed by eighteen native workers, five of whom have been ordained since 1956.[93] Another field of I. P. A. missionary activity is Mexico. In addition, the denomination publishes one of the oldest Pentecostal periodicals, *The Bridegroom's Messenger,* a publication which was started in 1907. Furthermore, the group maintains the Beulah Heights Bible

86 Founded in 1921 by Mrs. Elizabeth A. Sexton, her daughter Dr. Hattie M. Barth, and Paul T. Barth.

87 Philip Wittich established this association in 1914.

88 L. Sigsbee Miller, "The International Pentecostal Assemblies," *Pentecostal Evangel,* XLV (Aug. 18, 1957), 20.

89 *Idem.*

90 *Religious Bodies: 1936,* II:2, p. 1338.

91 One church in Tennessee reported having seven members; another in Oregon had seventeen. *Ibid.*, p. 1339.

92 Landis, *Yearbook,* p. 76.

93 International Pentecostal Assemblies, *Minutes* (Aug., 1960).

Institute in Atlanta, Georgia, and the William Carter Bible College at Greensboro, North Carolina.

About the only characteristic which appears to differentiate the I. P. A. from the other Pentecostals is a strongly worded policy regarding the participation of its members in war.

> While we believe that government is ordained of God, and that God's children should be "Subject unto the higher powers," according to Rom. 13:1–7, yet, as the Word of God admonishes us to "follow peace with all men," to "Love our enemies" and to "Resist not evil," we believe war to be at variance with the principles of the Gospel, and that God's children should not take up arms against their fellowmen. Matt. 5:39–48; Heb. 12:14.[94]

Open Bible Standard Churches, Incorporated. This fast-growing segment of the American Pentecostal movement, which has its national headquarters at Des Moines, Iowa, emerged in 1935 as a result of the amalgamation of two revivalistic bodies which had similar beliefs regarding doctrine and polity: the Bible Standard, Incorporated, and the Open Bible Evangelistic Association.

Fred Hornshuh and A. J. Hegan, the founders of the Bible Standard group, had been directors of the Lighthouse Temple in Eugene, Oregon. About 1914, this Pentecostal Church had been affiliated with Florence Louise Crawford's Apostolic Faith Mission in Portland, Oregon. The relationship became strained, however, when both Hornshuh and Hegan objected to the requirement that remarried divorcees separate before being admitted to church membership. In addition they objected to the parochialism of a mission which claimed to be the *only* true church, thus preventing it from fellowshiping with other Pentecostal bodies.[95] In 1919, when they saw that Mrs. Crawford would not entertain their pleas for a more temperate view regarding these matters, Hornshuh and Hegan, together with three others—Messrs. Hansen, Neat, and Thomas—withdrew to organize the Bible Standard Church. Fred Hornshuh, who was elected moderator, also

[94] International Pentecostal Assemblies, *General Principles* (Atlanta: Lee's Printing, n.d.), p. 11.

[95] Kendrick, *Promise Fulfilled,* pp. 167 f.

published the *Bible Standard Magazine* and founded the Bible Standard Training School.[96]

In Des Moines, the Pentecostal witness was largely the result of revivals which Aimee Semple McPherson had conducted there in 1927 and 1928. In the short space of two years three congregations had come into being: (1) The Foursquare Gospel Lighthouse, occupying quarters formerly belonging to the Grace Methodist Church; (2) a second Church, seating 1,500, under construction on Locust Street; (3) and a segment of the Foursquare Gospel Lighthouse at the original location (Fifth and Grand Streets) under the leadership of Rev. J. R. Richey, a recent arrival from California.[97]

However, Richey, an able organizer and preacher, was disenchanted with Mrs. McPherson. It was largely through his influence, then, that in 1932 the Iowa and Minnesota divisions of the Foursquare Church voted to withdraw from the parent body. Kendrick merely states that the "action was taken because of unhappiness resulting from certain practices within the Foursquare fellowship."[98] Everett Moore, however, pinpoints the practices as follows: (1) the inconsistency of Mrs. McPherson's life with her message; (2) the unfavorable publicity associated with the infamous kidnaping incident; and (3) the demand by Mrs. McPherson that all churches deed their property to the general organization which she controlled.[99]

Thirty-two ministers voted to separate and reorganize under Iowa law as the Open Bible Evangelistic Association. Three years later, on July 26, 1935, the amalgamation with the Bible Standard Church was effected. In 1946, an alteration of the charter was made, and the name of the group was changed to its present form—Open Bible Standard Churches, Incorporated.

Whereas the International Church of The Foursquare Gospel follows the episcopal pattern of church government, allowing its churches little choice in the selection of their pastor,[100] a modified congregational policy is the organizational pattern of the Open Bible

[96] *Ibid.*, p. 166.
[97] *Ibid.*, p. 165.
[98] *Idem.*
[99] Moore, "Handbook," p. 77.
[100] *Ibid.*, p. 71.

Standard Churches. Local congregations are sovereign units. The highest governing body is the General Conference, an annual meeting of all licensed and ordained ministers, together with one lay delegate from each church. A thirty-three-member General Board of Directors, consisting of area superintendents from the five geographical divisions of the church, executive officers, and department supervisors, handles the regular business of the church. An Executive Committee, which is made up of six elected officials, oversees the administration of the ten departments within the association.[101]

At the present time, the denomination numbers 261 churches (concentrated, for the most part, in the Central, Midwest, and Pacific Coast areas), 265 ordained clergy, and 26,000 members.[102] The church dispatched its first missionary to India in 1926. Since that time, it has expanded its missions program, maintaining about fifty men and women in these foreign centers: Guinea (West Africa), Liberia, Argentina, Jamaica, Cuba, Trinidad, Japan, and Puerto Rico. It also supports three Bible training schools—the Bible Standard College in Eugene, Oregon; Dayton Bible Institute in Ohio; and Open Bible College in Des Moines.

Cultic Branches

Most of the Pentecostal groups that have been described thus far are in general agreement on matters of faith and practice. There are a few deviant branches, however, which ought to be described in order that our catalogue of American Pentecostalism be as complete as possible. These groups on the outer fringe include a few cultic factions which indulge in some rather bizarre practices.

A cult has been described variously as (1) a religious movement which is oriented about a leader with a charismatic appeal, (2) one which has not existed long enough or has not become large enough to challenge the existing order, and (3) one which is looked upon as

[101] R. Bryant Mitchell, "Open Bible Standard Churches," *Pentecostal Evangel,* XLV (Sept. 29, 1957), 26.

[102] Landis, *Yearbook,* p. 75.

curious or mysterious or at least an odd form of religious expression.[103] In *The Church as a Social Institution,* David O. Moberg defined a cult as a loosely organized, impermanent group of people seeking satisfaction through some form of personal religious thrill.[104] Within Pentecostalism there are a number of marginal groups that fit the aforementioned descriptions, although as Elmer T. Clark warns his readers, "these are by no means representative of the Pentecostal movement."[105] One such group is the United House of Prayer for All People; another is the snake-handling cults which are ensconced in the mountainous regions of Virginia, Kentucky, and Tennessee.

The United House of Prayer for All People. Until the death of its leader—Bishop Charles Emmanuel Grace—in January, 1960, The United House of Prayer for All People was one of the largest deviant groups of Negro Pentecostals in this country: more than 300 churches in 60 cities, and an estimated three million followers.[106] (These statistics are somewhat incredible: an average of ten thousand members per church!)

For decades The United House of Prayer was a one-man-dominated organization. Bishop Grace, whose real name is thought to be Marcelino Manoel da Graca,[107] was the undisputed head and direct source of all major decisions. He founded the church in New England (West Wareham, Massachusetts) in 1919, when he constructed a House of Prayer for the total cost of thirty-nine dollars.[108] By the time of his death, Bishop ("Sweet Daddy") Grace's churches dotted the eastern seaboard. Moreover, at that time, the fortune of the one-time railroad cook-immigrant cranberry picker—who had been born in 1881 on Brava, Cape Verde Islands off the West African coast—[109]

[103] Purnell H. Benson, *Religion in Contemporary Culture* (New York: Harper & Row, 1960), pp. 613 ff.

[104] Englewood Cliffs, N.J.: Prentice-Hall, 1962, p. 88.

[105] *Small Sects,* p. 98.

[106] Cf. Gordon L. Hall, *The Sawdust Trail,* p. 163; "Sweet Daddy's Sugar," *Newsweek,* LV (Feb. 15, 1960), 32.

[107] J. LaFarge, "Incredible Daddy Grace," *America,* CIII (Apr. 2, 1960), 5.

[108] An article in The New York *Times,* Jan. 13, 1960, p. 47, places the founding in Charlotte, N.C., in 1926.

[109] LaFarge, "Incredible Daddy Grace," p. 5.

was estimated to be about thirty million dollars in cash, not including additional millions in real estate and securities.[110] Furthermore, it is common knowledge that "Sweet Daddy" Grace owned and administered, among other things, a soap factory, a coffee plantation, an insurance company, and apartment buildings.

What was the appeal of this man who answered to no board of presbyters and who privately boasted that he would not tolerate any minister who was smart enough to question his (Grace's) undisputed authority? According to one observer, it was that "his rites brightened dulled lives, became a focal point of hope for the frustrated and emotionally starved and offered excitement and thrills for everyone."[111]

In the Houses of Prayer primitive emotions find release. Services begin with congregational singing, accompanied by piano or band and interlarded with shrieks, handclapping, and stamping.[112] As the tempo and volume increase, members advance to the front of the auditorium to dance on the sawdust-covered floor; others flit about the aisles and passageways. Some collapse and fall prostrate to the floor; some speak in tongues. Many raise their arms and cry. And the Bishop was not apt to discourage adulation; in fact, it is reported that his admonitions consisted of shifting the attention of his adherents from God to himself.

> Never mind about God. Salvation is by Grace only. . . . Grace has given God a vacation, and since God is on His vacation, don't worry Him. . . . If you sin against God, Grace can save you, but if you sin against Grace, God cannot save you.[113]

In the Houses of Prayer, healing was dispensed. Daddy Grace's famed miracle soap not only cleaned the body but also reduced fat and healed sickness.[114] *Grace Magazine* (which sold for ten cents)

[110] The New York *Times,* Aug. 26, 1961, p. 2.

[111] Richard Mathison, *Faith, Cults and Sects of America* (Indianapolis: Bobbs-Merrill, 1960), p. 242.

[112] A rather complete description of a typical service appears in Arthur H. Fauset, *Black Gods of the Metropolis* (Philadelphia: University of Pennsylvania Press, 1944), pp. 27 f.

[113] *Ibid.,* pp. 112 f.

[114] Mathison, *Faith, Cults,* p. 241.

would, when applied, heal any ailment and even extract a tooth.[115]

Moreover, deficiencies of an inadequate education were miraculously overcome. Although 84 per cent of those that attended services conducted by the cult never got beyond the eighth grade, by purchasing Bishop Grace's "Gospel Stationery" (two sheets and two envelopes for five cents) they would be "supernaturally enabled" to compose a good letter.[116]

All in all, relatively little is known about Bishop Grace or the United House of Prayer for All People,[117] for as Elmer Clark has pointed out, "the group has no literature that can be trusted."[118] That the Bishop was undisputed head of the cult is evident. The task of the preachers was simply to carry out his instructions, conduct services, preach, and "perhaps most important of all," wrote Arthur H. Fauset, "to raise money."[119]

In outward form and pretension, the belief, practice, and polity of the United House of Prayer resembles a Pentecostal group of the perfectionistic type; that is, it believes in conversion, sanctification, and the ministry of the Holy Spirit. However, when the group is examined more closely, "the beliefs boil down to a worship of Daddy Grace."[120] Dr. Eddy writes:

> Bishop Grace allowed his disciples to believe that he is eternal and that he was present at the crucifixion of Christ. . . . Once I asked him outright if he were God. He replied somewhat evasively, "People say I am." Regardless of what he believed about himself, his followers looked upon him with worshipful regard. In every sanctuary, they have pictures of him in the flowing robes and the sacred bleeding heart associated with Christ.[121]

[115] Albert N. Whiting, "The United House of Prayer for All People: A Case Study of a Charismatic Sect" (unpublished Ph.D. dissertation, American University, 1952), p. 73.

[116] Fauset, *Black Gods,* p. 30.

[117] One of the most complete participant-observer types of investigation has been conducted by Dr. G. Norman Eddy of the Boston University College of General Education. His findings are recorded in an unpublished manuscript, "The True Believers: Some Impressions of American Deviant Religions," pp. 36–45.

[118] *Small Sects,* p. 122.

[119] Fauset, p. 24.

[120] *Ibid.,* p. 26.

[121] Eddy, "True Believers," p. 44.

Elsewhere, Elmer T. Clark analyzes The House of Prayer as being "theologically chaotic."[122]

In February, 1960, a month after "Sweet Daddy" was stricken in Los Angeles, Walter McCollough of Washington, D. C., was elected his successor. The next two years literally teemed with problems for the tall, thin, middle-aged Bishop. First, James Walton of Philadelphia, in the name of the House of Prayer, filed suit against Bishop McCollough, charging him with illegally disposing of the church's assets and requesting that the court require him to give an accounting. Lawyers for the Bishop argued that Walton represented a "splinter group" of the church and that he had no authority to sue.[123] After hearing evidence, District Judge George Hart ordered the Walton group which had been "interfering in a manner not justified" in the activities of the United House of Prayer to stop using the name of the church.[124]

Then after a year had nearly elapsed Judge Hart ordered the more than thirty millions of dollars in church assets frozen, and declared the office of bishop vacant, ruling that McCollough had been illegally elected.[125] Apparently the General Assembly, in violation of the church's constitution, had been improperly convened: all of the church elders had not been notified.

Finally, an additional suit was filed in Atlanta, accusing Bishop McCollough of using church funds "to maintain himself 'in unbelievable luxury' after illegally seizing the bishopric."[126]

The legal problems involving the Bishop and the denomination, described by the press as a vast religious organization of three million or more members throughout fourteen states, were resolved on May 9, 1962.[127] Judge Hart ruled that he would restore full control of the United House of Prayer to Bishop McCollough, who had rewon his post in an election on April 7. Furthermore, the judge released the Bishop from all previous restrictions and turned over to him the man-

[122] *Small Sects,* p. 123.
[123] The New York *Times,* Oct. 7, 1960, p. 71.
[124] *Ibid.,* Oct. 18, 1960, p. 79.
[125] *Ibid.,* Aug. 26, 1961, p. 41.
[126] *Ibid.,* Oct. 3, 1961, p. 34.
[127] *Idem.*

agement and assets of the far-flung membership.[128] However, it is too early to tell, as Dr. Eddy has observed, whether the cult has diminished or increased under Bishop McCollough's leadership.[129]

The Snake-Handlers. Whereas The United House of Prayer for All People is a Negro cult that is oriented about a charismatic leader, the predominantly white snake-handling cults concentrate their attention on a bizarre practice.

George Went Hensley is acknowledged to be the founder of snake-handling religion. After reading Mark 16:17 f.,

> And these signs will accompany those who believe: in my name they will cast out demons; they will speak with new tongues; they will pick up serpents, and if they drink any deadly thing, it will not hurt them; they will lay their hands on the sick; and they will recover.

"Little George," as he became known, felt compelled to test this biblical passage, so one day in 1909 he climbed White Oak Mountain, which rims Grasshopper Valley (Tennessee) on the east, in search of a large rattlesnake. A few days later, while conducting evangelistic services at nearby Sale Creek, Hensley cited the passage in Mark, thrust the rattler at the people, and challenged them to take it up as a test of their faith.

For about ten years, until Garland Defriese, one of Hensley's converts, was bitten, snake-handling meetings continued unabated in members' houses or in improvised brush shelters. The faithful "carried their Bibles and their snakes to meeting, chanted, spoke in tongues, prayed, and suffered ecstatic seizures."[130]

Following the Defriese incident, LaBarre relates that "the practice of snake-handling went into a state of suspended animation"[131] at Sale Creek. Meanwhile, Hensley relocated, first as pastor of the East Pineville Church of God and later as the one to introduce snake-handling at the Church of God at Pine Mountain.[132] It was of this group

[128] *Ibid.,* May 9, 1962, p. 34.
[129] "True Believers," p. 69.
[130] Weston LaBarre, *They Shall Take Up Serpents* (Minneapolis: University of Minnesota Press, 1962), p. 12.
[131] *Idem.*
[132] About seventeen miles from Harlan, Ky.

that the general public first heard when in the summer of 1938 the Associated Press sent out a story about snake-handling religion and the trial of three members of the Pine Mountain Church of God. John Day, whose wife was a member of the cult, had the men arrested, charging that reptile handling was a breach of the peace. In the trial that was subsequently held at Harlan, Kentucky, all three were acquitted.[133]

That the snake-handling cult had spread was made manifestly clear by the reports of several tragedies and near-tragedies that were carried by the various wire services and reported in The New York *Times* during the summer and fall of 1940. In Adel, Georgia, Rev. W. T. Lipham and Albert Rowans (father of a five year old girl who along with a half dozen others had been bitten by poisonous snakes at religious meetings) were booked and subsequently imprisoned on charges of assault with intent to murder.[134] During the same month of August, in Moscow, Ohio, three cultists were bitten by a copperhead snake "at the height of a frenzied religious service."[135] The *Times* dispatch quoted "Brother" Robert Sears, a railroad worker and pastor of the True Church of God, as saying: "We'll use snakes in our services whenever the Lord requires." He further declared that Mrs. Ethel Shelby, the forty-eight year old nurse who had been bitten on the right arm and who had received a timely antitoxin, was in the hospital because "she didn't feel the power of the Lord as the snake was passed to her." Later in August, from Hazard, Kentucky, came news that Jim Cochran, thirty-nine year old father of several children, died eighteen hours after being bitten on the right hand at Sunday services at the Holiness Church in Duane.[136] While from Leslie County came the report that Mrs. Clark Napier, forty year old mother of seven, died on August 22, after being bitten at services in Hyden.[137] Finally, on September 21, there was news of the passing

[133] Keith Kerman, a reporter who had been sent to Kentucky by the St. Louis *Post-Dispatch,* later recorded his observations in a chapter in *Eve's Stepchildren* (ed. by Lealon N. Jones, Caldwell, Idaho, 1942), pp. 93–102.

[134] The New York *Times,* Aug. 1, 1940, p. 18; Aug. 3, p. 28; and Aug. 4, p. 31.

[135] *Ibid.,* Aug. 6, 1940, p. 21.

[136] *Ibid.,* Aug. 27, 1940, p. 13.

[137] *Idem.*

of Robert Cordle of Richlands, Virginia, from a snake bite received in the religious services of a "New Light" congregation in Tazewell County.[138]

In 1943, Raymond Hays, a snake-handling preacher from Kentucky and a convert of George Went Hensley, came to Grasshopper Valley, Tennessee, with a box of rattlesnakes and copperheads, reviving a practice which had fallen into disrepute after the near-fatal accident to Garland Defriese. As a result of Hays's meetings, the Dolly Pond Church of God with Signs Following was organized and Tom Harden was elected its leader.[139] Weston LaBarre refers to this church as the "Mother Church of snake-handling in the South," and describes it as a building of "rough lumber, unpainted, with the two-by-four studs exposed in the undecorated interior."[140] By 1945, this church, with Tom Harden and George Went Hensley—respectively the preacher and the prophet of the cult—in the vanguard, opened services just beyond the city limits of Chattanooga.[141] Harden and Hensley were quickly arrested and fined for disorderly conduct. For refusing to pay the fine, they were sentenced to serve on a road gang. The case was appealed, and the charges were subsequently dismissed.

As accidents continued to recur among the snake-handlers, public opinion became aroused. Bills were passed in the Tennessee, Virginia, and Kentucky legislatures "against the handling of snakes in the public performance of religious ceremonies."[142] The result was that the cult was slowly forced to relocate in a number of the other southeastern states. About 1946, for example, a Rev. Gordon Miller led a group of snake-handlers in Euharlee, Georgia.[143] Bill Parsons

[138] *Ibid.*, Sept. 22, p. 3. In his article "Rattlesnake Religion" which appeared in *Christian Century,* LXIV (Dec. 10, 1947), 1517 f., John A. Womeldorf declared that "at least thirteen deaths are on record [since 1940] and the probability is that there are a great many which are unrecorded."

[139] Dolly Pond is a remote mountain hamlet some thirty miles from Chattanooga. Harden—a tall, slender, sharp-featured man of thirty—was the son of Enoch Harden, a convert of George Hensley and a disciple of Raymond Hays. See LaBarre, *They Shall Take Up Serpents,* p. 15.

[140] *Ibid.*, p. 16.

[141] *Ibid.*, p. 24.

[142] The first bill was passed by the Tennessee legislature in Feb., 1947. *Ibid.*, p. 26.

[143] See *Time,* L (Sept. 8, 1947), 25, for an account of how Miller baited Ernest Davis to drink from a "salvation cocktail" (strychnine).

directed the activities of The Holiness Faith Healers near Stone Creek, Virginia,[144] Benjamin R. Massey and the Rev. "Col." Hartman Bunn initiated snake-handling services at the Zion Tabernacle in Durham, North Carolina,[145] and Rev. Beauregard Barefoot has been active in the vicinity of Tallahassee, Florida.[146]

The characteristic features of a snake-handling service include a hymn sing. Such songs as "Dust on the Bible," "I Got Happy Down in My Heart," "The Great Speckled Bird," "I'm Gettin' Ready to Leave This World, I'm Gettin' Ready for Gates of Pearl," and "What a Beautiful Thought I Am Thinking"[147] create an atmosphere in which the "spirit begins to move," causing some members to "jump up and down, caper about, and kick the wooden box containing the snakes."[148] Next, as the chanting becomes more emotional, the worshipers clap or shout phrases like "Praise the Lord," "Thank God for Jesus," "Hallelujah to Glory." A ten-minute prayer period follows during which everybody prays aloud simultaneously. Some members go up to sick persons, applying a "healing hand" to the head of the ailing brother or sister, and pray for divine healing power on his or her behalf. Others speak in "unknown tongues." All is in readiness for the climax. The "power is strong within the congregation, heightened by the clichéd preaching."[149] A rope is stretched by a member to separate the spectators from the devout, and the visitors are warned that snakes are about to be produced. One of the cultists snatches a reptile from the angry knot in the opened box.[150]

Cymbals, tambourines, foot-stamping and hand-clapping provide the

[144] Womeldorf, "Rattlesnake," p. 1517.

[145] LaBarre, *They Shall Take,* p. 34.

[146] *Ibid.,* pp. 113–25.

[147] Archie Robertson, *That Old-Time Religion* (Boston: Houghton Mifflin Co., 1950), pp. 173, 179.

[148] In LaBarre's book (p. 19), there is a statement to the effect that "the box has been kicked in a kind of half-jocular sin-baiting, because the snake represents the Devil, whom the Spirit of God allows the true believer to overcome."

[149] Examples of such preaching are contained in Robertson, *Old-Time Religion,* pp. 169–71; LaBarre, *They Shall Take,* pp. 7 f.

[150] According to LaBarre (*ibid.,* p. 19), this is conceded a supreme test of faith, for the constantly jolted reptiles, thoroughly aroused, are most likely to strike.

rhythm for the worshipers of both sexes who pass serpents from hand to hand while jerking violently all over.[151]

Some take off their shoes and tread on the snakes barefooted.

Although the snake-handling usually lasts about half an hour, the service continues for an hour more. During this time, while songs like "Jesus Is Getting Us Ready for a Great Day" are being sung, some of the female cultists may "dance in the Spirit," or male "saints" may feel impelled to hold their hands in the flames of a kerosene torch or a miner's acetylene lamp.[152] Some may crawl up the aisle on hands and knees to confess their sins and to testify in front at the mourner's bench.[153]

Bona fide statistics regarding the number of groups which conduct snake-handling services as well as the total number of adherents to the cult are nonexistent. It is reputed, for instance, that groups in Kentucky do more snake-handling than those in other states and that the cult of Grasshopper Valley (Tennessee) is the center of contemporary snake-handling.[154] Moreover, it is known that since 1935 The Shrine of Divine Healing near Stone Creek, Virginia—located in the great landlocked area where Virginia, Kentucky, and Tennessee meet —has been another headquarters for the snake-handlers.[155] Based on reports of those who have been bitten by snakes, one can assume that in addition to those places already mentioned, snake-handling churches have existed, and perhaps still exist, in the following places: Long Beach, California; Fort Payne, Alabama; Rising Fawn (near Trenton), Georgia; Savannah, Tennessee; Lester's Shed (near Altha), Florida; Blue Hole (southeast of Manchester), Kentucky; Nolan, West Virginia; and Jolo, West Virginia.[156]

The size of the congregations varies. It is reported that on August 2, 1955, in a remote mountain clearing about fifty yards from the Virginia border near Harlan, Kentucky, some 4,000 people gathered

[151] *Ibid.*, p. 13. Womeldorf ("Rattlesnake," p. 1518) adds that "accompanying the handling of snakes is the offbeat music of guitars playing old revival tunes such as 'Devil in a Box,' 'Wicked Polly,' and 'Ring Them Bells of Love.' "

[152] LaBarre, p. 22.

[153] *Ibid.*, p. 33.

[154] *Ibid.*, p. 32.

[155] Womeldorf, "Rattlesnake," p. 1517.

[156] LaBarre, *They Shall Take*, pp. 46–50.

for snake-handling services.[157] Furthermore, The Shrine of Divine Healing (Stone Creek, Virginia) drew 2,000 people a week for ten weeks in 1945, and 5,000 at a "national snake handling demonstration."[158] On the other hand, LaBarre relates that the Pine Mountain Church of God (about seventeen miles from Harlan, Kentucky) is composed of "forty adult members . . . mostly poor farmers."[159]

Like their fellow Pentecostals who attend a "normative" church like the Assembly of God, Church of God (Cleveland, Tennessee), or Pentecostal Holiness Church, the snake-handling cultists believe that the Holy Spirit confers supernatural gifts such as *glossolalia* and the ability to heal by prayer, anointing with oil, and the laying on of hands. Moreover, like some of the more puritanical Pentecostals, those who handle snakes likewise forbid theatergoing, dancing, smoking, drinking,[160] immodest dress,[161] and the cutting of women's hair. Members refer to each other as "saints" and men often greet each other with a "holy kiss" and call one another "honey." However, radically different from most other Pentecostals are the snake-handlers' convictions (1) that taking medicine, either "store-boughten" or prescribed by a doctor, is considered a sure sign of lack of faith in God's ability to cure the sick, as promised in Mark 16:18, the text on which the cult is founded; (2) that handling snakes and drinking "deadly things" are sanctioned in the concluding verses of Mark's gospel; and (3) that "baths of fire" or handling fire is justifiable, based on a reading of such Old Testament passages as Isaiah 43:2[162] and Daniel 3:25.[163]

Difficult as it may be to believe, even the snake-handling cult has been rent by schism. The division occurred in 1945, at the time that

157 *Ibid.*, p. 47.

158 Womeldorf, p. 1518.

159 *They Shall Take,* p. 12.

160 Drinking tea, coffee, or even soft drinks such as Coca-Cola is proscribed, according to LaBarre, *ibid.*, p. 17.

161 It is interesting that most men wear open-necked shirts. They argue that *no* Bible text can be discovered which says Jesus or the apostles ever wore a necktie.

162 "When you walk through fire, you shall not be burned, and the flame shall not consume you."

163 "But I see four men loose, walking in the midst of the fire, and they are not hurt; . . ."

Tom Harden and George Went Hensley were imprisoned for holding snake-handling services near Chattanooga.[164] Preacher C. D. Morris of the Faith Tabernacle in La Follette, Tennessee, offered his church to members of the "persecuted" snake-handling faith as a sanctuary from the law. However, in making the offer, Morris stipulated "that snakes be handled in an orderly fashion, and by one person at a time."[165] Because of their belief in extreme local autonomy, many people resented Morris' almost Pauline-like attempt to regulate the mode of snake-handling. "From this period," writes LaBarre, "derive two branches of the faith in the southeastern states, one according to the Morris plan and another the original Hensley cult. The latter seems to have spread more widely in subsequent times."[166]

To conclude, since snake-handling seems to occur in the obscure and remote areas of the South, since its ethos is essentially rural and thus yearly in greater conflict with the increasing urbanism of the "New South," and since it is continuously entangled with the law in the Southeast, its extinction appears to be inevitable.

164 See above, p. 153.
165 LaBarre, *They Shall Take,* p. 25.
166 *Idem.*

CHAPTER 10

A Survey of Pentecostalism in Other Lands (I): North and South America, the Near East, Africa, and the Far East

Ever since Edwin Gaustad published his graphically documented *Historical Atlas of Religion in America,* many more individuals know about the phenomenal growth of American Pentecostalism during the last fifty years. Unfortunately, however, only a mere handful is aware that the development of Pentecostalism in other parts of the world has been equally remarkable. Because of the paucity of such information in English, it seemed suitable to devote two chapters to a continent-by-continent chronicle. In this chapter we shall consider the development of Pentecostalism in the non-European countries; Chapter 11 will survey the expansion of the Pentecostal movement on the Continent.

North America

Canada. The Pentecostal Assemblies of Canada, initially an organization of charismatic Christians in eastern Canada, was granted a Dominion charter in Montreal on May 17, 1919. Two years later, this body joined the Assemblies of God (USA), thus becoming the Eastern Canadian District Council of the Assemblies of God.[1]

[1] The definitive work on the PAOC is Gloria Kulbeck's *What God Hath Wrought* (Toronto: Pentecostal Assemblies of Canada, 1958), 362 pp.

In western Canada, the first move toward organization resulted from a convention that was held in 1919 at Moose Jaw, Saskatchewan. During this gathering, representatives of the Assemblies of God (USA)—Hugh Cadwalder and John W. Welch, the General Superintendent—persuaded the Canadians from the four western provinces to unite under the name "Western Canada District Council of the Assemblies of God" and to accept Cadwalder as their chairman.[2]

Shortly thereafter, it became evident that it would be highly impractical for the Canadian Pentecostals to operate as an organic part of an American denomination; therefore, it was decided to dissolve the union.[3] Since that time in the early 1920's, when the Pentecostal Assemblies of Canada had but 2 districts, 26 pastors and 8 missionaries, and 28 churches,[4] the denomination has grown until it now numbers 700 churches, a membership well over 75,000, and 579 ordained ministers serving in 7 district conferences.[5] In addition, there are sizable foreign language conferences serving the large concentrations of French, Slavic, German, and Finnish-speaking Pentecostals. The active missionary program of the Pentecostal Assemblies, in addition to the 117 active missionaries who serve abroad, includes an intensive effort in the Canadian Northland among the Eskimos and Indians who have settled from James Bay to Alaska. Those in the North Pacific are reached by Pentecostal missionaries who man "gospel boats" or pilot their own planes.[6]

Unlike the Americans, the Canadian Pentecostals did not stress their differences relative to faith and practice, and, therefore, did not proliferate so much. In the early days of the Pentecostal revival, writes Gordon Atter, "there was a considerable latitude as to doctrines preached within Pentecostal circles."[7]

[2] E. N. O. Kulbeck, "The Pentecostal Assemblies of Canada," *Pentecostal Evangel,* XLV (Aug. 4, 1957), 20.

[3] Atter, *Third Force,* p. 96, suggests that the separation was partly due to national influence and partly due to a difference of policy.

[4] *Ibid.,* p. 97.

[5] Anthony Ferry, "Oh, Sing It, You Precious Pentecostal People!" *Maclean's* (Nov. 3, 1962), 20; also Atter, *Third Force,* pp. 97, 204.

[6] For an interesting account of these labors in the Canadian Northland, see Atter, *Third Force,* pp. 258–62.

[7] *Ibid.,* p. 98.

Training schools for ministers were slow to develop in Canada, not only because of the antipathy which most Pentecostals had toward any form of education during the early years of the movement's history, but also because Canadian students who desired training could obtain it at the various American Bible institutes. The first resident institute, providing a three-year theological course, opened in Winnipeg during 1925. It was under the supervision of Dr. James E. Purdie, former rector of St. James' Anglican Church in Saskatoon, Saskatchewan. Ten years later, Bethel Bible Institute (which has been renamed Central Bible College) was founded in Saskatoon. In 1939, Ontario Bible School (now Eastern Pentecostal Bible College in Peterborough, Ontario) opened, and in 1941, British Columbia Bible Institute, located in North Vancouver, British Columbia, came into being. In that same year, the three-year French language Berean Bible Institute was organized for the purpose of training Pentecostals to minister to the French Canadians.

i

During 1921, when Canadian Pentecostals were contemplating affiliation with the Assemblies of God (USA), a small group of ministers protested rather vigorously, primarily on doctrinal grounds. The leader of this faction was Franklin Small of Winnipeg. Although one of the charter members of the original Pentecostal Assemblies of Canada, Small had become a strong supporter of the "Oneness" theory of water baptism, which had nearly decimated the Assemblies of God in the States. When that body repudiated the doctrine, and when the Canadians decided to merge with the Americans, Small, gaining the support of some strong churches in western Canada, proceeded to organize The Apostolic Church of Pentecost, receiving a Dominion charter in 1921.

In 1953, Small's group effected a merger with the Evangelical Churches of Pentecost,[8] so that today, counting the accessions as a

[8] This religious group was originally chartered in 1927 in the Province of Saskatchewan under the name *Full Gospel Missions,* but changed its name in 1948, when it applied for and was granted a Dominion charter. See Atter, *Third Force,* p. 103.

result of the union, the church comprises 125 churches, 157 ministers, and 15,000 adherents—mainly in the areas of Canada that are west of the Great Lakes. It supports 50 missionaries on 11 mission fields, operates the Full Gospel Bible Institute at Eston, Saskatchewan, and publishes a denominational periodical, *The End Times Messenger*.

In the early 1920's, The Apostolic Church of Pentecost was strongly "New Issue" ("Oneness," or "Jesus Only"), writes Gordon Atter; but in recent years this trend has become less marked. "Since the union in 1953, there are many trinitarians in their ranks. Their basis of fellowship is rather broad."[9]

ii

The Apostolic Church is an extremely small Canadian group, included only for the sake of presenting as complete a survey of Pentecostalism as possible. Its appearance in Canada is the result of English influences. During the early years of the Pentecostal Revival in Great Britain, when the faction led by W. O. Hutchinson began to indulge in certain fanaticisms, some of its number withdrew. They selected Dan P. Williams as their leader and established their headquarters in Penyfroes, South Wales. This dissident body referred to itself as the Apostolic Church.

It is rather difficult to describe the exact nature of this church's emphasis, since even the evaluations that have been offered by British Pentecostals are somewhat obscure. After the theological jargon has been deciphered, the principal tenet of the Apostolic Church is the belief that if, as Pentecostals claim, there has been the recovery of an experience which was practiced by the church in Apostolic times, namely, the *glossolalia* and the *charismata,* then there must also be a recovery of the offices which characterized the government in the early Christian Church, namely, those of apostles and prophets. In short, the Apostolic Church actually designates certain of its charismatically gifted men as "Apostles," believing them to have the same rights and prerogatives as those possessed by the Apostles during the first Christian era.

[9] *Idem.*

The Apostolic Church sent out missionaries to Canada where its success has been rather inconspicuous. Gordon Atter attributes only thirteen churches to it, and states that they are "scattered from the Great Lakes to the Maritimes."[10]

Newfoundland. Because Newfoundland did not become part of Canada until the Confederation in 1949, the organizational development of the Pentecostal Assemblies of Newfoundland has been separate from that of the Pentecostal Assemblies of Canada. Nevertheless, there has always been the closest fellowship between the two bodies. For example, the overseas missionaries of the Newfoundland church have been sent out under the auspices of the Pentecostal Assemblies of Canada; moreover, the Newfoundland body has a representative on the Board of Governors of the Eastern Pentecostal Bible College at Peterborough.

The work in Newfoundland is the result of the evangelistic efforts of a Bostonian, Miss Alice Garrigus. Since her pioneering days, Pentecostalism has spread so that there are now 110 churches with 15,000 members served by 169 preachers.[11]

One of the unique features of the Pentecostal work in Newfoundland is that since each denomination is permitted to operate its own schools, the Pentecostals have about fifty of them, all of which have excellent teaching staffs.[12] In still another way, the Newfoundlanders are different from their Pentecostal brethren on the mainland: there churches are less democratic. Church boards are a rarity.[13]

Mexico. It is Kenneth Scott Latourette's opinion that Mexican Protestantism has been characterized mainly by the following features: (1) it has been strongest in the cities and the villages near the American border; (2) it has owed its origin chiefly to American missionaries; (3) it has drawn its adherents primarily from the Mestizos,[14] small traders, manual laborers, schoolteachers, and students.[15]

[10] *Ibid.,* p. 105.
[11] *Ibid.,* p. 204.
[12] *Ibid.,* p. 104.
[13] *Idem.*
[14] The Mestizos are a fusion of the aboriginal Indians and their Spanish con-

In sharp contradistinction, the Pentecostals have grown "with a minimum of 'mission money' and in some cases with none at all,"[16] to become the largest body of Evangelicals in Mexico. They total 146,000.[17] Moreover, the people embracing Pentecostalism were, for the most part, men and women of the masses: peons on haciendas, common people on ranchos, in pueblos and the ciudades. A typical example is La Iglesia Apostolica de la Fe en Cristo Jesus. It began in 1916 when a Mexican laborer was converted in an American Pentecostal meeting. He returned to Mexico, witnessed to his countrymen, and invited a minister from the States to come and baptize all those who had confessed faith in Christ.

> The American did this and returned . . . , leaving the new church with Scriptures and the Holy Spirit in true apostolic fashion. That 1916 beginning has by 1962 grown to a denomination of 9000 [some say 30,000] full members, over 100 ordained ministers, and with the church buildings costing to date at least 1,000,000 *pesos*.[18]

In addition to La Iglesia Apostolica, the other Pentecostal groups with missions in Mexico include the following: the Interdenominational Pentecostal Church, the Independent Evangelical (Pentecostal) Church, International Church of The Foursquare Gospel, the Swedish Pentecostals, the Miepi, and the Assemblies of God.[19] The last-named organization, founded in 1931 and registered with the government as the Assemblies of God of Mexico, is "a strong indigenous church, directed entirely by nationals."[20] A 1962 report indicated that it had 182 ordained or licensed ministers and 115 lay workers who supervise 625 organized churches and missions that have a constituency of

---

querors. They comprise at least 60 per cent of Mexico's inhabitants. See "Down in Mexico," *Pentecostal Evangel,* L (May 27, 1962), 25.

15 Latourette, *The Twentieth Century Outside Europe,* Vol. V of the "Christianity in a Revolutionary Age" series (New York: Harper & Row, 1962), p. 179.

16 Donald McGavran, *Church Growth in Mexico* (Grand Rapids: Eerdmans, 1963), p. 114.

17 *Ibid.,* p. 33.

18 *Ibid.,* p. 115.

19 *Ibid.,* pp. 130 f. lists these groups as having a total of 87,000 communicants.

20 "Down in Mexico," p. 26.

18,000.[21] Five Bible schools which were founded by Mexican nationals exist for the training of workers, and since 1946, The Latin American Orphanage has provided a shelter and an elementary education for hundreds of children.

South America

In the estimation of observers like John Alexander Mackay, ex-President of Princeton Theological Seminary, the expansion of Pentecostalism in Latin America—especially Argentina, Brazil, and Chile—has been literally phenomenal.

Argentina. A group of Italians from Chicago brought the message of Pentecost to Argentina in 1909, witnessing primarily among colonies of their fellow countrymen who had settled there. In 1921, missionaries from Sweden and Canada arrived and began a work in Buenos Aires which subsequently spread to other large Argentine towns. By 1962, despite great persecution,[22] there were 50,000 Pentecostal believers in that country, a ratio of 1 to 318.[23]

One of the important reasons for the success of the Pentecostals in Argentina is the River Plate Bible Institute, which was founded in 1946 by the Union of Assemblies of God in Argentina. Principal Verne Warner of the Pentecostal Assemblies of Canada is in charge of the 11-member faculty and the small student body of nearly 30. The school has graduated 140 students, 90 of whom at least have entered the ministry.[24]

The Church of God (Cleveland, Tennessee) is reported to be the largest Pentecostal Church in Argentina, and one of the strongest Protestant groups.[25]

Brazil. From the earliest days of the Pentecostal revival, Brazil has

[21] *Idem.*

[22] See John H. Dring, "Persecution and Opposition," *Pentecost,* No. 42 (Dec., 1957), p. 15.

[23] "Argentine Survey," *Pentecost,* No. 59 (Mar.–May, 1962), p. 12.

[24] *Idem.*

[25] Charles W. Conn, *Where the Saints Have Trod* (Cleveland, Tenn.: The Pathway Press, 1959), p. 156.

been a center of activity for both American and Scandinavian missionaries. The first Pentecostal Church in Brazil was organized in Pará in 1910, with eighteen members, when Gunnar Vingren and Daniel Berg, Swedes living in the United States, arrived to conduct a program of missionary evangelism. By 1916, when Samuel Nystrom and his wife came from Sweden, there were already about 200 or 300 believers, with the largest church having a modest membership of 60.[26] Since that time the Pentecostal movement has grown until it now has more than 3,000 churches with a membership in excess of one million.[27] The principal concentration of Pentecostals is in Rio de Janeiro, Recife, Pará, and Manáos.

One of the two largest Brazilian Pentecostal bodies is the Congregacioni Christiani. It was founded by Louis Francescon in 1910. Having observed the divisions which frequently decimated the ranks of American Pentecostals, Francescon quickly established a policy of complete separation—almost isolation—between his group of Pentecostals and all other bodies. As a matter of fact, he even avoided using the word "Pentecostal" in the title of his denomination.

Despite the fact that some of Francescon's views may be construed as parochial, his labors in Brazil have been highly successful. He has been instrumental in founding a Pentecostal group which has 1,400 congregations with a membership of 500,000. The church which he pioneered in São Paulo is now a huge temple seating 5,000.[28]

Das Assembléias de Deus Do Brasil equals the Congregacioni Christiani in size. It reports 2,000 assemblies and outstations with a membership of 800,000. It broadcasts a program known throughout Brazil as "Voz Evangelica das Assembléias de Deus,"[29] publishes a biweekly religious periodical—*Mensageiro da Paz* (*Messenger of Peace*), and sends missionaries to Portugal and among the Indians in Goyaz.[30]

[26] Nystrom, "Miracles," p. 6.

[27] Atter, *Third Force*, pp. 216 f., citing Dr. A. Marcus Ward in the Methodist *Recorder*.

[28] David J. duPlessis, "1400 'Christian Congregations' (Pentecostal) in Brazil," *Pentecost*, No. 54 (Dec., 1960–Feb., 1961), p. 5.

[29] Emilio Conde, "Phenomenal Growth in Brazil," *Pentecost*, No. 44 (June, 1958), p. 1.

[30] Nystrom, "Miracles," p. 6.

Since 1951, the Church of God (Cleveland, Tennessee) has actively engaged in the task of evangelizing Brazil. Reports in the *World Christian Handbook* indicate that it has 65 places of worship and a membership of 1,050.[31] In addition, the Norske Pinsevenners Ytremisjon has 20 places of worship, serving a constituency of 5,050,[32] and the International Church of the Foursquare Gospel has 155 places of worship and a total Christian community of 26,532.[33]

Chile. Chile is perhaps the most Pentecostal of all the South American countries; over two-thirds of the Protestant inhabitants are Pentecostals.[34]

The largest single group is the Iglesia Metodista Pentecostal, with its 800 places of worship and 600,000 members.[35] This organization is the outgrowth of the charismatic revival in Valparaiso which subsequently reached all parts of Chile.[36]

In 1932, the Methodist Pentecostal Church divided when one of the younger pastors secured control of part of the denomination. The schismatic group became known as the Iglesia Evangelica Pentecostal. According to recently published statistics, it has 400 places of worship and serves a total Christian community of 300,000.[37]

Since Dr. Hoover's death in 1936, the Pentecostal movement has become largely indigenous and has been plagued by frequent dissent, the result of reaction to two evils which have crept in:

> One, the absolutist control gained by the superintendents and the small groups surrounding them over the affairs of the denomination—particularly in regard to finances; the other, a perverted concept of the nature and manifestation of the Holy Spirit, which had come to be placed above the correctives offered by Scripture and common sense.[38]

Two of these dissenting groups—Mision Iglesia Pentecostal and the Iglesia Pentecostal de Chile, with a combined membership of

[31] H. W. Coxill (ed.), *World Christian Handbook* (London: World Dominion Press, 1962), p. 129.
[32] *Idem.*
[33] *Ibid.,* p. 130.
[34] Atter, *Third Force,* p. 52.
[35] Coxill, *World Christian Handbook,* p. 133.
[36] For an account of this event see above, pp. 51–53.
[37] Coxill, *idem.*
[38] Tschuy, "Shock Troops," p. 1118.

20,000—were admitted as members of the World Council of Churches at its assembly at New Delhi in 1961.[39]

Among the foreign missionary agencies which have workers in Chile are the Assemblies of God (35 places of worship, serving 3,400 members).[40] The Church of God (Cleveland, Tennessee) has 21 organized churches, 16 missions, 38 workers and 840 members. Its main churches are in Santiago, Valparaiso, Antofagasta, and El Salto. The Church of God Bible School in Santiago is an effective ministerial training center at which students from 10 other church groups are enrolled.[41] In addition, the Church of God of Prophecy has 2 small missions; the International Church of the Foursquare Gospel, 31; the Norske Pinsevenners Ytremisjon, 2; and the Svenska Fria Missionen, 22.[42]

Colombia. In the country of Colombia, the Iglesia Evangélica Pentecostal Unida (an affiliate of the United Pentecostal Church whose headquarters are in St. Louis, Missouri) has the most thriving Pentecostal work: 70 churches with a Sunday School attendance of 5,000.[43] The Iglesia Internacional del Evangelio Quadrangular (associated with the International Church of the Foursquare Gospel) claims to have the largest congregation in the Republic of Colombia. Its Barranca Bermeje Church in the Department of Santander, which was closed by the Colombian authorities in 1953, has an average attendance of 1,100.[44]

Very small missionary works are also conducted by the Asambleas de Dios, Iglesia de Dios, and the Iglesia Evangélica Pentecostal.

The Near East

Egypt. In the entire Middle East only in Egypt have the evangelistic efforts by various Pentecostal organizations been really successful. A

[39] See an article "The Significance of the Chilean Pentecostals' Admission," in the *International Review of Missions,* LI (Oct., 1962), 480–482.

[40] Coxill, *World Christian Handbook,* pp. 132 f.

[41] Conn, *Where the Saints Have Trod,* p. 196.

[42] Coxill, *loc. cit.*

[43] Cf. *ibid.,* p. 134 and Atter, *Third Force,* p. 220.

[44] "Pentecostal Church Forcibly Closed in Colombia," *Pentecost,* No. 37 (Sept., 1956), inside front cover.

few—in some cases solitary—missions have been established in Israel, Iran, Jordan, Syria, Lebanon, and Turkey.

Pentecostal doctrines were brought to Egypt in 1908, when an American missionary, George S. Brelsford, established a mission at Assiout. Two years later, Ansel Post and H. E. Randall opened religious works in Alexandria and Cairo respectively. In that same year, 1910, Lillian Trasher founded the Assiout Orphanage,[45] which, during the last half century has cared for 8,000 boys and girls. By 1913, the missionary staff in Egypt was augmented by the arrival of five couples: the John Crouches, Andrew Crouches, Roy Scotts, Hugh Cadwalders, and Charles Doneys.

These and other missionaries succeeded in founding 170 places of worship which today serve a constituency of 20,000.[46] Of the many Pentecostal groups that have missions in Egypt—Church of God (Cleveland, Tennessee), Church of God of Prophecy, the Pentecost Faith Mission, and the Assemblies of God (USA)—the last-named organization has the largest number of missions: 120 assemblies with a total membership of 12,000.[47] The work is under the direction of an Egyptian national, Ayad Shenonda, and is strengthened by the Middle East Bible School at Port Said. This ministerial training school, which opened in 1953, enrolls about 20 students, and has 41 alumni who are full-time Egyptian ministers.

Africa

Central Africa. Very early in the twentieth century Pentecostalism appeared in Africa, especially around the region formerly called the Belgian Congo. Here missionaries came from America, Great Britain, Scandinavia, Switzerland, and New Zealand.

In September, 1915, two young Englishmen from Preston—W. F. P. Burton and James Salter, arrived in the Congo as the first representatives of the Congo Evangelistic Mission. During the years that followed they were instrumental in having the Scriptures translated into

[45] For a fuller account of this outstanding work see Gee, *Upon All Flesh,* pp. 57–62; and Frodsham, *With Signs Following,* pp. 143–53.

[46] Coxill, *World Christian Handbook,* p. 65.

[47] Atter, *Third Force,* p. 197.

Luban and in expanding the work of the Assemblées de Dieu du Congo–Est so that today it includes 300 places of worship and serves a total Christian community of 21,535.[48]

The missionary activity of the Assemblies of God (USA) centered around Gombari and Botongwe. At present, the American denomination lists 80 places of worship, serving a total Christian community of 48,196.[49]

In addition to these major branches of the Pentecostal movement, it is known that Swedish missionaries evangelized the territory around Uvira and that the Swiss penetrated the regions still farther north.[50]

The total Pentecostal membership in the Congo, as of 1960, was 105,000.[51] And as early as 1935, when Donald Gee visited Central Africa and recorded his observations in his book, *Upon All Flesh,* the work has been almost wholly indigenous.[52]

West Africa. Of all the countries in West Africa, Nigeria has been most receptive to the Pentecostal message. Latest statistics show that there are 170,000 Nigerian Pentecostals, most of whom are affiliated either with The Apostolic Church of England or the Assemblies of God of Nigeria.[53]

The Apostolic Church of England has established 1,061 churches to which 90,000 Nigerians belong. It commenced its missionary program in 1931, and has developed a church which is governed completely by the 201 ordained Nigerian pastors and 234 evangelists. The largest mission station is at Bodo, in Ogoni Province, where a huge 1,500-seat Apostolic Temple has been constructed. In the town of Ilesha, The Apostolic Church maintains 6 churches as well as a teacher-training center.

In 1940, the American-based Assemblies of God sent their first missionaries to the Ibo tribe, one of the four major Negro tribes in Nigeria. From the outset these missionaries guided the Nigerians in

[48] Coxill, *World Christian Handbook,* p. 61.

[49] *Idem.*

[50] Gee, *Upon All Flesh,* p. 66.

[51] Atter, *Third Force,* p. 227.

[52] P. 66.

[53] Atter, p. 227. In addition, the Church of God (see Conn's *Where the Saints Have Trod,* pp. 285–90), Congregational Holiness Church, and International Church of The Foursquare Gospel have followers.

the organization of their churches both on the local as well as on the national level. In 1947, all of the districts of the church united, calling themselves the Assemblies of God in Nigeria and electing Nigerians to the highest posts of leadership. "The individual assemblies have become self-supporting and self-governing, and, through the collections of special monthly missionary offerings, send national missionaries to other unevangelized Tribes."[54] The Assemblies of God in Nigeria operates 600 places of worship,[55] and ministers to about 25,000 believers.[56]

Union of South Africa. The largest concentration of Protestants on the African continent is in the Republic of South Africa (3,752,-495).[57] It is no wonder, then, that a variety of Pentecostal groups are also rather firmly entrenched there. The largest ones are the Full Gospel Church of God, the Apostolic Faith Mission, the Assemblies of God in Southern and Central Africa, and the International Assemblies of God.[58]

Pentecostalism was introduced to the South Africans in 1908 by two Americans, John G. Lake and Thomas Hezmalhalch, who laid the foundation for the Apostolic Faith Mission. However, it was Peter Louis leRoux who, as president of the Mission for twenty-nine years, was the one person most responsible for its becoming the largest Pentecostal group in South Africa. In 1962, records of the Apostolic Faith Mission listed 210 European (Afrikaans-speaking) Assemblies with a membership of about 70,000. These figures do not include the native, Indian, and Colored churches which have approximately 100,000 members.[59]

The Apostolic Faith Mission, which is at least 90 per cent Afrikaans, is an entirely indigenous organization.[60] One of its chief

[54] "Pentecostal Progress in Nigeria," *Pentecostal Evangel,* XLVII (Mar. 29, 1959), 22 f.

[55] Atter, *Third Force,* p. 200.

[56] Coxill, *World Christian Handbook,* p. 77.

[57] Special issue on Africa published by *Christianity Today,* VIII (July 31, 1964), 18.

[58] Coxill, pp. 92 f.

[59] Atter, *Third Force,* p. 201.

[60] Donald Gee, "One in Twenty-five in South Africa is Pentecostal," *Pentecost,* No. 38 (Dec., 1956), p. 1.

activities is conducting missionary work in Kenya, Nigeria, and Rhodesia. In addition, since 1955, it has maintained the Apostolic Bible College. This school, which is under the direction of Principal Charles J. H. Bennett and a faculty of five lecturers, is responsible for training new ministers for the denomination.[61]

The Full Gospel Church of God in South Africa is second in size only to the Apostolic Faith Mission. Archibald Cooper, its founder, came to South Africa to participate in the Anglo-Boer War (1899–1902). During that time he was converted in a revival conducted by Gypsy Smith and remained to found a church in Durban. With less than 100 members in 1910, this denomination today ministers to a constituency of 130,000.[62]

During the 1930's the Full Gospel Church experienced unprecedented growth following the penetration of the western Cape region by its evangelists and its program of conducting huge camp meetings at Pretoria, Vereeniging, Benomi, Germiston, and Florida.

Originally, the ministry of the Full Gospel Church was primarily to Europeans, that is, those of British or Dutch extraction, but today it also serves the Bantu, Colored, and Asiatic residents.[63] As a matter of fact, it has the largest Christian Protestant Asiatic Church in South Africa[64]—Bethesda Temple in Natal. This church which has an aggregate membership of 13,000 (mostly Indians), oversees 63 branches throughout the Union, and even one in India.

In addition to maintaining a number of strong Afrikaans churches on the Rand, supervising W. J. duPlooy's industrial mission school in North Transvaal, and missionizing Portuguese East Africa, the Full Gospel Church operates the Berea Bible Seminary at Kroonstad, of which T. D. Mooneyham is Principal.[65]

The third large Pentecostal group is the Assemblies of God in South Africa. Until 1961, it was an interracial group composed of

[61] "South Africa," in *Pentecost,* No. 51 (Mar., 1960), p. 15.

[62] "Full Gospel Church in Southern Africa," *Pentecost,* No. 43 (Sept.–Nov., 1960), p. 11.

[63] "Bantu" or "Natives" are the "Pure Blacks" of South Africa; the "Colored" are racially mixed; and the "Asiatics" are from India.

[64] Joan Goddard, "Opening of the New 'Bethesda' in Durban," *Moving Waters,* reprinted in *Pentecost,* No. 47 (Mar., 1959), 1.

[65] Gee, "One in Twenty-five," p. 1.

approximately 100,000 members and supervised by about 150 missionaries from the following countries: America, Canada, Britain, Ireland, Germany, Sweden, Norway, and even Australia.[66] Since 1961, however, in keeping with the nationalistic trends, some radical changes have been made in the original constitution of the Assemblies of God in South Africa. For example, the African division now has its own administrative officers. It is a self-contained and self-administered fellowship (in which no foreign missionaries hold office) with approximately 35,000 members. In addition, there is a white division as well as an Indian and Colored Assemblies of God, each with its own organization and each completely free of supervision by foreign missionaries.[67]

"It is the wish of the majority of Africans," reports a British missionary, that non-Africans "offer their services to the African church in those specialized fields of ministry such as teaching and training the African in the Word of God, but to withdraw from organizational and administrative positions."[68] Thus the African executive board has no white members, and the missionaries themselves no longer have any offices in South Africa. They have been advised by N. B. H. Benghu, the outstanding Zulu pastor and chairman of the African Assemblies of God,[69] to remain neutral, not to take part in "indabas" (quarrels) between Africans, to forget the methods and countries of their origin, and to leave all organizing to the African nationals.

The Far East

Australia. In contrast to the other parts of the world, Pentecostalism in Australia developed rather late. There were isolated cases of

[66] Atter, *Third Force,* p. 200. It must be noted that in 1963 the American Assemblies of God missionaries, on the advice of their superiors in Springfield, Mo., resigned from the Assemblies of God in South Africa because of some of its strange doctrinal standards. Those who withdrew formed a group called the International Assemblies of God.

[67] "Radical Changes in African Constitution," *Pentecost,* No. 58 (Dec., 1961–Feb., 1962), p. 6.

[68] *Idem.*

[69] There is a short biographical account of Benghu in *Pentecost,* No. 59 (Mar.–May, 1962), p. 7.

charismatic phenomena in the State of Victoria during the first decade of the twentieth century, but there was no widespread Pentecostal revival until American and British evangelists like Smith Wigglesworth (1921), Aimee Semple McPherson (1922), and A. C. Valdez (1925)[70] arrived to conduct large campaigns in Melbourne, Victoria; Sydney, New South Wales; and Brisbane, Queensland. As a result of the revival ministry of Valdez in Melbourne, as well as of his recognition that a trained ministry was imperative if Australian Pentecostalism were to survive, The Victorian Bible Institute was established at Richmond, a suburb of Melbourne.[71]

The Apostolic Faith Mission of Australia, the first organized body of Pentecostals, was established in 1927; its headquarters were in North Melbourne. Because of certain unpublicized errors[72] together with the inconsistent Christian testimony in the personal life of one of the outstanding evangelists, some of the assemblies in the northeast decided to organize themselves as The Assemblies of God, Queensland. Under the leadership of Pastor George Burns, a former Church of Christ minister, and C. G. Enticknap, Pentecostalism became solidly established in the Brisbane area. In 1936, a Bible School was established, and Henry Wiggins came from Britain to assume the post of Principal.

A Unity Conference was held in Sydney in 1937, to which delegates from both The Assemblies of God, Queensland and The Pentecostal Church of Australia came. They decided to form a united fellowship, embracing the whole of Australia and to adopt the name, Assemblies of God in Australia.[73] C. L. Greenwood, head of The Pentecostal Church of Australia, and C. G. Enticknap were appointed respectively Chairman and Vice Chairman.

The amalgamation proved successful. The Pentecostal movement expanded throughout the Commonwealth. In 1947, the National Conference voted to establish the Commonwealth Bible College. It

[70] Frodsham, *With Signs Following*, pp. 219–22, has a full treatment of the Wigglesworth and Valdez meetings.

[71] Atter, *Third Force*, pp. 114–16.

[72] Gordon Atter suggests that certain Pentecostalists embraced the principles of Christadelphianism.

[73] "Assemblies of God in Australia," *Pentecost*, No. 41 (Sept., 1957), p. 5.

sent missionaries to India and Japan. It promoted an active ministry among the Australian aborigines, but its greatest activity has been among the natives of New Guinea, a mandated territory of Australia. The first mission was established in 1950 in the Sepik River area by Mr. and Mrs. H. Davidson. At present, about 30 missionaries are engaged in operating about 40 mission stations.[74]

In addition to the work of the Assemblies of God in Australia, the Apostolic Church of Wales has a few churches in various states, and so has the British-based Elim Foursquare Gospel Church—especially in New South Wales. Altogether, it is estimated that there are about 15,000 Pentecostals in Australia.[75]

India. Most of the Pentecostal churches in India are still under missionary supervision. They are independent, locally governed groups which as late as 1959 had no united voice on the national or governmental level. The National Christian Council of the Evangelical Fellowship of India, for example, refused to recognize the Pentecostals.[76]

Pentecostal missionary societies represented in India include the Assemblies of God (USA and Great Britian), the Apostolic Church of Pentecost (Canada), the Pentecostal Holiness Church (USA), together with others from Sweden, Norway, and Australia.[77] Most of their effort seems to be concentrated in southwestern India (Maharashtra). Assemblies of God missionaries from the United States, as well as from England, have established Bible Schools for the training of Christian workers at Junnar.[78] For some years, Lief Sandal, a Norwegian missionary, has labored in Bombay. In Kirkee, near Poona, there is the Zion Church which is maintained by the Australian Assemblies of God.[79]

One of the most flourishing missionary endeavors has been that

[74] Atter, *Third Force,* p. 268.

[75] *Ibid.,* 227.

[76] "All-India Pentecostal Fellowship," *Pentecost,* No. 44 (June, 1958), p. 5.

[77] Cf. *Pentecost,* No. 59 (Mar.–May, 1962), p. 14; and Coxill, *World Christian Handbook,* pp. 152–61.

[78] *Pentecost,* No. 55 (Mar.–May, 1961), p. 15.

[79] *Idem.*

supported by the Assemblies of God (USA). It is reported that there are at least 400 churches in South India with a total membership of 20,000. In addition to the aforementioned school in Junnar, the South India Assemblies of God operates Tamil Bible Institute in Madura, Bethel Bible Institute in Panalur Tranancose, and Southern Asia Bible Institute in Bangalore. Students from these schools have been largely responsible not only for extending the influence of the Assemblies of God but also for founding many of the so-called "independent" Pentecostal churches throughout India.

The work of the Assemblies of God in North India is an outgrowth of the Pentecostal revivals that occurred in the early 1900's at the orphanages directed by Pandita Ramabai in Mukti and Fannie Simpson in Calcutta, and it is presently concentrated in large industrial areas such as Calcutta, Jabalpur, and Assanol. At the present time the Assemblies of God reports having 50 churches with a membership of 5,000.

One of the significant by-products of the missionary efforts of the Assemblies of God in India has been the extension of Pentecostalism throughout East Pakistan. It is reported that Abdul Munshie, who has been called "the apostle of Pentecost to East Pakistan," and who has conducted outstanding revivals among the outcast Hindus, the caste Hindus, and the Moslems, was stimulated to embrace Pentecostalism through the witness of Assemblies of God missionaries—Rev. and Mrs. Maynard Ketcham and Rev. and Mrs. Charles Woolver. Largely as a result of Munshie's evangelistic efforts, 15 churches and at least 20 "preaching points" have been established. It is estimated that there are nearly 5,000 Pakistani Pentecostals.

The largest Pentecostal groups in India, however, are the independent, indigenous India Pentecostal Church and the Pentecostal Church of God of Andra Pradesh. The former group was founded in 1923 by K. E. Abraham and today totals 500 churches with 100,000 members.[80] In the state of Kerala, where it has 200 churches, the India Pentecostal Church operates Hebron Bible School.[81] The

[80] Cf. Atter, *Third Force,* p. 111; Coxill, *World Christian Handbook,* lists more modest figures: 300 churches and 9,000 full members (p. 157).

[81] *Pentecost,* No. 64 (June–Aug., 1963), p. 11.

Pentecostal Church of God of Andra Pradesh[82] was begun in 1936 by P. Abraham Samuel. Following years of hardship and opposition, in 1959 it was able to claim 250 churches, 450 working stations, and 20,000 members.[83] Under Samuel's direction, Zion Bible College is maintained at Bezwada.

Indonesia. Two American missionaries—Groesbeck and van Claver—introduced Pentecostalism to Indonesia, when they landed on the Island of Bali in 1921. They had been sent from Seattle under the auspices of Bethel Temple, Inc.[84]

It is reported that during this time a Balinese princess was miraculously healed and that this aroused much interest in Pentecostalism. Only a short time thereafter the Pentecostal missionaries encountered severe opposition from the Dutch authorities and were forced to relocate in East Java.[85] Here, in 1923, the first persons to embrace Pentecostalism were Mr. and Mrs. F. G. van Gessel. Mr. van Gessel, a member of the Shell Oil Company staff, together with Groesback and van Claver, established the first Pentecostal church in Indonesia at Tjipu. When the Americans left the country in 1926, van Gessel resigned his post with Shell to become minister at Tjipu as well as at Surabaya.

One correspondent from Indonesia has stated that converts whom van Gessel trained have done much to acquaint their country with Pentecostal faith and practice.[86]

It is necessary to mention that about this time (1922) a gifted European missionary, Johann Thiessen, commenced his ministry at Bandung, West Java. He is acknowledged to have founded the Gerakan Pentakosta (Pentecostal movement), the oldest Pentecostal organization to which 460 churches belong. Its headquarters

[82] Andra Pradesh is reputed to be the fourth largest state in India.

[83] Cf. "Thousands at Convention in India," *Pentecost,* No. 48 (June, 1959), p. 6; and Coxill, p. 159.

[84] Letter from S. B. P. Pardede, an Indonesian theological student at the Commonwealth Bible College in Queensland, Australia, Sept. 2, 1964.

[85] Atter, *Third Force,* pp. 52, 158; also Steiner, *Mit folgenden Zeichen,* p. 87.

[86] Pardede, "Letter."

are in Djakarta, the capital of Indonesia, and its many congregations dot Java and the Celebes.

In 1935, Bethel Temple dispatched W. W. Patterson and others to establish a Bible school at Surabaya. A few years later when the Japanese subjugated Indonesia, many foreign missionaries were interned, others were transferred by their mission boards, and a diffusion of Pentecostalism resulted. The movement split into a variety of denominations among which are the following:

1. Geredja Pantekosta Di Indonesia (Pentecostal Church of Indonesia) has 1,000 churches and a membership of 250,000. It maintains four Bible schools and publishes a religious journal *Pusaka Rohani (Spiritual Inheritance).* S. B. P. Pardede observes that the highly centralized system of church government practiced by this group has resulted in many divisions. "It is rather difficult," he writes, "to supervise the assemblies that spread throughout the 3,000 islands country [*sic*] from the Central HQ."[87]

2. The second largest body of Indonesian Pentecostals is the Geredja Bethel Indjil Sepenuh (Full Gospel Bethel Church), which claims to have 500 churches and 150,000 members. It operates a Bible School, a Minister's Training College, and a Correspondence School that serves 2,250 Indonesians. Unlike the Geredja Pantekosta, this group "gives great independence and autonomy to her local assemblies. Each assembly is free to have fellowship and cooperation with whosoever [*sic*] they will."[88] Whereas American Pentecostals shun the National Council of Churches, Geredja Bethel is a full member of the Indonesian Council of Churches.

3. The other smaller groups which together with the aforementioned churches account for the estimated 1,000 wholly indigenous Pentecostal churches,[89] serving 500,000 constituents, are the Sidang Djemaat Aliah (Assemblies of God), Geredja Pantekosta (Pentecostal Church), and Geredja Isa Aimasih (Church of Jesus Christ).

[87] *Idem.*

[88] *Idem.*

[89] "The Indigenous Pentecostal Work in Indonesia," *Pentecost,* No. 38 (Dec., 1956), p. 11.

Japan. In 1963, the Pentecostals celebrated their fiftieth anniversary of witness in the "Land of the Rising Sun." Their first mission was started in Tokyo in 1913 when the Assemblies of God (USA) sent Mr. and Mrs. C. F. Juergensen and their daughters, Marie and Agnes, to Japan. Soon they were joined by six other Americans: Mr. and Mrs. B. S. Moore, who established a work in Yokohama, Mr. and Mrs. John Juergensen, Miss Jennie Wengler, and Miss Mae Straub.[90]

Because of the Pacific War, as the Japanese refer to World War II, the growth of Pentecostalism was retarded. In the spring of 1949, however, 16 national workers and 7 missionaries from Great Britain, Canada, and the United States met and organized the Assemblies of God in Japan. At the time, there were but 13 churches in the association, and only three of these were self-supporting. Today there are 74—at least one on each of the main islands of Hokkaido, Honshu, Kyushu, and Shikoku—and two-thirds of these churches pay their own pastor. There are over 120 national workers, almost all of whom are graduates of the Central Bible Institute in Tokyo.[91]

The policy of the Nihon Assenburiizu Kyodan (Assemblies of God in Japan) has been to train national leaders to assume the responsibility for the churches in their country. That is why it has invested much in its Tokyo facilities—eight large buildings which house the radio recording studio, the Sunday School and literature department, dormitories, and a large auditorium seating 1,500.

According to the latest *World Christian Handbook,* the following Pentecostal groups are engaged in missionary work among the Japanese: Assemblies of God (USA and Great Britain), Church of God (Cleveland, Tennessee), International Church of The Foursquare Gospel, Nihon Pentekosute Kyodan (Japanese Apostolic Mission), Norske Pinsevenners Ytremisjon, Pentecostal Church of God of America, Shito No Shinko Kyodan (Apostolic Faith), Svenska Fria Missionen, the Open Bible Standard Mission, and the United Pente-

[90] Dorothy C. Haskin, "Fifty Years of Pentecost in Japan," *Pentecostal Evangel,* XLIX (Oct. 29, 1961), 11.

[91] Raymond Brock, "Japan Observes Centennial of Protestant Missions," *Pentecostal Evangel,* XLVII (Sept. 27, 1959), 26.

costal Church. The total number of Japanese Pentecostals is about 10,000.[92]

New Zealand. In 1922, while traveling throughout Oceania, Smith Wigglesworth conducted a Pentecostal revival in this dominion, and it led to the establishment of The Pentecostal Church of New Zealand. Soon thereafter (1924), the largest Pentecostal group—the Assemblies of God General Council in New Zealand—was also founded. During the last four decades, a large number of "independent" churches have likewise appeared. Seventeen of these thrive in many large cities and towns and unlike the other 37 churches are unaffiliated with any national or international Pentecostal organizations.

According to statistics published in 1960, there are only 10,000 Pentecostals in New Zealand.[93]

[92] In addition to Coxill, *World Christian Handbook,* pp. 167–76, see "Tokyo," in *Pentecost,* No. 47 (Mar., 1959), p. 9.

[93] Atter, *Third Force,* pp. 55, 115, 226.

CHAPTER 11

A Survey of Pentecostalism in Other Lands (II): The European Continent

European scholars like Nils Bloch-Hoell estimate that there are probably one million Pentecostals on the Continent. Amazingly enough, at least half of these are in Iron Curtain countries. Predominantly Catholic Italy also has a sizable number of Pentecostals. So do the Scandinavian countries, especially Sweden which has a larger percentage of Pentecostals than any other country in the world. In the remaining countries, however, Pentecostals have had to struggle to maintain a witness, particularly in the British Isles where our survey begins.

British Isles

Apostolic Church. Prior to World War I, most British Protestants who embraced the Pentecostal viewpoint remained within their own denominations and by their lives and witness tried to persuade others to accept the Pentecostal blessing too. This proved to be an impractical way of sharing a religious experience, for the opposition to Pentecostalism had become too widespread. Therefore, some Pentecostals agitated for a more aggressive distinctly Pentecostal program of evangelism both at home and abroad. Others urged the adoption of a clearly Pentecostal mode of organization. In November, 1908, for example, a group of Pentecostals, led by W. O. Hutchinson, separated themselves, forming the Apostolic Faith Church which attempted to give precedence to the Holy Spirit in *all* matters, including the guidance of the church by means of glossolalic utterances of certain "gifted" people who even bore New Testament names like "Apostle" and "Prophet." The emphasis, strongly reminiscent of ancient Montanism, developed certain eccentricities. To quote Donald Gee: "Sincerity can become deeply fanatical, . . . and unhappily this occurred among these friends. The subsequent extremes would make sorry reading."[1] As a result of these extravagances, a nucleus withdrew from the Hutchinson group in 1916 to form one of the first strong Pentecostal denominations in Britain—the Apostolic Church of Wales—which "gained considerable momentum, and although predominantly a Welsh movement it . . . spread throughout the British Isles, and finally overseas, especially in Denmark, West Africa, and latterly Australia."[2]

The growth of the Apostolic Church is generally ascribed to its claim to possess a " 'fuller vision' concerning church order and government." It placed strong emphasis upon prophetic utterances in matters pertaining to the governing of the church. That is, it waited for the direction of the Holy Spirit, employing the media of the gift of tongues and interpretation of Spirit-inspired proclamations in a known tongue, to determine how certain issues which arose in the church should be handled. In the early days of Pentecostalism, when there was an absence of strong spiritual leadership and when people were attracted by the thought of supernatural oversight, the Apostolic Church made rapid advances. While doing so, it also created innumerable local divisions within Pentecostalism in England and in Scotland.[3]

At the present time the Apostolic Church has about 240 churches.[4] (There are no available figures regarding the size of the church or

[1] Gee, *Pentecostal Movement,* p. 73.

[2] *Ibid.,* p. 106.

[3] According to Gee (*idem*), "The Apostolic Church was notorious for proselyting."

[4] Atter, *Third Force,* p. 107.

the number of pastors.) It has had especially good results from its missionary endeavors in Nigeria, where it commenced its work in 1931. The church in West Africa numbers 1,061 assemblies with a total membership that approximates 90,000. The Apostolic Churches in Nigeria are "indigenous, self-supporting, and self-propagating." Apart from the 11 white missionaries whose function is purely supervisory, the church has 434 ordained African ministers and evangelists.[5]

Elim Church. As one studies the development of Pentecostalism in Great Britain, it is interesting to note that great emphasis was placed upon extending the message of Pentecost among foreigners (the first distinctively Pentecostal organization was the Pentecostal Missionary Union, founded in 1909), but little was done about evangelizing the homeland. It was to rectify this imbalance that a young Welshman, George Jeffreys, began to conduct evangelistic campaigns that were conspicuously successful, especially at Monaghan in Northern Ireland. There in 1915, after Jeffreys had been joined by Ernest Darragh, William Henderson, Robert Mercer, Frederick Farlow, and a Miss Treight, the Elim Evangelistic Band was first organized.[6]

The Band spent three years evangelizing Ireland, then in October, 1918, it changed its name to the Elim Pentecostal Alliance. By the end of 1919, seventeen workers were associated with it. Gee, while describing the period between 1920 and 1924 as a difficult and discouraging time for British Pentecostals, hastens to add:

> The brightest element for the moment was the steady progress of the virile "Elim" work on the line of an aggressive evangelism that at last really did begin to move the masses, not only in Ireland, but in England and Wales too.[7]

George Jeffreys was invited to come from Ireland and to establish an "Elim" work in England. This he did in 1920, uniting with his brother, Stephen. For the next decade the Jeffreys, either singly or together, held outstanding revival campaigns at Leigh-on-Sea, Essex,

[5] *Ibid.*, p. 199.

[6] Gee, *Pentecostal Movement*, p. 97.

[7] *Ibid.*, p. 111. Gee explains that the leadership wavered, doctrinal controversies predominated, and revival enthusiasm became more sentimental than actual.

London, Grimsby, Hull, Glasgow, Aberdeen, Dundee, and Edinburgh, to mention but a few of the cities which they evangelized and in which Elim churches were subsequently established. Today the Elim movement has 290 churches, 258 ordained clergy, and a membership in excess of 20,000.[8]

Since the majority of the Elim churches came into existence through the influence of George Jeffreys' revivals, it is natural that they should look to him for leadership.

> The people who had been called forth largely lacked the ability to provide stable local leaders and evolve a genuine democratic polity for their organization, so that for a continuing movement to be established it was inevitable, in these circumstances, that stable organization had to rise at the centre and be imposed at the periphery.[9]

When Jeffreys moved on, the organization which had grown up around him provided the necessary guidance for the local group. British sociologist, Bryan R. Wilson, a student of the Elim Church, informs us that Jeffreys' "agents took control and later became the agents of the bureaucratic organization which grew up under the shadow of his charismatic prestige."[10]

Of the three major Pentecostal bodies in Britain, then, Elim has the most centralized form of government. Ultimate authority rests with the Annual Conference,[11] which includes all ministers in the movement and an equal number of lay members. The full conference appoints the executives of the denomination—President, Secretary General, Field Superintendents, and all other officers—controls the finances, determines matters of church government, and so forth. The Executive Council, which is composed of nine ordained ministers, manages and transacts all matters between the annual sessions of the Conference to whose authority it is always subject. Herein, says Wilson, the real power of the Elim Church resides.

[8] Coxill, *World Christian Handbook,* p. 209.

[9] Wilson, *Sects and Society,* p. 63.

[10] *Idem.*

[11] *Ibid.,* p. 65. The pattern is similar to that in the Methodist Church: the Representative Session (laymen, ministers, and denominational officers) make regulations governing Elim; the Ministerial Session (laymen excluded) has ultimate authority on matters like admission, ordination, disciplining of ministers, etc.

Thus in spite of the theoretical control by the representative conference, there can be little doubt that most of the activity of the movement is controlled and regulated by a relatively small number of administrators at the central headquarters.[12]

Elim is also organized into district presbyteries, but very little power is exercised at this level because of the close relationship between local churches and Elim headquarters. On the local level there is no congregational polity. All problems are resolved by the Church Session (minister plus deacons who are elected biennially by a church meeting, and elders who are appointed for a two-year term by the minister).

On matters of doctrine, the Elim position is different in a few points from the views held by other Pentecostals. For example, whereas most Pentecostals stress speaking in tongues as *the* initial evidence of a Holy Spirit baptism, the Elim Church states: "Through Jesus men may obtain Holy Ghost baptism, which is an additional blessing promised to every believer, and which is *manifested by speech in tongues, prophecy, or similar charismata.*"[13] (Italics mine.) Elim also recognizes the laying of hands on the sick and anointing them with oil as an ordinance.[14] Most Pentecostals practice but two rites: communion and baptism.[15]

Elim's missionary activity is best described by a statement appearing in one of their pamphlets: "So great is the interest in foreign missions that we have one missionary supported on the field overseas for every six churches in the homeland."[16] What this means is that Elim has about fifty missionaries, most of them laboring in Tanganyika, the Union of South Africa, and India.

The church also operates the Elim Bible College at "Elim Woodlands" in Clapham Park, near London and publishes the *Elim Evangel* for its 6,000 subscribers.

Assemblies of God. The Assemblies of God in Great Britain and

[12] *Ibid.*, p. 66.
[13] *Ibid.*, p. 17.
[14] *Ibid.*, p. 19.
[15] Except for those who practice feet washing as an ordinance.
[16] *Introducing the Elim Church* (London: Evangel Press, n.d.).

Ireland, which together with the Elim Church represents the majority of British Pentecostals, would not be in existence, perhaps, if some Welshmen had not wounded the national pride of their English colleagues by threatening to affiliate with an American denomination.

From the very beginning of the Pentecostal revival, the churches in Wales had constituted a sizable segment of British Pentecostalism. In the early 1920's, however, their ranks had been decimated by the proselyting tactics of the Apostolic Church. Since there was no British Pentecostal organization to which they could turn for leadership, in desperation they applied to America, desiring to be admitted as the Welsh District Council of the Assemblies of God. "This stung the English brethren into action," writes Donald Gee.[17]

Thomas Myerscough of Preston, who had been affiliated with English Pentecostalism from the days of the first revival in Sunderland, was too old to launch the project, so he linked his prestigious personality to the energetic, businesslike Assemblies of God pastor, J. Nelson Parr of Manchester. An announcement was circularized, scheduling a preliminary conference for early February, 1924. There was sufficient interest shown, and by May a decision was made to frame a constitution and to elect 7 men to function as an Executive Presbytery. About 70 churches—half of them from South Wales—united to form the Assemblies of God in Great Britain and Ireland.

Gee reports that "there had been strong hopes that the Elim Alliance would unite with the 'Assemblies of God,' and representatives of Elim visited the Conference at Highbury in May [1925]."[18] But Elim finally declined the offer to merge on the grounds that "the blessing of God which had rested so conspicuously upon their chosen methods might be jeopardized if they became merged with a body working on a different governmental basis."[19] The impasse was this: Elim stood for centralized government; the Assemblies of God for local government.

In matters of Church Order and Government Assemblies of God seek to follow as simply as possible the New Testament pattern. They . . . are

[17] *Pentecostal Movement,* p. 128.
[18] *Ibid.,* p. 130.
[19] *Idem.*

united together only in a perfectly voluntary fellowship that involves no centralized legislative government whatever, and leaves each local Assembly entirely free to own its own property, call its own pastor, and manage its own affairs without let or hindrance.[20]

During the past four decades the Assemblies of God has expanded. Today it is the largest Pentecostal group in Britain and Ireland, claiming to have 510 churches, and 20,000 full members.[21] Its practices differ somewhat from its American namesake in several ways. (1) Perhaps influenced by the Plymouth Brethren or the Anglican Church, the Assemblies of God in Britain celebrates communion every Sunday morning. During this service there is little or no preaching. (2) Rarely does a British Assemblies of God church have an "altar call" or an "after service" for those seeking the Pentecostal "experience," a procedure that is quite common in both American and Canadian churches. British "tarrying meetings" (they call them "waiting meetings" or "receiving meetings") are separate from all other services conducted by the church to which the public is invited.[22]

The Benelux Countries

Belgium. This predominantly Roman Catholic country has about 100,000 Protestants;[23] and of this total, only 3,000 are Pentecostal.[24]

Douglas R. Scott, a converted bandleader who became a British missionary, came to Belgium in the early 1930's to conduct revival meetings in Antwerp, Liege, Charleroi, and Paturages.[25] In the last-named city, which is in the heart of the Belgian coal-mining district, Scott succeeded in wooing Pastor De Worm and the congregation of the Evangelical Reformed Church into the Pentecostal camp.

On the whole, the growth of Pentecostalism during the 1930's was unspectacular; and following the outbreak of hostilities in 1939, its activity ceased entirely. Since the conclusion of World War II, how-

[20] Gee, *The Story of a Great Revival,* p. 10.
[21] Coxill, *World Christian Handbook,* p. 208.
[22] Atter, *Third Force,* p. 108.
[23] Kenneth Scott Latourette, *The Twentieth Century in Europe,* Vol. IV of Christianity in a Revolutionary Age Series (New York: Harper & Row, 1961), p. 380.
[24] Atter, *Third Force,* p. 164.
[25] Cf. Gee, *Upon All Flesh,* p. 30; and Steiner, *Mit folgenden Zeichen,* p. 70.

ever, the Elim Missionary Society of England, the Assemblies of God (USA), and the Svenska Fria Missionen have all sent missionaries to Belgium. It was mainly as a result of their labors that the Union of Pentecostal Churches in Belgium has emerged. Heading this organization of forty churches is Pastor Alfred Amitie. Belgian Pentecostals are especially proud of their Emmanuel Bible Institute which, since its founding in 1959, has provided instruction for students from France, Spain, Italy, Morocco, Switzerland, Algeria, and Germany.[26]

The Netherlands. A Pentecostal witness in the Netherlands began in 1907–1908 when Mr. and Mrs. G. R. Polman of Amsterdam experienced a Holy Spirit baptism. At that time, Polman was pastoring only a mission. It subsequently became too small, and in 1920 a beautiful new auditorium was built at Kerstraat.

When Pastor Polman died in 1931, P. van der Woude assumed the leadership of the small Dutch Pentecostal movement. He settled in Rotterdam and built up a rather impressive congregation of 500. In 1933, Peter Klaven, who is presently the chairman of the Dutch Pentecostals, returned from his missionary work in the Dutch East Indies to assume the pastorate of the Amsterdam assembly. Shortly another church was established at Haarlem, but until the end of World War II, Pentecostalism in the Netherlands was nothing more or less than a "fringe" religion. In recent years, however, it has shown remarkable growth and in 1962 the Broederschap van Volle-Evangelic Gemeenten claimed to have 45 pastors, 60 congregations, and a membership of about 10,000.[27]

An especially successful impact by Pentecostalism upon Holland resulted from an extensive divine healing revival which T. L. Osborn, an American, conducted in the summer of 1958. Employing the means of mass evangelism, he was able to reach crowds of 15,000 in The Hague. Gee, reporting from Holland in 1961, wrote of Osborn's efforts: "It stirred the whole country. It compelled the attention of the church ministers [Dutch Reformed]."[28] As a result of those meetings,

[26] Atter, *Third Force,* p. 165.
[27] *Ibid.,* p. 180.
[28] Gee, "What I Found in Holland," *Pentecost,* No. 56 (June–Aug., 1961), p. 7.

some of the ministers in the Dutch Reformed Church have personally testified that they have "spoken in tongues."[29]

The expansion of Pentecostalism has been so rapid that there are more assemblies than qualified men to serve them. To correct this, the Dutch—counseled and financially assisted by the Assemblies of God (USA)—opened the Nederlandse Pinksterbijbelschool at Groningen, a city in northern Holland. The Bible Institute is directed by E. A. Graf, formerly a pastor at Stadskanaal.[30] To be sure, it is a modest effort, for the school is able to accommodate only fifteen students; nevertheless, it is helping to correct the pastor-church imbalance which has plagued Dutch Pentecostalism during the past decade.

SCANDINAVIA

Denmark. The Danish Pentecostal movement gained its initial thrust from a revival conducted by the Norwegian pastor Thomas Ball Barratt during June, 1907. It was during these meetings that actress Anna Larssen was converted. She left the theater, married, and did evangelistic work in Copenhagen and its environs. A lasting tribute to her efforts is the existence of two flourishing churches: one with a membership of 500; the other with a membership of 1,000—the largest Free Church in Denmark.[31]

In the 1920's Danish Pentecostalism received an additional boost when Smith Wigglesworth arrived from England to lead a campaign in Copenhagen.

> For three weeks thousands daily attended the meetings. Each morning 200 or 300 were ministered to for healing. Each evening the platform was surrounded. Again and again as each throng retired, another company came forward seeking salvation. Many were baptized in the Holy Ghost.[32]

It was in this revival that another outstanding theatrical personality, Anna Lewini, was won to the Pentecostal cause. She later departed for missionary work in Ceylon.

[29] *Ibid.*, p. 6.

[30] V. G. Griesen, "Global Conquest Helps Open Holland Bible School," *Pentecostal Evangel*, XLVIII (Aug. 14, 1960), 13. See also "Pentecost in the Netherlands," *Pentecostal Evangel*, XLIX (Nov. 26, 1961), 17 f.

[31] Atter, *Third Force*, p. 165.

[32] Frodsham, *With Signs Following*, p. 74.

It is generally agreed that the initial progress which Pentecostalism made was vitiated by the influx of workers from the English-based Apostolic Church who introduced doctrinal differences that caused widespread dissension.[33] Be that as it may, at last count the Apostolic Church appeared to be the most active Pentecostal group in Denmark: it had 70 assemblies ministering to a constituency of 9,000.[34]

Finland. As was the case in most of the Scandinavian countries, the Pentecostal revival in Finland was the result of Thomas Ball Barratt's evangelistic endeavors. He visited that country in 1911, and a revival swept through the land.

During this time Finland was under Russian occupation, and there was bitter opposition from the Russian Orthodox clergy because a few Russian marines had been "contaminated" by the new religion. Some Pentecostals were arrested; others were imprisoned; but as Eino I. Manninen, the present leader of the Finnish Pentecostals, once said, "The Finnish people possess *sisu* [a steel-like perseverance]." They remained stanchly Pentecostal.

The Finns, like all Scandinavian Pentecostals, have no central organization. Thus the titular head of the movement is generally the pastor of the largest church: in Norway, Thomas Ball Barratt; in Sweden, Lewi Pethrus; and in Finland, Eino I. Manninen, pastor of the large 3,000-member Saalem Church in Helsinki.[35]

In the absence of an official body that would unite the Finnish Pentecostals in one body, each local church functions independently of every other church. The local congregation voluntarily cooperates with other congregations on missionary projects; it also unites with other churches twice a year for nationwide meetings.[36]

Finland was impoverished by World War II, for exorbitant reparations were demanded from her. Nevertheless, the postwar years have been a period of substantial growth for the Pentecostals. They have built many new churches, and rebuilt others. Today there are about 200 Pentecostal assemblies, attended by 40,000 people, who are served

[33] Atter, *Third Force,* p. 165.
[34] Coxill, *World Christian Handbook,* p. 202.
[35] Atter, *Third Force,* p. 174.
[36] Eino I. Manninen, "Pentecost in Finland," *Pentecostal Evangel,* LI (Nov. 10, 1963), p. 7.

by 300 pastors and evangelists.[37] These figures make it the largest group outside of the State Church (Suomen Evankelis-Luteritainen Kirkko). "A certain strained condition between the State Church exists all the time," says a Finnish Pentecostal spokesman, "because we have given up the infant baptism, and because most of our members have severed from the State Church and are now registered in the civil register."[38]

For a relatively small religious group, the Finnish Pentecostals are zealously missions conscious. They have 172 missionaries on foreign soil: of these, 29 are in Japan, 26 in Kenya, and 21 in Tanganyika.[39] These men and women are not sent out by a central missionary society, but are dependent upon local congregations for their support. The Finns also have a missionary ship, *Ebenezer,* which plies the waters around Ceylon and India. It is used "as an evangelistic centre to reach places with the gospel that might not be open to the more permanent settlement."[40]

Norway. As in Finland, 90 per cent of the Norwegian population is affiliated with the State Church (Norske Kirke). Thirty other churches constitute the remaining 10 per cent of the total. The largest of these thirty groups is the Norske Pinsevenners.[41] As a matter of fact, the largest dissenter congregation in Norway—Filadelfia—was founded in Christiania (Oslo) in 1916 by Thomas Ball Barratt. Dedicated in 1938, it is a majestic, modern church, with a seating capacity for 2,500. At that time, in addition to this church, there were three other Pentecostal congregations in Oslo, having a combined membership of 1,350.[42]

All told, there are 350 Pentecostal churches in Norway, serving a

[37] *Idem.*
[38] *Idem.*
[39] "Finland's 172 Missionaries," *Pentecost,* No. 66 (Dec., 1963–Feb., 1964), p. 10.
[40] *Idem.*
[41] Latourette, *The Twentieth Century in Europe,* p. 323.
[42] These figures are nearly 30 years old; they were obtained from William S. Johnson, "Pentecostal Work in Norway," *Pentecostal Evangel,* XXVI (Oct. 15, 1938), 5.

membership of 40,000.[43] Since 1913, when Barratt (formerly a Methodist pastor) was rebaptized, the Pentecostal movement in Norway has been largely baptistic both in its view of baptism as well as in its conception of congregational organization.[44]

Sweden. In January, 1907, Lewi Pethrus, pastor of a Baptist church in Linköping, Sweden, read an account of Barratt's revivals in Norway. Intrigued, he traveled to Christiania, experienced a Holy Spirit baptism there, and returned to his church "with a transformed ministry."[45]

In a short time, *glossolalia* manifested themselves in St. Johannes Church in Stockholm; in Skövde, where John Ongman, pastor of the large Filadelfia Free Church in Örebro, encountered the experience; and in Store Mellösa. In the winter of 1906–1907, the revival penetrated the Bethel and Bethany Baptist Churches in Gothenburg, and Barratt was invited to conduct special meetings there.

By 1910, a unique Pentecostal-Baptist assembly was formed in Stockholm. It took the name Filadelfia and called Lewi Pethrus as its pastor. Three years later, however, the church was excluded from the Stockholm District Association of Baptist Churches, not because of its emphasis upon the charismatic gifts, but because it practiced "open communion."[46] The Pentecostals felt that the Baptist Union's insistence on "closed communion" laid an undue stress on the matter of formal membership to a particular congregation. The Baptists, in turn, regarded the Pentecostal position as vague and inimical to good order and discipline.

The Stockholm incident was the summons for thousands of believers throughout Sweden who had long favored Pentecostal principles but had remained in the Swedish Baptist Union, the Methodist Church,

[43] Steiner, *Mit folgenden Zeichen,* p. 35; and Coxill, *World Christian Handbook,* p. 215.

[44] Bloch-Hoell, *Pinsebevegelsen,* p. 430.

[45] "Fifty Years of Pentecostal Revival in Sweden," *Pentecost,* No. 42 (Dec., 1957), p. 6.

[46] World Council of Churches, "The Pentecostal Movement and the Swedish Baptist Union, 1907–1920," *Bulletin,* VI, No. 1 (Spring, 1960), 3–12, treats the entire controversy.

and the Swedish Mission Covenant Church to separate and form free and independent Pentecostal churches. To this day, there is among Scandinavian Pentecostals what Gee calls "an almost fierce sentiment against all central organization."[47] The churches are locally organized. Each Monday they have a church meeting which is for members exclusively.

> These close meetings are a strong feature of the Pentecostal assemblies all over Northern Europe, and are hallowed times of unique Christian fellowship, when worship, business, sharing, discipline and missionary reports often seem to reproduce pages out of the New Testament. A solemn breaking-of-bread service at one of these strictly guarded meetings is something to remember. You separate, feeling that you might have been in Ephesus or Corinth. The same Spirit with His same gifts still abides.[48]

The Pentecostal churches in Sweden are united solely by their annual conventions which are inspirational rather than legislative. One in Nyhem has an average attendance of 18,000 to 20,000—4,000 of this number being young people under twenty years of age. The annual "Preacher's Week" attracts 990 ministers from all over Sweden.[49] Of course, the patriarchal figure of Lewi Pethrus, who successfully directed the activities of the world-famous Filadelfia Church in St. Eriksplan, Stockholm—with its membership of over 6,000—has given tone and leadership to Swedish Pentecostalism.

In 1962, there were 600 churches in Sweden, ministering to a total Christian community of 115,000.[50] The figure of 2,200 ordained clergy seems rather high, but at least half of that number are evangelists (many of them women) who conduct religious services all over the country right up into Lapland.[51] The Swedish Pentecostals support 410 missionaries, conduct a high school for their youth at Kaggeholm Castle, publish a daily newspaper, *Dagen,* as well as a religious weekly, *Evangelii Härold.*

[47] Gee, *Pentecostal Movement,* p. 176.
[48] Gee, *Upon All Flesh,* pp. 16 f.
[49] Atter, *Third Force,* p. 192.
[50] Coxill, *World Christian Handbook,* p. 218.
[51] Gee, *Upon All Flesh,* p. 17.

BALTO-SLAVIC COUNTRIES

Bulgaria. Pentecostalism was brought to Bulgaria in the 1920's by John E. Varonaeff, an American of Russian-Ukrainian extraction who had received the baptism of the Holy Spirit in New York City during the early days of the revival.[52] According to Gordon Atter, Varonaeff was responsible for singlehandedly opening eighteen Pentecostal churches in Bulgaria,[53] this despite severe opposition from both the Bulgarian Orthodox Church and the agrarian Communist agitators.

By 1933, the Pentecostals finally gained recognition with the Bulgarian government.[54] With support from an American Pentecostal missionary society which concentrated its efforts in eastern Europe—the Russian and Eastern European Mission[55]—Bulgarian Pentecostals established 30 good-sized assemblies besides many smaller groups. By 1935, the Pentecostals in Bulgaria numbered 5,000.[56]

But even during these years, the political youth movement was a menace to the Pentecostals; it often broke up meetings, meting out physical harm to attendants.[57] Finally with the outbreak of hostilities in 1939, the Pentecostals, together with all other denominations, were required to endure untold suffering as Bulgaria first sided with Germany and was then overrun by Russia.

It was under Soviet supervision that the Communist-dominated Fatherland Front government was set up and the monarchy was abolished. In 1947 the Communists established a puppet regime whose constitution was patterned after the Russian one, and these were some of the events that followed: prayer and religious instruction were abolished in schools, as was worship in the armed services; limitations were put on the activities of the "established" church

[52] Atter, *Third Force,* p. 83.

[53] *Idem.*

[54] Gee, *Upon All Flesh,* p. 22.

[55] *Idem.* According to Gee, it was founded in 1925. Its headquarters were located in Chicago, and its director of European affairs was G. H. Schmidt. The society supported 18 Bulgarian workers during the height of the depression.

[56] *Idem.*

[57] *Idem.*

(Bulgarian Orthodox); the leader of the Bulgarian Pentecostals, Pastor Popoff, was imprisoned because of his alleged "Western connections." He spent fifteen years in jail, being released finally in the winter of 1962. Under these conditions, the number of Pentecostal meeting places dwindled to one, although in 1962 the *World Christian Handbook* still estimated that there were 5,000 Pentecostals in Bulgaria.

Poland. The Pentecostal movement in Poland is the product of two influences:[58]

1. A revival which occurred in western Poland in 1910 among the German-speaking Poles at Cieszyn, Trzync, and Grodeck resulted in the formation of the Zwiazek Stanowczych Chrescijan (Union of Resolute Christians). At the outset, the churches in this organization were rather small; they were frequently persecuted by the Roman Catholics; and, for the most part, they were financially destitute. In time, however, the Polish Pentecostals prospered: chapels were built; a monthly periodical, *Glos Prawdy* (*Voice of Truth*) was first published in 1920; and a hymnal *Spiewnika Pielgrzymka* (*Songs of a Pilgrim*) was produced. Members of this group traveled to other parts of Poland and helped to establish churches in Warsaw and Malopolska (near Austria). However, the Nazi occupation of Poland from 1939–1945 very nearly obliterated this branch of Pentecostalism. What remained was forced to unite with other equally fragmentary Protestant groups to form the United Evangelical Church of Poland.

2. The evangelistic efforts of Poles who had emigrated to the United States, had been exposed to Pentecostalism, and returned to the "old country" to carry on a witness among their countrymen likewise resulted in the expansion of the movement, especially to those living in the central and eastern districts of Poland.[59] Leading this contingent was G. H. Schmidt of the Russian Eastern European Mis-

[58] Data drawn from *Kalendarz Jubileuszowy* (Warszawa: Prezydium Zjednoczonego Kosciola Ewangelicznego, 1963), pp. 85–90. Also W. Dawidow, "Kosciol Chrzescijan Wiary Ewangeliczney" (unpublished Th.M. thesis for the Protestant Faculty of the Warsaw University); abstracted for this writer by the author on Nov., 1963.

[59] See Gee, *Upon All Flesh,* p. 19, for an account of a service in which he participated while visiting eastern Poland (White Russia).

sion (REEM). For about a decade these Pentecostals avoided any organization. In 1929, however, they united as the Christian Church of the Evangelical Faith (Kosciol Chrescijan Wiary Ewangelicezney) and selected Arthur Bergholc, who had received his ministerial training in England, to lead them. Headquarters were established in the city of Lodz; multilingual religious periodicals were edited for the various Slavic peoples who had settled in Poland,[60] and a Bible institute was opened in Danzig in order to prepare a corps of trained pastors and evangelists.

There are data available which indicate that in 1935 this branch of the Pentecostal movement in Poland had 66 pastors (subsidized wholly by American organizations like REEM and the Assemblies of God), about 500 places where the full gospel was preached, and a membership of 20,000.[61] The Nazi invasion, however, forced the disbanding of the Christian Church of the Evangelical Faith, and the only churches to survive were those located in White Russia. The Pentecostals in the eastern Ukraine united with either the Baptists or the Methodists.[62]

After the war, while the government did permit non-Roman Catholics complete freedom of worship, it did require that smaller groups, like the Pentecostals, amalgamate. Therefore in 1953, the Pentecostals who composed the Christian Church of the Evangelical Faith joined the other Pentecostal body (the Union of Resolute Christians) and two other equally small non-Pentecostal denominations to form the United Evangelical Church. In this united body, there are 84 local churches, 124 mission stations, 61 chapels, 23 prayer halls, 1 home for the aged, 158 ministers, and 10,000 members.[63] What proportion of these figures is exclusively Pentecostal is a matter of sheer conjecture.

Russia. Surprisingly enough, it was only after the Communists came to power in Russia that Pentecostalism began to expand. Its growth

[60] *Przystep* for the Poles: *Ewangelskij Holos* for the Ukrainians; and *Priidet Primiritel* for the Russians.

[61] Gee, *Upon All Flesh,* p. 20.

[62] *Kalendarz,* p. 89.

[63] Atter, *Third Force,* p. 187.

was facilitated when the Soviets permitted John E. Voronaeff to enter the Ukraine in 1922. Preaching chiefly among the Baptists and other "Evangelical Christians," this dynamic evangelist succeeded in winning thousands to Pentecostalism, so that by 1926 the Pentecostal movement in the Soviet Union had 350 congregations with 17,000 believers.[64] Soon an organization was established—the All Ukrainian Council of Christians of the Evangelical Faith—with headquarters in Odessa. However, this phenomenal growth was halted by a wave of religious persecution. In 1928, for instance, 800 Pentecostals were imprisoned, among them Pastor Voronaeff, who has never been heard from since.[65] The others, because they lost their rights of citizenship, were forced to migrate from place to place in order to survive.[66]

Needless to say, there was little activity by the Pentecostals during the thirties. It was not until 1939, when the Pentecostal churches from eastern Poland came under Soviet control, that the movement experienced a renaissance. The active Pentecostal organizations which had emerged in the Ukraine and Byelorussia were forced by the Nazi authorities to unite with the Baptists and Evangelical Christians. Even after their liberation, the Russians, finding the German policy of dealing with united groups a simple one from an administrative standpoint, forced about 400 Pentecostal congregations to remain in the Council of Evangelical Christian Baptists.

The Evangelical-Baptist-Pentecostal alliance has not been very successful, especially from the Pentecostal viewpoint. A group which emphasizes the "leading of the Spirit" as much as it does, and one which is used to giving free expression to religious emotion, would certainly chafe under the restrictions put upon it by the more formal segments of the congregation. To alleviate the tension, many Pentecostals have seceded, creating problems for the Council.

> In the Ukraine, Byelorussia, Moldavia and even in other areas of Latvia and the Bryansk Province of the Russian Federation it became one of the main tasks of the travelling senior presbyters to mediate in

[64] Kolarz, *Religion in the Soviet Union,* p. 332.

[65] His wife was subsequently imprisoned for twenty years. For a detailed account of this event, see "Release of Mrs. Voronaeff," *Pentecost,* No. 54 (Dec., 1960–Feb., 1961), p. 3.

[66] Gee, *Upon All Flesh,* p. 25.

mixed congregations, to curb the zeal of the Pentecostalists, or to bring the independent Pentecostals back into the fold. The Evangelical Christian-Baptist Council in Moscow was repeatedly forced to deal with the "Pentecostal problem."[67]

Kolarz informs us that in these controversies, the Soviet authorities support the Baptists, regarding them as the more docile and the Pentecostals as dangerously fanatical. It is not surprising, therefore, to hear of instances where the government ejected pastors like Ivan Panko from the Ukraine, because they felt him to be an agitator. During the Khrushchev regime many Pentecostals were sentenced to ten-year prison terms, not only believers from the well-known areas like the Ukraine or Byelorussia, but also those from Crimea, Lithuania, the Kaliningrad Province, and Moscow.[68] Many who are presently in jail had served time under Stalin's rule, so persecutions are nothing new to them.

In spite of the fact that Pentecostal leaders are branded as criminals and hooligans by the Soviet press,[69] that they are imprisoned for allegedly indulging in dangerous religious fanaticisms and debauchery, for alienating the youth from Soviet life, and for being hostile to the State, army, Party, trade unions, and Soviet education,[70] Pentecostalism has continued to spread, and rather rapidly at that. Kolarz tries to explain this seeming paradox by suggesting that Pentecostalism's growth is caused by the fact that it attracts the poor. It is "more proletarian even than the Baptists."[71] Furthermore, its dynamism attracts the young:

> There is something romantic and revolutionary about the Pentecostal Movement in the Soviet Union. In the first place, the movement is banned and it demands some courage to belong to it. Moreover, the Pentecostal meetings take place in circumstances which appeal to young people . . . mountains . . . forests . . . half-dark rooms . . . , and all meetings are secret and conspiratorial. What the underground gatherings of illicit political circles did for another generation, the Pentecostal prayer meetings have done for certain young Soviet people in the fifties.[72]

[67] Kolarz, *Religion in the Soviet Union,* p. 333.
[68] *Ibid.,* p. 336.
[69] *Ibid.,* p. 334.
[70] *Ibid.,* p. 336.
[71] *Ibid.,* p. 335.
[72] *Idem.*

According to J. Nelson Parr, who visited Russia in 1960, there are 250,000 Pentecostals in Russia.[73]

Yugoslavia. Before World War II, most Yugoslavians belonged to the Greek Orthodox Church. Because it controlled the religious activities in the country, no evangelical groups were permitted to develop. In the postwar period, under Marshal Tito's regime, all churches have been granted equal right to conduct religious services. Thus it is that the Kristova Pentekostna Crkva (Christian Pentecostal Church) functions in Yugoslavia under the leadership of Ludwik Ullen and Dragutin Volf. There are about 1,016 adherents who meet in 60 "prayer halls" throughout Yugoslavia;[74] the larger congregations are in Osijek, Banat, Novi Sad, Zagreb, and Belgrade.

The devotion of both clergy and believers is impressive. Many Pentecostals come to worship on foot or on bicycle from distances up to fifteen miles. Their prayer sessions last until three in the morning. There is no Bible training institute for educating young pastors; therefore, Dragutin Volf (pastor of the church in Novi Sad) translates correspondence course materials that have been donated by the Assemblies of God (USA), prints them on a duplicating machine, and distributes them to the Yugoslavian pastors.

AUSTRIA, GERMANY, AND SWITZERLAND

Pentecostalism first appeared in Austria in 1923, the result of a missionary effort by the Filadelfia Church in Stockholm, which sent two workers to Vienna. Two assemblies were opened during the first year, but were soon amalgamated. Another assembly was opened in Kärnten which developed rather well, acording to Swiss Pentecostal historian, Leonhard Steiner.[75] And he should know, because it was his Swiss Pentecostal Mission which sent missionaries to evangelize the district of Salzkammergut during that period. They succeeded in

[73] "J. Nelson Parr Reports on Russia," *Pentecost,* No. 53 (Sept.–Nov., 1960), pp. 1 f.

[74] Gustav Kinderman, "Pentecostal Brethren in Yugoslavia," *Pentecost,* No. 52 (June–Aug., 1960), p. 10. See also Dick Fulmer, "Pentecost in a Communist Country,"*Pentecost,* No. 64 (June–Aug., 1963), p. 9.

[75] *Mit folgenden Zeichen,* pp. 66 f.

establishing small churches at Fuschl, Bad Ischl, Salzburg, and St. Wolfgang. From here the revival spread to Frankenburg.

In 1936, the authorities forbade the Pentecostals in Vienna and Salzkammergut to congregate. Furthermore, they ordered Swedish missionaries to leave the country. This was a foretaste of the impending crisis. Pentecostal believers were forced to gather for worship in the homes of their elders until after the "Anschluss," when Karl Fix of the Deutschen Volksmission entschiedener Christen reopened the work in Vienna.

During and immediately following World War II, the Pentecostal work in Austria passed through countless crises. Finally in 1946, various leaders who had been scattered by the conflict called for a general convention to be held at Sattledt. There the Austrians united under the name Freie Christengemeinden Philadelphia. The selection of the word "Philadelphia" indicates that the Scandinavian influence had had a lasting effect on the Austrian work. Shortly thereafter, however, the phrase "in Österreich" was substituted for it. In 1954, when Steiner authored his *Darstellung der Pfingstbewegung,* there were but 700 Pentecostal adherents in Austria with the largest congregations located in Vienna, Linz, Salzburg, Groz, and Knittelfeld.

Interestingly enough, as small as it is, Austrian Pentecostalism is divided into two other branches: the Österreichische Zeltmission whose headquarters are in Kärnten, and the Germeinde bibelglaubiger Christen whose religious center is in Frankenburg. Statistics regarding Pentecostalism's advance in this predominantly Roman Catholic country are unimpressive. At most, there are only 2,000 Pentecostals, perhaps 6 ordained clergy and about 20 places of worship.[76]

i

The leaders of the Pentecostal revival in Germany were former Lutheran pastors: Jonathan Paul from Berlin, C. O. Voget from Breslau, Karl Ecke, Emil Humburg, and Martin Genische, a gifted musician.

During the early 1900's, the industrial city of Mülheim-Ruhr in the

[76] Cf. Atter, *Third Force,* p. 164; Coxill, *World Christian Handbook,* p. 199.

Rhineland became a famous center for large Pentecostal conferences, and it was there that the Christlichen Gemeinschaftsverbands Mülheim (Mülheim Christian Alliance) was organized. Led by Emil Humburg, the Mülheim Alliance developed into a 600-church movement in the period prior to World War II. One of its greatest accomplishments was the publication of a hymnal, *Pfingst Jubel* (*Pentecostal Songs*), which is still utilized by German-speaking Pentecostals around the world.

One of the characteristics of the Mülheim Pentecostals was a penchant for "prophetic introspection." As Gee describes it, one gathers that it was a sort of oral analysis of an extremely personal nature which was often embarrassing to the person whose inner-soul condition was being analyzed. Certain men and women claimed to have insights, or Spirit-inspired visions which allowed them to make these revelations. Needless to say, this is the sort of practice that can very easily degenerate into sheer fanaticism. It apparently did, and, as a sort of protest movement, a second strand of Pentecostalism began to develop in Germany—the Freie Pfingstgemeinden (Free Pentecostal Churches)—under the leadership of Pastor Strunk of Leipzig and Pastor Bartknecht, supported by a group of American missionaries who taught at the Pentecostal Bible Institute in Danzig. As Hitler grew in power, it was necessary for the Freie Pfingstgemeinden to affiliate with the Baptists in order to continue their work.

With the conclusion of World War II, a new church was established in Hamburg; it was pastored by Paul Rabe, and its polity was modeled after the Scandinavian form of church government—complete autonomy of the local congregation. Oscar Lardon opened a similar "free" assembly in Altoona. Alwil Rothenburg oversaw several in the Berlin area. At the same time, many Americans, feeling that Germany was a mission field, set up tents and conducted numerous revival meetings on the border of the Russian Zone. Ben Kummerfield, Richard Ruff, Harold Herman, Willard Cantelon from America, as well as German businessman Herman Zaiss, drew large crowds to their "canvas cathedrals." Thousands of converts were won to the Pentecostal movement, and a need for organization arose. At last in 1953, all of the "free" assemblies united to form the Arbeitsgemeinschaft der Christengemeinden in Deutschland (Fellowship of the Christian Assemblies in Germany). The polity of this group is similar to that of the Assemblies of God (USA). Today about 150 churches are included in this Fellowship which operates the Bibel Schule Beröa in Erzhausen bei Darmstadt. The group engages in a foreign missions program, as well as in vigorous outdoor evangelistic projects.

In southern Germany, there is a third Pentecostal group, the Volksmission, which is directed by Karl Fix. Its headquarters are in Stuttgart, the same city in which the Pentecostals have a large sanctuary seating 1,000. There are about 150 churches associated with the Volksmission.

Before Hitler's rise to power, the Church of God (Cleveland, Tennessee) sponsored a German-American pastor, Herman Lauster, permitting him to return to his homeland and engage in the work of evangelism. For a few years he was able to elude the Gestapo; then he was apprehended for conducting religious services that were unauthorized. He was imprisoned, but the work that he had done in the Swabian section of Germany was established. In the postwar years, 46 churches have sprung up in the vicinity of Württenberg as a result of Lauster's evangelistic efforts. The Gemeinde Gottes has about 1,000 members; it conducts a Bible School; and it publishes the *Bote de Gemeinde Gottes,* a German edition of the *Church of God Evangel.*[77]

ii

Reports about the Pentecostal revival that was taking place in western Europe reached the German-speaking areas of Switzerland in the early 1900's. These were followed by personal visits of two lady missionaries from Norway, as well as by Thomas Ball Barratt, who came from Norway to conduct meetings in Switzerland. By 1910, there was sufficient interest manifested by the Swiss to host a Pentecostal convention in Zurich to which the outstanding European Pentecostals came to minister: Paul from Germany, Boddy from England, and Polman from Holland. This conference helped to establish Pente-

[77] Charles Conn's history of Church of God missions, *Where the Saints Have Trod* (pp. 237–45), has a complete account of Lauster's ordeals in Germany. It is both factual and fascinating.

costalism in Switzerland, for soon thereafter men like A. Reuss, P. R. Ruff, Christian Siefer, and H. Steiner emerged to assume the pastorates of small Pentecostal assemblies.

In the early twenties, Smith Wigglesworth of England conducted some highly successful evangelistic-healing meetings at Berne, Neuchatel, Lausanne, Vevey, and Geneva.[78] They did much to extend the influence of Pentecostalism, so much so that in 1921, the Swiss Pentecostal Missionary Society (Schweizerische Pfingstmission) was organized to "school, send out, and support missionaries."[79] Before the year ended, their first representative was off to Basutoland in South Africa, and since that time nearly two dozen other missionaries have been commissioned by this rather small society.[80]

To safeguard the doctrinal development of Pentecostalism so that the fanaticisms which sometimes accompanied it in other countries would not arise in Switzerland, as well as to insure the independence of the local churches, a Council of Elders (Aeltestenrat) was formed in 1926. This Council together with delegates from all the Swiss missions constitutes the General Assembly which meets annually to elect a chairman as well as secretaries for home and foreign missions. For years the leader of this Council has been Karl Schneider of Winterthur.

The Swiss Pentecostal Mission is the largest Pentecostal body in that country. Up-to-date figures are rather difficult to obtain, but a conservative estimate would be 100 assemblies with about 3,000 communicants.[81] Their official organ is *Die Verheissung des Vaters* (*The Promise of the Father*). Among the other groups are the Eglises Evangéliques de Réveil, which maintains a number of thriving churches in French-speaking Switzerland, and which has a constituency of 1,000;[82] the Freien Christengemeinden; and the Gemeinden für Urchristentum with centers respectively at Aach-Hoffeld and Signau.[83]

[78] Frodsham, *With Signs Following,* pp. 99 f.

[79] L. Steiner, "Pentecost in Switzerland," *Pentecostal Evangel,* XXXV (Feb. 15, 1947), 7, 13.

[80] Steiner, *Mit folgenden Zeichen,* p. 63.

[81] Steiner, "Pentecost," p. 7.

[82] Fritz Blanke, *Kirchen + Sekten* (Zürich: Zwingli Verlag, 1959), p. 70.

[83] Steiner, *Mit folgenden Zeichen,* p. 65.

LATIN EUROPE

France. There have been small groups of Pentecostals in Paris and Le Havre since 1909,[84] but 1931 really marks the beginning for Les Mouvements de Pentecôte in France. In that year, Douglas R. Scott, sensing a missionary call to Africa, arrived in Le Havre for a period of intensive language study. He was invited to preach at the establishment of Mlle. Biolley, an elderly Swiss woman, who operated a temperance restaurant which doubled as a meeting place for those interested in the message of Pentecost.[85] In lamentable French, it is reported, Scott preached the gospel and offered to pray for the sick. The results were phenomenal: scores were converted and many were healed.[86] Soon two churches of 200 to 300 people were established in Le Havre. The intended short stay of Scott extended to a period of eight years, during which time he evangelized many areas of France and saw the revival spread from the channel port of Havre to Rouen, Paris, Marseille, Toulon, Nantes, and Dieppe. In 1939, just before leaving for the Belgian Congo—his original destination—Scott wrote about the Pentecostal revival in France:

> At this time, nine years after the foundation of the Pentecostal work in France, we . . . have now 51 established assemblies and gospel meetings, some of which are very strong in numbers, and others just commencing. Each of these assemblies sees a continual stream of conversions, baptisms in water, baptisms in the Spirit, and miracles of healing. In fact, the revival goes on steadily and gradually, without any special evangelistic effort.[87]

As to organization, here is André Nicolle's comment: "We had no sort of Movement or organized Assembly in those days; we just 'went ahead' in faith, with nothing but the promises of God to guide us."[88] Eventually, though, after constant communication with the British

[84] *Ibid.*, p. 67.
[85] H. Ch. Chéry, *L'Offensive des Sectes* (Paris: Les Éditions du Cerf, 1954), p. 335.
[86] Frodsham, *With Signs Following,* pp. 85–92, has accounts of the healings which allegedly occurred at Havre and elsewhere.
[87] *Ibid.,* p. 91.
[88] Atter, *Third Force,* p. 171.

Pentecostals, the assemblies that were scattered throughout the Channel area, the north of France, and the Riviera took the name Les Assemblées de Dieu. Like its British and American namesakes, it permits each church to have complete autonomy in matters of local polity. There is no hierarchy: each church has a pastor, whom it has called, and a Council of Elders which assists the pastor in any administrative problems. Pastors meet for a National Congress from time to time, primarily for fellowship and the discussion of perplexing pastoral problems, not for the purpose of legislation.[89]

At the present time, there are about 266 Pentecostal places of worship throughout France,[90] established in 61 departments. Most of them are located in les Alpes-Maritimes, les Bouches-du-Rhône, le Calvados, l'Eure, le Pas-de-Calais, la Seine, la Sein-Maritime, and la Seine-et-Oise.[91] There are about 30 additional meetings for worship and evangelization in North Africa.

One hundred eighty ordained ministers (and probationers) serve in metropolitan France; 13 in North Africa. The French Assemblies of God supports 21 missionaries in the territories of the communauté Française in Africa; it publishes *Viens et Vois* (*Come and See*) for its 5,000 subscribers; and it maintains l'Institut Biblique du Château des Croisers at Andrimont, Belgium, for its fledgling preachers.

A recent Pentecostal outburst among the Gypsies of France has awakened even the most apathetic Frenchman to the existence of the movement.[92]

Les Assemblées de Dieu comprise 90 per cent of all French Pentecostals. The other 10 per cent is scattered among groups like La tendance Jeffreys, L'Eglise apostolique, Le "Latter Rain," La Première Pentecôte, and a few Pentecostal Baptists.[93]

Italy. Among the many Protestant groups that exist in Italy are the

[89] *Idem.*

[90] Gérard Dagon, *Petites Églises et Grandes Sectes* (Paris: Société d'Evangélisation, n.d.), p. 34.

[91] *Idem.*

[92] Cf. Kenneth Ware, "Revival among the Gypsies," *Pentecostal Evangel,* XLIX (Oct. 22, 1961), 8; C. Le Cossec, "World Pentecostal Gypsy Mission," *Pentecost* No. 66 (Dec., 1963–Feb., 1964), p. 13.

[93] Chéry, *L'Offensive,* pp. 359 f.

Waldensians, the oldest group which traces its history from A.D. 1200, and the Pentecostals, the largest evangelical body.[94]

An Italian Pentecostal from Chicago, Giacomo Lombardi, arrived in Rome in 1908. He was soon followed by P. Ottolini, who established Pentecostal assemblies at Turin and Milan in 1910; and by a Californian, S. Arena, who emigrated to Sicily in 1919. These men overcame both hostility and indifference, and by 1929 were instrumental in establishing 149 Pentecostal assemblies in Italy.[95] But the work which had grown steadily for three decades was driven underground by severe persecutions resulting from the Lateran Treaty between the Fascists and the Vatican State.[96]

> The first official act of persecution by the government was the revoking of the decree of appointment of the pastor at Rome. Not only did this act remove the right of free exercise of religious activity in Rome but it brought all the other Pentecostal churches automatically under the same decree. All churches were to be closed and all activities suspended. The purpose of the Ministry of the Interior in taking such action was evident; the police were to consider the Pentecostal work a dangerous body from a political, social, and psychical viewpoint.[97]

Until 1944, when the liberation armies freed Italy, there was not a single Pentecostal church open. The Italian Pentecostals met "in caves, open fields, or in private homes behind closed doors."[98] By 1946, however, churches were rebuilt; a year later, they organized under the name Assemblies of God of Italy. Nevertheless, Pentecostals continued to be harassed until 1954, when the Federal Council of Evangelical Churches in Italy succeeded in pressuring the Supreme Court to rescind the circular of April 9, 1935, which prohibited Pentecostals from meeting for public worship.[99]

The Assemblies of God of Italy maintains close contact with three organizations in the United States: (1) the Christian Churches of

[94] "Pentecost in Italy," *Pentecostal Evangel,* XLIX (Oct. 29, 1961), 22.
[95] Fiorentino, "Summary," p. 9.
[96] "Pentecost in Italy," p. 22.
[97] Fiorentino, "Summary," p. 9.
[98] Donald Sheley, "A Visit to Italy," *Pentecostal Evangel,* XLV (Feb. 10, 1957), 27. See also "Pentecost in Italy," p. 22.
[99] The official registration of this decree was delayed until 1960. Until that time, Pentecostals had no right to perform marriages or funerals, or to hold property.

North America which contributes liberally toward the support of national workers; (2) the Italian Branch of the Assemblies of God (USA), which underwrites the cost of translating and printing gospel literature, as well as improving the work of Sunday Schools; and (3) the Assemblies of God (USA), which has been responsible for building the six-story Rome Bible Institute that can accommodate 100 students.

Pentecostal churches in Italy still encounter local persecution. They find it virtually impossible to rent halls for public worship as a result of pressure put on landlords by the Roman Catholic clergy. Thus congregations are forced either to build or to purchase buildings. This they have done, and the number of congregations has tripled within the past decade. Today there are nearly 600 churches, ministering to 100,000 communicants.[100]

The Italian Pentecostals publish a monthly religious journal, *Risveglio Pentecostale,* and maintain a home for twenty-five orphans in Tolupara-Mentana, a suburb of Rome.

Portugal. The existence of Pentecostalism in Portugal is largely the result of efforts made by the Svenska Fria Missionen, which sponsors 110 places of worship for some 3,300 communicants.[101] Since the Scandinavian influence predominates, there is no central organization of Portuguese Pentecostals. Each local assembly governs itself. Conferences are held in Aveiro, patterned after the famous "Nyhem" conventions in Sweden. The largest Pentecostal churches are located in Lisbon[102] and Oporto; the outstanding Pentecostal leader is Pastor Alfredo Machado.

Spain. Pentecostals are unwelcome in Spain. They are often unable to secure permits to hold religious services, and without such a permit it is illegal to have a congregation of more than six members. Moreover, it is unlawful to propagandize in any form outside the confines

[100] "Pentecost in Italy," p. 22.

[101] Coxill, *World Christian Handbook,* p. 217. The Assemblies of God has 86 places of worship and 3,500 communicants.

[102] According to *Pentecost,* No. 66 (Dec., 1963–Feb., 1964), p. 15, this assembly, the largest in Lisbon, seats 1,500.

of the church; no sounds must emanate from the building; it cannot bear any signs that would advertise services. Pentecostals as do all Spanish Protestants find much difficulty in getting married.

If they have been baptized Catholic as an infant and later turn Protestant they are denied the right of a Catholic marriage and at the same time they cannot get clearance from the Catholic Church for a civil marriage.[103]

The Assemblies of God (USA) has established four small works in Spain: a Church at La Coruna, which opened in 1946, has 80 members and is pastored by a Spaniard; an American missionary, Roy Dalton, leads a congregation of 100 at Ronda; a small congregation of 25 members constitutes the church in Barcelona;[104] and a small mission exists at Gijon. Latest reports estimate that there are perhaps no more than 400 Spanish Pentecostals.[105]

[103] W. K. McIntyre, "Renewed Hope in Spain"; quoted in Atter, *Third Force,* p. 191.

[104] Even though this assembly has existed for eighteen years, it has been unable to obtain a worship permit from the Barcelona authorities.

[105] Atter, *Third Force,* p. 51.

CHAPTER 12

Pentecostalism Since World War II: Significant Trends

ERA OF COOPERATION

Relations between Pentecostals and Christians of other Protestant denominations have always been somewhat strained, but they were at their lowest ebb right after World War I. The Church of the Nazarene, for instance, dropped the word "Pentecostal" from its official title in order to distinguish itself from the fanatical glossolalics. In England, Oswald Chambers, a leader in the Keswick movement, referred to the "Tongues Movement" as a "Satanic Counterfeit." The Methodist Church in Norway and in Chile took a firm stand against the Pentecostal Revival.[1] And at their 1928 Chicago convention, American Fundamentalists overwhelmingly adopted this resolution:

> Whereas, The present wave of modern Pentecostalism, often referred to as the "tongues movement," and the present wave of fanatical and unscriptural healing which is sweeping over the country today, has become a real menace in many churches and a real injury to the same testimony of Fundamental Christians,
>
> Be it Resolved, That this convention go on record as unreservedly opposed to Modern Pentecostalism, including the speaking with unknown tongues, and the fanatical healing known as general healing in the atonement, . . .[2]

[1] Bloch-Hoell, *Pentecostal Movement,* pp. 67, 82, 120 f.

[2] Brumback, *Suddenly from Heaven,* pp. 282 f., citing the *Pentecostal Evangel* (Aug. 18, 1928).

Then in the early 1940's, a remarkable change began to take place. Some influential Pentecostal leaders began to question the isolationistic stance which their movement had taken during the preceding two decades, and their inquiries were not in vain. In 1943, a number of the major Pentecostal denominations joined the National Association of Evangelicals which, in a sense, was the successor to the Fundamentalist movement that had repudiated Pentecostalism in 1928.

Pentecostals Unite with Other Evangelicals. What caused the deep-seated hostility which had existed for about twenty years (1920–1940) between Pentecostals and non-Pentecostals to abate? The reasons for the thaw are, admittedly, none too clear. Perhaps the war had something to do with it. Pentecostal ministers received commissions as chaplains and served with distinction in many battle theaters. Pentecostal denominations, especially the Assemblies of God, carried on varied social and evangelistic activities for their own servicemen, as well as for those of other faiths.[3]

Perhaps the remarkable advances which the Pentecostals had been making in foreign missions over a period of thirty years commended them to their fellow Christians. Perhaps, as Donald Gee put it, non-Pentecostals finally realized "that the Pentecostal churches had come to stay, and that fellowship with them was not only possible, but desirable."[4] Perhaps, it was the aftereffect of statements issued by leading Pentecostals in which they descried past evidences of isolationism, exclusivism, and fanaticism within their movement.[5]

Whatever the reasons, the first tangible sign that a new epoch in relations between Pentecostals and non-Pentecostals was being ushered in was the gathering of a group of key evangelicals in Chicago on May 3–6, 1943. Despairing of what they felt were modernistic

[3] Although hundreds of thousands of dollars were spent to publish *Reveille,* a paper for service personnel, there was no attempt to capitalize on it. The name of no Pentecostal group appeared anywhere. See Brumback, *Suddenly from Heaven,* p. 314. For an account of British Pentecostal ministries, see Gee, *Pentecostal Movement,* pp. 197 f.

[4] Gee, "The Contribution of the Pentecostal Movement to the Church Universal," in the *World Pentecostal Conference Souvenir Brochure,* ed. by H. W. Greenway (London: The British Pentecostal Fellowship, 1952), pp. 10 ff.

[5] *Idem.*

trends in the Federal Council, they met to form an association of Bible-believing Christians that was "large enough and broad enough to include whole denominations, schools, . . . and missionary organizations."[6] What is really significant, though, is that for the first time in decades the Pentecostals had been invited. Not only that, they had come. One hundred and six representatives from the Assemblies of God alone responded and attended the Constitutional Convention.[7] The Church of God (Cleveland, Tennessee) sent five delegates.[8] One of the participants, obviously relieved, reported later: "We were not asked to compromise one iota of our distinctive Pentecostal testimony."[9] All the Pentecostals were able to subscribe to the simple statement of faith that was adopted by the National Association of Evangelicals. All were convinced that irrespective of denominational affiliation, background, or intellectual attainment, Calvinists, Arminians, Holiness, and Pentecostals alike had finally "found a common bond in their love for the Lord Jesus and their belief in the fundamentals of the Christian faith."[10]

The newly established friendship between the Pentecostals and other Evangelicals was sealed with the appointment of two Pentecostals to a twenty-two-member Board of Administration, and the representatives reported back to their respective general conferences that "the cause seems to be a worthy one and should have the support of all true followers of the Lord Jesus Christ."[11]

However, such resolutions to affiliate with the National Association of Evangelicals were not going to be endorsed without opposition. Charles Conn relates that

> some of the Church of God preachers questioned the propriety of such close association with non-Pentecostals. Nevertheless, a majority of the delegates realized that there is but a hair's-breadth between the current of

[6] Harold Lindsell, *Park Street Prophet* (Wheaton, Ill.: Van Kampen Press, 1951), pp. 113–18.

[7] J. Roswell Flower, "The Basic Unity of Evangelical Christianity," *Pentecostal Evangel,* XXXI (June 19, 1943), 8.

[8] Conn, *Like a Mighty Army,* p. 260.

[9] Stanley Frodsham, "Fifth Annual Convention of the NAE," *Pentecostal Evangel,* XXXV (May 10, 1947), 6.

[10] Flower, p. 8.

[11] *Idem.*

conviction and the shoals of bigotry. . . . It is easy to confuse separation from the world with aloofness toward all that is unlike oneself—and then regard the misunderstanding as a virtue. An aggressive, vital, evangelistic church is in danger of such absorption in its own affairs that it loses its outside perspective and looks askance at all others than itself.[12]

Needless to say, the decision of the Evangelicals to invite Pentecostals to the Chicago convention, and the subsequent decision of the major Pentecostal groups to join the NAE, did much to eliminate the discord which had for so many years characterized relations between Evangelicals who were Pentecostal and those who were not.[13] It is also necessary to emphasize the fact that the union of Pentecostals with American Evangelicals actually antedated any formal mergers by Pentecostal groups themselves.

Pentecostals Establish a Global Fellowship. From the earliest days of the Pentecostal revival, certain of its leaders have pleaded for some sort of organic unity. In 1911, for example, Pastor Thomas Ball Barratt of Norway issued his "An Urgent Plea for Charity and Unity." He acknowledged that there is a spiritual union among Pentecostals, but he recommended the creation of a simple, practical outward form as an expression of this union.[14] To allay the fears of those who had been shut out of various churches because of their Pentecostalism and who, therefore, had an antipathy toward any form of organization, Barratt wrote:

All we aim at is a real and brotherly cooperation within and between the various Pentecostal Centers. [Such as those he had established in Copenhagen, Gothenburg, and Christiania.]

We should not copy the ponderous machinery of some church systems, the complicated organizations and formal services prevalent there. . . . The Holy Spirit is clearly leading us on very simple lines these days, more in harmony with Primitive Christianity.[15]

After emphasizing that Pentecostals must guard against "the spirit of

[12] Conn, *Like a Mighty Army,* p. 261.

[13] From the outset, Pentecostals have served on several important commissions and boards of the NAE. In 1961, for instance, Cordas Burnett and Thomas Zimmerman of the Assemblies of God served as Executive Secretary and President, respectively.

[14] In *Word and Work,* XXXIII (Apr., 1911), 105.

[15] *Idem.*

religious anarchy, that ignores the humble and inspired work of God-given leaders, and a practical order of work and union" within the movement, he concluded:

> Must we everlastingly live our congregational lives in different communities, separated, not because of the growth and extension of the Kingdom, but because we cannot see alike in every question? . . . What is there to be done? We must either find some form of union, or stand as separate bodies, and aim at some form of alliance between these.[16]

Ten years passed before anything was done to implement Barratt's suggestion. Then at Amsterdam, in 1921, several Pentecostal leaders and groups came together for the first time. A tenseness developed, related Donald Gee, because "the German preachers determined to monopolise the Convention with a new teaching . . . that . . . was reinforced by frequent visions of an extremely personal nature for those present, and by prophecies."[17] The delegates from Sweden disagreed with what they interpreted to be an "over-balanced emphasis" and subsequently clashed with the German Pentecostals. Thus, except for brief periods of fellowship, nothing was accomplished to promote the cause of unity.

In the period between 1930 and 1940, additional Pentecostal Unity Conferences were sponsored by the Assemblies of God (USA); by a Mr. Naumann, described by Donald Gee as a consecrated Pentecostal businessman of London, who worked to persuade the leaders of various branches of Pentecostalism in the British Isles of "the need for a greater degree of unity";[18] and by Swedish Pentecostals.

The Assemblies of God invited representatives from Britain, Canada, South Africa, and other parts of the world to the General Council which was held in Memphis, in 1937. "There was an urgent desire for fellowship and unity," writes David J. duPlessis, and "it was decided that an attempt should be made to call a World Conference in London during the summer of 1940."[19] Meanwhile, in May, 1939, and January, 1940, a score of Pentecostal leaders, representing such

[16] *Idem.*
[17] *Pentecostal Movement,* p. 122.
[18] *Ibid.,* pp. 169 f.
[19] "World Pentecost," in *World Pentecostal Conference Souvenir Brochure,* p. 3.

British churches as the Apostolic Church, Assemblies of God, the Elim Church, and one or two independent groups, met in London. They hoped to achieve some sort of unity among the various Pentecostal groups in the British Isles.

Finally, from June 5 to 12, 1939, delegates from twenty different European countries came to Stockholm. They discussed many subjects, but "there were no resolutions that sought to crystallise into a form of words the mind of the majority."[20] To sum up, while all of these unity conferences provided an opportunity for fellowship and discussion, they studiously avoided making any suggestions concerning the merger of existing Pentecostal groups. Moreover, observes Gee, somewhat sadly, "Old party-cries were easily revived, and suggestions of compromise launched by sincere champions of imaginary crusades for vital truths."[21]

Needless to say, the outbreak of World War II postponed any thoughts that some Pentecostals might have had about uniting. After the cessation of hostilities, however, some of those who recalled the Unity Conference in Stockholm began to agitate for a world conference. American Pentecostals, wishing to help in the rehabilitation of their brethren on the Continent, also expressed a desire for such an organization. In countries like Italy, where the Pentecostals were engaged in a struggle with the government over the question of religious liberty, there was the feeling that a world conference "could speak and act with more authority and influence" than a mere local organization.[22] It was the proper time for the establishment of a worldwide Pentecostal fellowship.

A Prayer Convention was held at Basel in May, 1946; those who had gathered decided to schedule the first world conference of Pentecostals one year hence in Zurich, and to use as a theme I Corinthians 12:13—"For by one Spirit we are all baptized into one body." When that conference began, some of the Pentecostals who were deeply moved by the plight of their fellows in war-torn Europe disagreed with others as to the best methods to employ in achieving an effective re-

[20] Gee, *Pentecostal Movement,* p. 181.
[21] *Ibid.,* p. 171.
[22] *Ibid.,* p. 227.

lief program. A sizable delegation from Scandinavia adamantly opposed any organization beyond that of the local church.[23] Still others disagreed about the fundamental purpose for calling such a conference: "Some had come primarily for spiritual discussions; others for more practical purposes. . . . As a result there was confusion and frustration."[24] The only concrete results were the following: (1) an international center for coordinating the work of evangelism and relief among European Pentecostals was to be established in Basel; (2) an international missionary magazine, *Pentecost,* was to be published; it would include descriptions of the missionary and evangelistic outreach of the various branches comprising the Pentecostal movement.[25]

Commenting on that first convention to which almost every major Pentecostal body had sent a representative, David duPlessis wrote:

> Much of what had been accomplished . . . was not recorded in books on earth. Links of fellowship were forged that were stronger than conference resolutions. The need for unity and cooperation was impressd upon all with greater emphasis than ever before.
>
> . . . .
>
> It was soon evident that more international fellowship and closer cooperation were necessary for harmonious working, both at home among the older churches and on the foreign fields among the younger churches.[26]

Because no basis for international fellowship and cooperation had been developed at Zurich, it was obviously necessary that other world conferences be convened. A second one was scheduled to be held in Paris, in May, 1949. At this meeting, another debate developed as to the form that the worldwide fellowship ought to take; however, it was resolved when a specially appointed fifteen-man committee submitted the following proposals: (1) that spiritual fellowship be maintained and strengthened by arranging for conferences in different lands

[23] *Ibid.,* p. 228.

[24] *Ibid.,* p. 229.

[25] Cf. Lester Sumrall, "International Pentecostal Conference in Switzerland," *Pentecostal Evangel,* XXXV (May 31, 1947), 6, 10–12; (June 7), 6 f.; and (June 21), 6 f.

[26] DuPlessis, "World Pentecost," p. 4.

at least every three years; (2) that a secretary be selected by each conference to serve the interests of all Pentecostal groups during and between such conferences; (3) that the conference select a committee of five which would advise and assist the secretary; (4) that the conference reaffirm its recognition of the inherent principles of spiritual unity and fellowship of Pentecostals and thus leave "inviolate the varied forms of church government," and recognize "that every freedom and privilege enjoyed by any church or group of churches shall remain their undisturbed possession";[27] and (5) that the conference "encourage fellowship and facilitate co-ordination of effort among Pentecostal believers throughout the world."[28]

In the ensuing years, the fears which earlier haunted so many Pentecostals regarding the propriety of a worldwide Pentecostal conference have subsided. Attendance at all subsequent gatherings—London (1952), Stockholm (1955), Toronto (1958), Jerusalem (1961), and Helsinki (1964)—has steadily increased. However, the meetings have devoted less and less time to controversial discussions and "business" and have stressed instead "warm fellowship, inspiring music, and outstanding preaching." The most recent conference in Helsinki was arranged so as to provide lectures during the morning sessions, testimonies and special music in the afternoon meeting, and evangelistic preaching in the evening services.[29]

National Alliances Evolve. According to some Pentecostals, a val-

[27] *Idem.*

[28] *Idem.* See also "Echoes of Paris" in *Pentecost,* No. 9 (Sept., 1949), p. 2.

[29] At the 7th triennial gathering in Helsinki (June, 1964), the theme of the lectures was Evangelism, and the following are the titles of some of the addresses: "Christ, the Foundation of World Evangelization Today," "God's Gift of Evangelists," and "The Holy Spirit in World Evangelization." See "The 7th Pentecostal World Conference," in *Pentecostal Testimony* (Aug., 1964), pp. 6–7, 10; and "3,200 Registered," in *Pentecostal Evangel,* LII (Aug. 2, 1964), 9.

From the thirty countries represented there came a variety of sacred music to entertain and edify the gathering; for example, the Swedish Preachers' Choir, the Evangel College (USA) Ensemble and Choir, and the French Gypsy Quintet.

The evening meetings were attended by upwards of 11,000 people. They heard sermons by preachers from the United States, South Africa, Germany, Sweden, and Norway.

uable by-product of the World Pentecostal Conference in 1947 was that it stimulated movements toward union among Pentecostals in North America and in the British Isles.

Be that as it may, one year later, eight Pentecostal denominations sent representatives to Chicago in the months of May and August to explore the possibility of "interdenominational Pentecostal cooperation and fellowship."[30] Little was accomplished excepting the fact that there was general agreement that another conference should be held in the fall for the purpose of effecting a formal organization. Such a gathering took place in Des Moines, Iowa, from October 26 to 28. A constitution was adopted which declared the purpose of the Pentecostal Fellowship of North America to be as follows:

> To give expression to the inherent principles of spiritual unity and fellowship of Pentecostal believers, leaving inviolate the existing forms of church government adopted by its members; and recognizing that every freedom and privilege enjoyed by a church or group of churches, shall remain their undisturbed possession.[31]

A thirteen-member Board of Administration was elected to oversee the affairs of the newly created fellowship. In addition, a chairman, two vice-chairmen, a secretary, and a treasurer were appointed. They constituted the Executive Committee and were *ex officio* members of the Board as well. Pentecostal groups which had sent observers were permitted a voting representation of one delegate for each 5,000 members up to 25,000, and one delegate for each 15,000 members thereafter. Delegates to this initial conference also made the following statement of objectives:

> 1. To provide a vehicle of expression and coordination of efforts in matters common to all member bodies, including missionary and evangelistic effort throughout the world.

[30] The largest groups to send delegates were the Pentecostal Holiness Church, Church of God (Cleveland, Tenn.), Foursquare Gospel Church, Open Bible Standard Churches, Assemblies of God, and the Pentecostal Assemblies of Canada. Smaller groups represented were the Elim Missionary Assemblies and International Pentecostal Assemblies. See Conn, *Like a Mighty Army,* p. 276.

[31] Kendrick, *Promise Fulfilled,* p. 211, citing *Pentecost,* No. 7 (Mar., 1949), p. 7.

2. To demonstrate to the world the essential unity of Spirit-baptized believers, fulfilling the prayer of the Lord Jesus "that they all may be one" (John 17:21).

3. To provide services to its constitutents which will enable them to accomplish more quickly and efficiently their responsibility for the speedy evangelization of the world.

4. To encourage the principles of comity for the nurture of the body of Christ, endeavoring to keep the unity of the Spirit until we all come to the unity of the faith.[32]

The success of the Pentecostal Fellowship of North America was assured, for by the time of the second convention in Oklahoma City (1949), the original total of eight participating Pentecostal denominations had swelled to fourteen, "representing a constituent membership of over 1,000,000."[33]

In the years that have passed since the formation of the Pentecostal Fellowship of North America in 1948–1949, the member bodies have done much to eliminate the suspicion and the hostility that had developed as a result of the sanctification controversy forty years before.[34] On the national level, for example, the PFNA has sponsored forums and seminars in which the representatives of various Pentecostal groups could exchange views on topics of mutual interest, namely, home and foreign missions, youth programs, radio evangelism, Christian education, and religious publishing. Locally, the PFNA has revived the idea of jointly sponsored religious rallies. In the Los Angeles area, for instance, the Assemblies of God, Foursquare Gospel Church, Pentecostal Church of God, Independent Full Gospel Churches, Pentecostal Holiness Church, and the Church of God (Cleveland, Tennessee) united to conduct a youth rally in the amphitheater of the Hollywood Bowl to which a crowd of 21,000 people came.[35]

[32] A pamphlet titled *Pentecostal Fellowship of North America;* revised and printed in 1962; and available from any one of the member denominations.

[33] R. O. Corvin, "The Pentecostal Fellowship of North America," *Pentecost,* No. 10 (Dec., 1949), p. 2.

[34] Brumback, *Suddenly from Heaven,* p. 315.

[35] Kendrick, *Promise Fulfilled,* p. 213, citing *Pentecostal Evangel,* XXXVI (Oct. 23, 1948), 13.

In commenting on such united evangelistic efforts, one Pentecostal wrote:

> It is no longer an unusual thing for 15,000 to 20,000 to turn out to the tent campaigns. . . . Very seldom does one find a Pentecostal Assembly in any city that does not fully co-operate with all the others in these city-wide campaigns.[36]

About the time that the PFNA was being organized, various British Pentecostal bodies likewise were turning their attention to the matter of union. They too wanted to dispel some of the vestiges of a rivalry in the 1930's, involving the three main Pentecostal organizations—Elim, Assemblies of God, and the Apostolic Church;[37] therefore, they strongly endorsed the idea of British Pentecostals uniting. There is a paucity of information concerning the British Pentecostal Fellowship, since its establishment in October, 1948; however, we do know that two of its significant achievements have been (1) the publication of a Pentecostal hymnal containing eight hundred selections, and (2) its sponsorship of the 1952 World Conference of Pentecostal Churches which convened in London.

Statistics regarding the British Pentecostal Fellowship are now nearly a decade old; however, they indicate that in 1956 about 1,000 churches, 60,000 members, and 800 ministers[38] from the following groups comprised the Union: Assemblies of God, Apostolic Church, Congo Evangelistic Association, Elim Foursquare Gospel Alliance, Elim Pentecostal Churches, European Evangelistic Society, International Bible Training Institute, Pentecostal Jewish Mission, and the United Apostolic Faith Church.

Although British Pentecostals have manifested a renewed interest in the matter of unity, they have stopped short of any formal amalgamation. Even the steps that have been taken, however, are regarded as having had a salutary effect on Pentecostalism in the British Isles. For example, in writing about themselves in a cooperative publishing venture—*What Is This Pentecostal Movement?*—British Pentecostals

[36] David duPlessis, "Pentecostal Movement Shares in the Present Revival in North America," *Pentecost,* No. 14, (Dec., 1950), 5. Cf. *Pentecost,* No. 20, (June, 1952), p. 16.

[37] Wilson, *Sects and Society,* p. 41.

[38] *Pentecost,* No. 38 (Dec., 1956), p. 14.

emphasize the fact that although they bear different names they "are one." Furthermore, although they retain their distinctive tenets, "they enjoy much inter-fellowship." They conclude with the statement that their "unity is much more impressive than their diversity."

Chilean Pentecostals Join the World Council. Although there are certain individuals like Donald Gee of England who have been interested in the World Council of Churches and the Ecumenical Movement since the days of the World Missionary Conference in Edinburgh (1910),[39] most Pentecostals frown upon any association with the World Council. Their primary objection is on theological grounds. As thoroughgoing Evangelicals who cling tenaciously to the doctrine of verbal inspiration, the validity of the supernatural elements contained in scripture, the substitutionary atonement, and the divinity of Jesus Christ, they feel unable to have "real fellowship" with those churches that compromise on these issues. Many churches within the World Council, the Pentecostals believe, do precisely that.[40]

Furthermore, many Pentecostals are suspicious of any kind of detailed organization. They feel that the "true Church" is spiritual, that it is composed of those who are "in Christ" by virtue of their being spiritually reborn; therefore they abhor any attempt to create a visible united church here on earth.

Finally, some Pentecostals still resent having any association whatsoever with the established denominations which opposed and ostracized them during the early days of their revival. Others regard participation in the World Council "as sharing in the subtle drift towards a final apostasy foretold in the Apocalypse."[41] Still another segment of somewhat provincial Pentecostals fears that fellowship with non-Pentecostals would inevitably result both in a weakening of the movement's distinctive testimony as well as in a diminishing of its spiritual power.

Nonetheless, as early as 1952 certain ecumenical-minded Pente-

[39] Gee, "The Pentecostal Churches and the WCC," *Pentecostal Testimony* (June, 1964), pp. 8–9, 35.

[40] Thomas Zimmerman, "20th Century Pentecost," *Pentecostal Evangel,* LII (Aug. 6, 1961), 28 f.

[41] Gee, "Amsterdam and Pentecost," *Pentecost,* No. 6 (Dec., 1948), p. 17.

costals issued statements such as the following one which David J. duPlessis[42] delivered before the International Missionary Council at Willingen:

> Within Pentecostal ranks there are some honest misgivings concerning some aspects of the ecumenical movement for church unions, but there also is a hearty recognition of a significant moving of the Holy Spirit in recent years to draw all true Christians closer together.
>
> . . . .
>
> After nearly half a century of misunderstanding and ostracism, for which they recognize they have not been entirely without blame on their own part, the Pentecostal Churches offer their fellowship in Christ to the whole of His Church in this grave hour of her history. They believe they have something to gain by larger fellowship with all who truly belong to Christ. They are greatly encouraged by many world-wide tokens that old prejudices are melting and a new era of mutual appreciation dawning. Brethren, let us receive one another, as Christ also received us to the glory of God.[43]

Nearly ten years after this pronouncement by duPlessis, at its New Delhi Assembly in November, 1961, the World Council of Churches admitted two groups of Chilean Pentecostals into membership: Iglesia Pentecostal de Chile and Mision Iglesia Pentecostal (Chile).

Although they represent only a small portion of the nearly 500,000 Chilean Pentecostals, their admission into the World Council led one Pentecostal observer to exclaim that he felt the World Council by this act was demonstrating to the world its recognition of the Pentecostal revival.[44]

The affiliation of the Chilean Pentecostals notwithstanding, there is no widespread movement on the part of other Pentecostals to unite with the World Council.

[42] DuPlessis is an ecumenical-minded Pentecostal who for years served the movement in the Apostolic Faith Mission of South Africa. A protégé of John Mackay, duPlessis has served on the staff of the Second Assembly of the World Council at Evanston, has attended the Third Assembly in New Delhi as a "Pentecostal observer," and has been disfellowshiped by the Assemblies of God (USA) for his ecumenical activities. See *The Spirit Bade Me Go;* it is published by him and available by writing 3742 Linwood Avenue, Oakland 2, Calif.

[43] In Norman Goodall (ed.), *Missions Under the Cross* (New York: Friendship Press, 1953), pp. 249–50.

[44] Gee, "Pentecostals at New Delhi," *Pentecost,* No. 59 (Mar.–May, 1962), p. 17, quoting duPlessis.

When letters were sent to various Pentecostal organizations asking this question: "In view of the recent entry of the Chilean Pentecostals into the World Council of Churches, do you foresee any changes in your attitudes toward the National Council, the World Council, or the Ecumenical Movement?" the responses were uniformly negative: "I foresee no change for us. Present feeling in our midst is very distinctively against Ecumenicity as touching a close unity with non-Evangelicals."[45] None whatsoever as far as the U. S. Pentecostals are concerned."[46] Perhaps the clearest statement of the current ecumenical stance of most Pentecostals is contained in the following excerpt from a sermon preached at the 1961 World Pentecostal Conference in Jerusalem by Thomas Zimmerman, General Superintendent of the Assemblies of God (USA):

> Within the past few weeks news releases have indicated that three Pentecostal denominations have applied to the World Council of Churches for membership—two in Chile and one in Yugoslavia. We are not personally acquainted with these groups, nor do we know their reason for joining hands with the World Council of Churches. But, brethren, these are not days in which to compromise!
>
> Regardless of efforts of the World Council of Churches and the National Council of Churches who assay to call us "brethren," *we are miles apart.* [Italics mine.] Nor can we afford to compromise with them on our more basic, sacred, God-given, heaven-blessed position, including the infallibility of God's Word, the Virgin Birth, the atoning death of our Lord and Savior, His resurrection, and His bodily return.[47]

Re-emphasis on Healing

The doctrine of divine healing has always been emphasized with Pentecostal churches, but the practice has occurred intermittently. In the years following V-J Day, however, the practice of praying for the sick was revived on a scale hitherto unknown. In the forefront of the movement were American Pentecostals: William Freeman, Oral

[45] A response from an official of the Pentecostal Church of Christ.

[46] The answer submitted by a representative of the General Council, Assemblies of God.

[47] Zimmerman, "20th Century Pentecost," p. 29. See also Frank M. Boyd "Ecumenicity—False and True," *Pentecostal Evangel,* L (Oct. 7, 1962), 4–5, 19.

Roberts, Tommy Hicks, O. L. Jaggers, and Gordon Lindsay. These men felt that "even a casual study of the New Testament makes it clear that divine healing was the chief cause for which Christ received the attention of the nation of His day."[48] Furthermore, they reasoned, the Great Commission that Christ gave to the Church included the command to heal the sick. Likewise, they were convinced that "the healing revival is the God-appointed means to reach the unsaved masses in the heathen lands, or where Protestant Christianity has a feeble hold."[49]

The cornerstone of "deliverance evangelism," as it was referred to among Pentecostals, is the belief that just as God wants everyone to be saved from sin, so also does He desire everyone to be well.[50] The task of the deliverance evangelists, therefore, is to proclaim this truth and to encourage their listeners to believe it.

Literally scores of such evangelists have arisen during the past decade and a half. Among them are men and women whose names have often appeared in the nation's religious and secular press: "Little David" Walker, William Branham, whose great campaigns stirred South Africa, Jack Coe, Harold Herman, whose revivals in Italy, Germany, and Korea have been extraordinarily successful. Most of these evangelists operate apart from any established Pentecostal denomination; most have incorporated as nonprofit religious organizations; most publish monthly journals which inform contributors about past and forthcoming revivals and are a medium for soliciting funds.[51]

[48] Gordon Lindsay, "The World-Wide Salvation Healing Revival," in Greenway, *World Pentecostal Conference Souvenir Brochure,* p. 51.

[49] *Ibid.,* p. 53.

[50] But all men are not saved, because they refuse to appropriate God's gracious provision for them. Likewise all men are not cured of their ills because they do not appropriate the healing which God has provided through Jesus Christ's suffering ("By his wounds you have been healed." I Pet. 2:24). A more detailed survey of this matter is found in Noel McNeill's unpublished manuscript, "As of a Rushing Mighty Wind: An Assessment of North America's Pentecostal Movement," p. 30.

[51] Evangelist and Mrs. M. A. Daoud head The Voice of Miracles and Missions, Inc.; they publish the *Miracles and Missions Digest,* and work principally in Madagascar. The Voice of Healing maintains headquarters in Dallas. Under the leadership of Gordon Lindsay, it publishes, helps foreign nationals to build churches through its Native Church Crusade (in 1962, for instance, 388 churches were built in this way), and assists missionaries to obtain equip-

Perhaps the most famous, as well as the most typical, of these evangelists are Oral Roberts, Tommy Hicks, and T. L. Osborn.

Oral Roberts. Except for Billy Graham, Oral Roberts is undoubtedly the best-known American evangelist. Born in Pontococ County, Oklahoma, on January 24, 1918, to a struggling revivalist preacher named Ellis and his wife Claudia, Roberts himself grew up to become an ordained minister in the Pentecostal Holiness Church. Since 1947, the period of his first somewhat modest campaigns in Tulsa,[52] Roberts has catapulted into international prominence. Each year he has conducted about a dozen week-long crusades in the United States; he has also directed longer ones in these countries: Australia, Formosa, Japan, Poland, Finland, Canada, and Puerto Rico.

In the early 1950's, Roberts founded and directed the Healing Wings Revival Ministry. In his campaigns, he used an immense fireproof tent which seated as many as 18,000 people.[53] From city to city, a staff of twelve transported it and other audio-visual equipment in eight stainless steel truck trailers. Since then, the Oral Roberts Evangelistic Association has emerged. Its center of operations is the seven-story Abundant Life Building[54] in downtown Tulsa which houses some 415 employees, Roberts' office, the editorial offices of *Abundant Life* (formerly *Healing Waters Magazine*), and an auditorium seating 1,500. International offices are also maintained in Britain, South Africa, Australia, and New Zealand.

In 1955, Oral Roberts launched his first television films, and a year later, the *Christian Century* reported:

Today he is heard on 600 radio stations and seen on 167 television stations weekly. Short-wave broadcasts beam his sermons to over a dozen

---

ment and to construct evangelistic centers in larger cosmopolitan areas. "Miracle Arm" LeRoy Jenkins directs a Faith Healing Clinic and Cathedral of Tomorrow in Tampa, Fla., and publishes *Revival.*

[52] Hayes B. Jacobs, "Oral Roberts: High Priest of Faith Healing," *Harper's,* CCIV (Feb., 1962), 40.

[53] The tent was 200′ x 360′. It had an aluminum preaching platform that held 60 people, a 60,000-watt lighting and public address system. It was worth $240,000. See "Deadline from God," *Time,* LXVI (July 11, 1955), 41.

[54] The three-million-dollar building, which opened in 1957, is a windowless, ultramodern, air-conditioned structure, faced with white marble and floodlighted at night.

foreign countries. According to a public relations release, "a recent estimate of his television, radio, and short-wave audience embraced almost a billion persons."[55]

The most recent venture by Roberts, himself only an intermittent student at Oklahoma Baptist University and Phillips University, is the establishment of Oral Roberts University. When it has been completed, it is reported that the school will be housed in facilities worth 25 million dollars and supported by an endowment of an equivalent amount of money. The long-range objective of the school is to train 1,000 ministers annually to be adepts in the type of evangelism which Roberts himself perfected.

Although *Time* demurs,[56] hundreds of people claim that they have been cured while attending Roberts' meetings. They testify to being "delivered" of ailments ranging from tuberculosis to menopause troubles. Be that as it may, it is generally conceded that more people have heard about the "full gospel" from Oral Roberts than from any other Pentecostal. "He seldom draws less than 12,000 and usually 15,000 to 16,000."[57]

Tommy Hicks. Whereas Oral Roberts' influence has been primarily in North America, the successes of Pentecostals like Tommy Hicks and T. L. Osborn have been abroad. Unknown to most people until the appearance of an article in *Christian Century,* was the fact that there was a greater response to Tommy Hicks's revival in Buenos Aires (1954) than to the campaign which Billy Graham conducted in London.[58]

The Hicks meetings started in Argentina just prior to Easter with about 5,000 people turning out to the *cancha* (stadium) of the Atlanta Soccer Club. By the end of May, the revival services had to be transferred to a larger *cancha,* "where the attendance never dropped below 60,000 a night, and on at least one night (May 24) was reported by the Buenos Aires papers to have passed 200,000."[59]

[55] W. E. Mann, "What About Oral Roberts?" LXXIII (Sept. 5, 1956), 1018.
[56] "Deadline from God," p. 42.
[57] Mann, "What About Oral Roberts?" p. 1018.
[58] "But What About Tommy Hicks?" *Christian Century,* LXXI (July 7, 1954), 814.
[59] *Idem.*

The lame, the blind, the deaf and dumb from all over this republic and from all social strata have struggled into the stadium to receive his touch. Hundreds in a single night have lined up to give a brief word of testimony at the microphone as to how they have been healed. Experienced ministers and missionaries from many countries say they have never seen anything like it.[60]

T. L. Osborn. Osborn's first successful salvation-healing revival was in 1951 in Camagüey, Cuba, where it is reported that as many as 30,000 gathered in the local ball park to hear an American evangelist with a Pentecostal background being interpreted by a "native Episcopal rector, fully in sympathy with the effort."[61] Osborn conducted another series of meetings in Ponce, Puerto Rico. There throngs of over 15,000 attended, with hundreds testifying to having been divinely healed from all manner of diseases.

From the Caribbean, Osborn's campaigns took him to Formosa and Japan (1956), Mombasa, and Holland (1958). Immense crowds flocked to Osborn's meetings in The Hague and in the northern city of Groningen. They stimulated such an avid interest in Pentecostalism that Donald Gee wrote three years later:

> It would be ridiculous not to recognize that this impressive new revival spirit in Holland stems from the immense campaigns conducted by T. L. Osborn in the summer of 1958. . . . I was shown the huge field in The Hague where something like 15,000 people gathered. After three years one can sense lasting effects.[62]

All told, Evangelist Osborn has ministered in almost fifty foreign countries.

Like Oral Roberts, Osborn has established an evangelistic association with headquarters in Tulsa and international branches in Sydney, Australia; Toronto, Canada; Birmingham, England; Wellington, New Zealand; Dusseldorf, Germany; and Zurich, Switzerland. The Association publishes a colorful monthly, *Faith Digest,* and makes extensive use of tapes, recordings, and films. Perhaps the really unique feature of Osborn's organization is the Association for Native Evangelism whereby contributors are asked to sponsor national pastors

60 *Idem.*
61 "The Great Healing Campaigns," *Pentecost,* No. 17 (Sept., 1951), p. 8.
62 "What I Found in Holland," *Pentecost,* No. 56 (June–Aug., 1961), p. 7.

who will be under the direct supervision of Pentecostal missionaries until such time as the native pastor's work is self-sustaining. According to one report, over 2,000 native evangelists have been supported by this program.[63]

Abatement of Sectarian Traits

Sociologists of religion claim that when sects such as the Pentecostals first emerge they tend toward religious extremism or radicalism. Eventually, however, they do mature and slough off their emotional excesses.[64] In time their cultural and economic standards invariably improve; their numbers increase; their church property becomes aesthetic. In short, they attain a level of denominational respectability.

When these larger groups achieve this status, seemingly tensions develop within them. There is always a faction which is convinced that the price that must be paid for "progress" is too dear: doctrinal compromise, loss of spiritual vitality, and especially an overemphasis on organization and education, which they feel has a stultifying effect upon, and is antithetical to, "true" religion. For a while such a faction remains within the larger group and endeavors, by agitation, to revive it. However, when the patience of an agitating faction is finally exhausted, it is then that a new sect is born.

During the past two decades, the Pentecostal movement has experienced these tensions. While some Pentecostal groups have become increasingly respectable—numerically, socially, economically, and psychologically—other Pentecostals, equating organization and scholarship with spiritual apathy and apostasy, have withdrawn to form new groups.

"Sects," writes Elmer Clark, "frequently . . . protest against elements which only wealth can secure—fine churches, organs, costly raiment, jewelry, indulgence in worldly amusements, and the like."[65]

[63] McNeill, "As of a Rushing Mighty Wind," p. 85.

[64] Cf. Walter G. Muelder, "From Sect to Church," *Christendom,* 10 (Autumn, 1945), 450–62; and H. Richard Niebuhr, *Social Sources of Denominationalism* (New York: Meridian Books Inc., 1960), pp. 17–28.

[65] *Small Sects,* p. 18.

The early Pentecostals frequently engaged in this kind of deprecation. It was caused, I think, by the types of people who were attracted to Pentecostalism then—the urban and rural poor, the socially rejected. Such people disdain outward appearances. To them, it is the inward that matters. Therefore, writes Donald Gee, "attractive, well-kept buildings, conveniently located [are] considered unworthy of attention in a 'spiritual' movement."[66] Such an attitude, although common among early Pentecostals, has changed remarkably during the past twenty years or so.

Churches Replace Temporary Quarters. Since World War II the allegiance of Pentecostal groups to the store-front or the second-floor mission has waned. Moreover, "the frame tabernacle so characteristic of early Pentecostal architecture has begun to give way to more permanent structures."[67] Current Pentecostal journals frequently feature new churches that have been built. The Central Assembly of God in Wichita, Kansas, for example, recently moved into a beautiful new sanctuary which accommodates over 1,000 people. It features an entry of diamond-shaped windows of cathedral tropicel, and it has spacious paved and lighted off-street parking facilities. Pentecostals in Grand Falls, Newfoundland, are planning an ultramodern structure that will cost approximately one million dollars. The Apostolic Church in England recently constructed the largest church building in Wales. In Tammerfors, Finnish Pentecostals claim to have the most beautiful church in northern Scandinavia. It was designed by the famous architect Bertel Strömmer.

Liturgical Order Supplants Charismatic Ardor. Another evidence of the process of maturation within certain segments of contemporary Pentecostalism is that worship services have become more restrained. And it is Liston Pope's opinion that as a sect approaches the status of a denomination, its communicants become less emotional and manifest a preference for a more formal and conservative type of

[66] *Pentecostal Movement,* p. 90.
[67] Klaude Kendrick, "The Pentecostal Movement," *Christian Century,* LXXX (May 8, 1963), 609.

service.[68] This type of transformation has been occurring almost imperceptibly within some of the larger Pentecostal groups whose meetings in earlier years were like this one which A. J. Tomlinson described in his brief autobiography, *Answering the Call of God:*

> Yesterday [May 27, 1909 (?)] was a wonderful day in the camp [meeting]. In the beginning of the service in the morning, one or two messages were given in tongues, and I gave the interpretation. Afterwards I was seized with two or three spells of weeping, and finally fell on my back under the overwhelming power of God. After screaming for a while as though my heart would break, I became a little more quiet . . . The meeting that followed during the day is indescribable. Men, women and children screaming, shouting, praying, leaping, dancing, and falling prostrate under God's overwhelming power. Wonderful![69]

Dr. W. C. Dumble of Toronto described a Pentecostal meeting which he attended in Los Angeles in 1906 thus:

> I had the rare joy of spending last evening at Pastor Bartleman's meeting, or more correctly at a meeting where he and Pastor Pendleton are the nominal leaders, but where the Holy Spirit is actually in control. Jesus is proclaimed the Head, and the Holy Ghost His executive. Hence there is no preaching, no choir, no organ, no collection, except what is voluntarily placed on the table, or put in the box on the wall.[70]

Such examples of Pentecostal services where there was no order of worship and where the emotions and charismatic outbursts were allowed free course have largely disappeared. Although a printed liturgy for divine services is still not used, a certain tradition has emerged. Most Pentecostal meetings are planned to include congregational singing, prayer, special musical selections (generally while the offering is being collected), Scripture reading, a sermon, and an "altar call."[71] At the midweek "Prayer and Praise" service, a greater informality abounds, as ample opportunity is given for members to testify.

[68] *Millhands and Preachers* (New Haven: Yale University Press, 1942), pp. 120–40.

[69] Pp. 14–15.

[70] In Bartleman's *How Pentecost Came,* p. 86.

[71] At the conclusion of the sermon, the American preacher typically invites those who desire to accept Christ, to tarry for the Spirit baptism, and those who hope to receive healing to come to the altar. British Pentecostals do not practice this.

More often than not, spontaneous outbursts of *glossolalia* which characterized Pentecostal meetings in earlier days have become subordinated to the ministry of the Word of God. Dr. Nils Bloch-Hoell relates an incident that took place in the Minneapolis Gospel Tabernacle (a church affiliated with the Assemblies of God) during his visit to this country in 1947.

Pastor Frank Lindquist was delivering his sermon when a woman in the audience began to "sing in the Spirit." He asked her to keep silent. She answered that she was impelled to sing by the Spirit. Lindquist insisted that she be quiet, maintaining that the Spirit that had impelled him to deliver the Lenten sermon could not very well contradict Himself.[72]

That a greater emphasis has been placed on teaching Pentecostals to control their emotionalism is evidenced by the appearance of admonitions such as this one:

> It has been well said that the Holy Spirit is a gentleman—He does not disturb meetings. There is a proper time and place for manifestations of the Holy Spirit and it is *not* a time when it will inject a harsh note into the meeting and disturb either speaker, singer, or audience. May God grant that we may never quench the Spirit, but may He also grant that we *do* quench emotional outbreaks that are not of His leading.[73]

As the authority and leading of the Spirit became subordinated, and as ardor became displaced by order, a natural consequence was the delegation of responsibility to church officials and various boards. For example, when the Assemblies of God were established in 1914, the leaders consisted of a chairman and a secretary whose "duties were, mainly, to arrange for and preside over the annual council meeting, to publish the minutes of the council sessions and to keep the Movement informed of Council activities throughout the year."[74] In addition, twelve representatives were appointed "to act in all necessary matters . . . as a Home and Foreign Missionary and Executive Presbytery."[75] Today, the denomination is administered by the follow-

[72] Bloch-Hoell, *Pentecostal Movement,* p. 162.

[73] Briggs P. Dingman, "Unction or Emotion?" *Pentecostal Evangel,* XXXIII (Dec. 1, 1945), 3.

[74] Brumback, *Suddenly from Heaven,* p. 177.

[75] *Ibid.,* p. 178.

ing full-time staff: a general superintendent, five assistant general superintendents, a general secretary, a general treasurer, eight national secretaries (in charge of strategic ministries such as youth, education, home missions, radio), and other supervisors. The total number of persons now employed at the Assemblies of God headquarters exceeds 600, and the location—the corner of Lyon and Pacific Streets in Springfield, Missouri—has been referred to as "Coronary Lane and Ulcer Boulevard." Not a few constituents ask: "Is the simple fellowship which the founders envisioned being overcome by ecclesiastical centralization? Is cooperation being exchanged for coercion?"[76]

Growing Interest in Education. According to Liston Pope, a religious group begins to discard its sectarian character when it starts to insist (1) on having academically qualified ministers and (2) on supporting a program of religious education rather than solely one of evangelism.[77] Since 1940, such changes in emphases have been occurring within Pentecostalism.

In the early days of the movement's history, there were few academically trained leaders. As a matter of fact, Charles W. Conn highlights the occasion when Sam C. Perry joined the Church of God (Cleveland, Tennessee) "because he was one of the first college men to preach in the Church of God, most of its preachers being self-educated or uneducated."[78] The paucity of educated men and the shortage of educational facilities in the Church of God were symbolic of a condition common to all Pentecostal groups in those early days. Antipathy toward education was predicated on the following grounds: (1) that education is harmful to spirituality;[79] (2) that the enormous cost of building, staffing, and maintaining educational facilities would require the diverting of funds from strictly spiritual enterprises such

[76] *Ibid.*, p. 322.

[77] Pope, *Millhands,* pp. 122–24; 139–40.

[78] *Like a Mighty Army,* p. 105. Perry became State Overseer in Kentucky, and eventually a member of the Supreme Council.

[79] In his *Pillars of Pentecost* (p. 129), Conn says: "Fortunately the attitude that education is harmful to spirituality is found only in isolated areas, and is not a general attitude."

as home and foreign missions;[80] (3) that henceforth ministers would be judged for their scholarship rather than for their spiritual leadership;[81] (4) that the words of Jesus as in John 16:13 ("When the Spirit of truth comes, he will guide you into all truth . . .") signify that the Holy Spirit personally instructs the believer; therefore, it is unnecessary to provide either religious or secular training;[82] finally (5) that since most of the people who joined Pentecostal churches came from the lower social and economic strata and in many cases had not advanced past the secondary school level themselves, they had little or no appreciation for education in general and for higher education in particular.[83]

However, as the movement grew, the climate of opinion changed. By the 1920's, most Pentecostal administrators realized that their converts as well as their youth were growing up without any training in Pentecostal-Christian principles. Some Bible institutes and Bible colleges began to spring up both here and abroad. Elaborate programs for Christian education on the local church level were likewise instituted.

It was not until after World War II, however, that a growing demand for "collegiate education in a Pentecostal atmosphere" was heard. Pentecostals were recognizing that a baccalaureate degree had become as necessary for their offspring as a high school diploma had been for them. During this time, Carl Brumback writes, "Almost two thousand applicants were turned away in one year from the crowded Bible Institutes."[84]

Articles such as the following began to appear in Pentecostal periodicals:

There are true values in culture and education. It would be almost

[80] "The primary purpose of the Movement was spiritual. . . . Since there was only so much money available, it was felt that we [Pentecostals] should concentrate on evangelization and not education." Brumback, *Suddenly from Heaven,* p. 327.

[81] In 1949, at its General Council in Seattle, Assemblies of God ministers and delegates unanimously passed the motion that a college degree would never be a requisite for ordination. *Ibid.,* p. 328.

[82] Kendrick, *Promise Fulfilled,* p. 117.

[83] *Idem.*

[84] *Suddenly from Heaven,* p. 327.

criminal folly arbitrarily to deny them to our rising generation because of a perverted idea that by means of such a denial we can preserve spiritual power and purity. We shall do no such thing. . . . Moreover, there are important spheres of service that demand men and women of wide learning and expert scholarship. . . .

Whether right or wrong, it is to be recognized that this desire for a more cultured ministry, either at home or abroad, marks a definite change from the early temper of the Pentecostal Revival—when we rather gloried in the fact that, on the whole, we were "unlearned and ignorant" men.[85]

It is no wonder, then, that in the last twenty years, nearly a score of Bible and liberal arts colleges have been established by various Pentecostal denominations. Before the war, the Assemblies of God had but one school of collegiate rank; today it claims two fully accredited colleges, and seven Bible colleges.[86] The Church of God has developed Lee College (in Cleveland, Tennessee) into a reputable junior college and has announced plans to inaugurate a four-year program shortly. Undoubtedly the most auspicious undertaking in the history of Pentecostal higher education has been the construction of Oral Roberts University whose Liberal Arts College and Graduate School of Theology opened last fall. The campus consisting of 220 acres is located one mile outside the Tulsa city limits. Buildings that have been erected include dormitories that will house 160 students apiece; a multipurpose building, consisting of classrooms, a dining hall, auditorium, and offices; and a six-story Learning Resources Center that is designed to house a library of 500,000 volumes. Publicity brochures indicate that the University hopes to have an eventual annual enrollment of 2,000 undergraduate and 1,000 graduate students.

Concern for Social Problems. Sects, assert some scholars, either tend to renounce or are indifferent to prevailing culture and social

[85] Donald Gee, "Unlearned and Ignorant," *Pentecostal Evangel,* XLIV (Nov. 16, 1946), 5.

[86] Southern California College at Costa Mesa is endorsed by the Western Association of Schools and Colleges and Evangel College (Springfield, Mo.) by the North Central Association of Colleges and Secondary Schools; the four-year Bible college program of Bethany Bible College (Santa Cruz, California) is likewise fully accredtied by WASC.

organization.[87] "None have any program of social reform," says Elmer T. Clark. "Not one takes an active part in the labor struggle; most . . . look upon such matters as political questions to be wholly avoided."[88]

Such generalizations adequately characterize the lack of social consciousness on the part of far too many Pentecostals during the early decades of the movement's existence. On the whole, most of them were aloof to the many serious problems that afflicted the society of which they were members. They maintained that an individual had to come to the Pentecostal church to seek a religious experience. That would change his life. Only in this manner could social reform be achieved.[89] More recently, however, there have been signs that Pentecostals are realizing the need to apply the principles of the gospel to the needs of society. They seem to be more willing to offer their services to the community and thus help to ameliorate its manifold problems.

A few have even entered politics. Such acts have not escaped criticism, but the responsible leadership is rallying to their defense.

> David SERVED his own generation by the will of God, and there are some among us in the Pentecostal Revival who feel called of God to serve our generation in the sphere of politics.[90]

Others are actively engaged in working with drug addicts and prostitutes in cosmopolitan centers like Brooklyn, Chicago, Boston, Los Angeles, and Toronto. The most successful leader in the establishment of Teen Challenge Centers has been the Rev. David R. Wilkerson.[91] He conducted his first series of meetings for teen-age gangs at

[87] *Millhands,* pp. 122–24. Also F. A. Shippey, "Sociological Forms of Religious Expression," *Religion in Life,* XXVII (Spring, 1958), 172–84; and R. A. Buchanan, "Church-Type and Sect-Type," *London Quarterly* (Apr., 1963), p. 3.

[88] *Small Sects,* p. 219.

[89] If one were to articulate the Pentecostal social philosophy, it might be this: one changes society by reforming the individuals who comprise it. Central to the reformation of individuals, needless to say, is the experience of conversion.

[90] Donald Gee, "Pentecost and Politics," *Pentecost,* No. 47 (Mar., 1959), p. 17.

[91] He recently wrote a book about his work: *The Cross and the Switchblade* (New York: Bernard Geis Associates and distributed by Random House, 1963).

the St. Nicholas Arena in Manhattan in 1958. At that time, 125 members of such feuding gangs as the "Mau Maus," "Egyptian Kings," "Hell Burners"—all members of Grand Gangsters, Inc.—were converted and subsequently rehabilitated.[92]

Since the pioneering venture of Wilkerson, Pentecostal workers have (at some hazard to their lives) invaded the "turfs" in Los Angeles, the Negro and Spanish sections of Chicago, Harlem, Coney Island, and Greenwich Village. That their efforts have been successful is attested to by statistics released in 1962. The Teen Challenge organization claimed that its records of the past five years showed that 80 per cent of those who remained in the Centers for at least two weeks experienced successful "withdrawal" from drug addiction.[93]

Another field of "social service" in which the Pentecostals have been both active and successful is ministering to the inmates of the nation's prisons. The Assemblies of God has a full-time National Prison Chaplain, who has counseled the prisoners of state and federal penal institutions in forty-six states. The philosophy of Arvid Ohrnell, who held that position for years, was: Christ dealt with individuals. Why should we hesitate to follow His example when dealing with the outcasts of society?

Self-criticism Voiced. A prominent characteristic of the sect mentality, it seems, is to claim for itself a pure revelation of truth in its entirety and to engage in constant criticism of all other religious organizations.[94] One of the most significant indications that the maturation process has commenced in a sect might be, then, when it shifts its critical attention from others to itself. As one reads the literature that has been produced by Pentecostals, especially during the past two decades, one becomes aware that they have begun to evaluate themselves rather critically.

Ten years ago, Charles W. Conn criticized his Pentecostal colleagues for condemning audio-visual techniques, education, and attractive churches:

[92] "Reaching Gangs for Christ," *Pentecostal Evangel,* XLVII (Mar. 22, 1959), 14.

[93] Cf. "Teen Challenge Marches On," *Pentecostal Evangel,* LI (Dec. 29, 1963), 11; McNeill, "As of a Sound," p. 120.

[94] Cf. Clark, *Small Sects,* p. 223; Pope, *Millhands,* pp. 122–24.

We hurt only ourselves when we resist things that are good and beneficial because we are afraid they may be worldly. There was a time when Pentecostal people looked askance at the radio, branding it as a worldly thing. Now we have accepted it as a device beneficial in getting the gospel to lost men. . . .

. . . .

To be frightened by progress is to be defeated. Hesitancy in accepting progress will bring stagnation. . . . We must utilize scientific advancement and take advantage of the conditions of our day. . . . We must accept progress as God's gift to aid us in our task.[95]

Pentecostal modes of worship were critically appraised by Donald Gee. He was fearful lest music, which has a central place in Pentecostal worship, be employed solely to stir the emotions. He cautioned that "danger . . . lurks in the catchy and popular chorus, the old-time favorite song in a massed congregation, the sentimental solo."[96] He observed that while all of these may be legitimately used, it ought to be realized that they are "sensuous thickets where . . . instead of being revealed, Christ becomes obscured by the very means we have ostensibly used to lift Him up."

Briggs Dingman, in commenting on the fact that the Pentecostal movement is often criticized for displaying too much emotion during the worship service, acknowledged that there is a sense in which there is some fairness in this criticism. Disliking the coolness and the lack of emotion in the non-Pentecostal churches, there is a danger of leaning too far in the other direction and becoming *too* emotional.[97] The ideal, Dingman advised, would be to "discern the golden mean" so that Pentecostal services would reflect the Lord's presence and "redound to His glory."

On another occasion, Gee described the view of earlier Pentecostals who took refuge in the fanatical idea that in some miraculous way the Holy Spirit would compensate for their deficiencies of scriptural knowledge, their disinterest in obtaining such knowledge, or their inability to communicate the little they did know. "That period

[95] "Pointing Out Some Pentecostal Perils," *Pentecostal Evangel,* XLIV (Oct. 28, 1956), 19–21.

[96] "Music and the Spirit-Filled Life," *Pentecostal Evangel,* XXIV (May 23, 1936), 6 f.

[97] "Unction or Emotion," p. 3.

has passed," he declared. "Conditions have changed. People today will not be satisfied with an incompetent ministry."[98] Furthermore, he suggested that Pentecostals be more critical of their own claims, for "in their doctrine of the 'initial evidence' it is easy to make more of the gift than the Giver and to bend energy in promoting the glossolalia until . . . it becomes the supreme end in view."[99]

Elsewhere Gee criticizes those in the healing and deliverance ministry for marring it by their commercialism, thriving on the credulity of the masses, and publishing exaggerated reports.[100] But perhaps the most comprehensive bit of self-criticism is contained in the following excerpt from one of his editorials in *Pentecost:*

> If we, as Pentecostals, now glory in our numerical growth and our riches in property, we need to take very much to heart the warning to the Laodicean church.[101]

Emergence of New Pentecostal Groups

According to J. M. Yinger, the history of the Christian Church abounds with the accounts of sects which shifted gradually into respectable denominations or churches.[102] From the preceding section, it is clear that in the second generation a large segment of the Pentecostal movement has undergone a transformation which has caused it to lose some of its sect characteristics and to take on the traits of a denomination.

For example, Pentecostals have become property owners rather than being propertyless. They have risen economically, and their churches have become more elaborate, their worship services more dignified. There is a greater demand for music of a professional

[98] "Why I Believe in Bible Schools," *Pentecostal Evangel,* XLVII (May 3, 1959), 6 f.

[99] "Wheat, Tares and 'Tongues,'" *Pentecost,* No. 66 (Dec., 1963–Feb., 1964), p. 17.

[100] "The Value of the Supernatural," *Pentecost,* No. 62 (Dec., 1962–Feb., 1963), p. 17.

[101] "Pentecostals at New Delhi," *Pentecost,* No. 59 (Mar.–May, 1962), p. 17.

[102] *Religion and the Struggle for Power* (Durham, N.C.: Duke University Press, 1946), pp. 18–19.

quality[103] and for an educated ministry.[104] The groups have grown in influence and numbers, and, in the process, they have developed an increasing amount of eccelesiastical "machinery." Prior concerns of meeting the needs of an adult membership have been subordinated to a stress on the religious education of the young. Those cultural standards which the fathers condemned, the children have embraced. The stress on the future, on preparing for the next world, has given way very largely to a principle of accommodation to the surrounding culture. All of these characteristics are evidences of the sect-to-denomination process—one which is bound to produce tension. And tensions have developed between the larger Pentecostal groups on the one hand and some others who, remembering the simplicity of the "early days," have become uncomfortable and have withdrawn to form new factions that advocate little or no organization, that stress the "leading of the Spirit" in place of a fixed order of worship and administration, and prefer isolation to compromise. In the postwar period, especially, a veritable spate of these "independent" Pentecostal groups has appeared: the New Order of the Latter Rain, The World Church, Wings of Healing, Full Gospel Fellowship of Ministers and Churches, International, and the Gospel Assemblies—to mention but a few representative types.

As stated earlier, most of these newer divisions of Pentecostalism came into being because their leadership believed that the older and larger churches had modified or abandoned many of the "Pentecostal" practices that were prominent during the beginning of the revival. They were especially concerned that "the depth of worship and the operation of the gifts of the Spirit so much in evidence in earlier decades were not so prominent in the thirties and forties."[105] To remedy this fault, an organization called the New Order of the Latter Rain came into being in 1947. It originated with Rev. George Hawtin and Rev. Percy Hunt, and its first prominent center was the Sharon

[103] Typical of the larger Pentecostal Churches, the First Assembly of God in Memphis has a Minister of Music who directs a ninety-voice robed choir.

[104] No longer will the speak-as-the-Spirit-moves-you-type preaching do, as Oliver Whitely points out in *Trumpet Call of Reformation* (St. Louis: Bethany Press, 1959), p. 23.

[105] Brumback, *Suddenly from Heaven*, p. 331.

Bible Institute at North Battleford, Saskatchewan. Here, says Noel McNeill, a Canadian Pentecostal,

> there was such an effusion of Divine Power in healings, miracles and utterance gifts [prophecy] that wide attention was attracted. Thousands flocked from every part of the continent and the world to special "Camp-meeting-Conventions."[106]

The meetings were publicized as a new outpouring (i.e., Latter Rain) of the Holy Spirit upon a movement that had become dry and barren.

What had started out as a counteraction to the growing denominationalism of the Pentecostal movement became an organization of come-outers, replete with tenets of faith and a charismatic leadership. Its major emphases were (1) that the gifts of the Spirit were to be conveyed only through the "laying on of hands" by certain individuals; (2) that these individuals were selected by prophetic directive (tongues and interpretation) to be "Apostles," and that their utterances regarding faith and practice were to have an authority at least equivalent to that of Scripture; (3) that doctrinal statements be rejected and "all organization be branded as "Babylonian";[107] and (4) that the larger "apostate" Pentecostal churches be violently attacked for their backslidden condition.

Interestingly enough, whereas many Protestant churches had found it necessary to denounce the excesses of the Pentecostals in the early 1900's, the larger Pentecostal bodies were compelled to announce their disapproval of the New Order of the Latter Rain in the late 1940's. The result: some of the larger Pentecostal bodies lost influential ministers and churches to the schismatics.

New sects generally arise in protest of the abuses, real and imagined, which they feel are present in the well-established religious organizations. This fact accounts for the emergence not only of a group like the New Order of the Latter Rain but also of the following "independent" Pentecostal groups.

The Full Gospel Fellowship of Ministers and Churches, Inter-

[106] McNeill, "As of a Rushing," p. 27.

[107] Cf. Brumback, *Suddenly from Heaven,* pp. 331–32; McNeill, "As of a Rushing," p. 28; and M. D. Beall, "The Babylonish Garment," *Latter Rain Evangel,* XIII (Nov., 1963), 10–14.

national reflects a rebellion against the bureaucratic machinery of the older, more highly organized Pentecostal denominations. It emphasizes that

> it . . . shall never have any ecclesiastical authority. It shall not have and shall never attempt to exercise a single attribute of power or authority over any church, or over the messengers of the churches in such wise as to limit the sovereignty of the churches under one sovereign, the Lord Jesus Christ.[108]

O. L. Jaggers, formerly a minister in the Assemblies of God, founded The World Church because he felt that the *charismata* no longer had precedence among the larger Pentecostal groups.

Dr. Thomas Wyatt, after his "appointment with God" in the wilderness of Judea,[109] realized that the "deliverance gospel" preached by many Pentecostals was perhaps too limited, for it emphasized only healing and salvation. In 1942, Wyatt conceived of an organization, Wings of Healing—with its adjunct, The Twelve Legions—which would serve "all mankind, regardless of color, class, or creed" and which would be "active on the frontiers of human want around the world."[110] Wings of Healing is undenominational and nonsectarian, striving "to meet the needs of all men, spiritually, physically, economically, and socially."[111] Dr. Wyatt's organization is one of the very few Pentecostal groups that take an interest in politics and economics.

Perhaps the best illustration of antiorganization sentiment is the existence in the Midwest of some 60 churches with 7,000 members who, according to Noel McNeill, reject "the use of any name" and which refuse

> to incorporate . . . because . . . prophetically they believe that all churches recognized by civil powers make up the Harlot Church while they alone constitute the true Body of Christ.[112]

[108] From the *Constitution* of the Full Gospel Fellowship cited in Walter J. Hollenweger, "Handbuch der Pfingstbewegung" unpublished Th.D. dissertation, Zürich, 1965), Vol. III, p. 778.

[109] See his account in *Keys to the Kingdom* (Hollywood: Oxford Press, 1961), p. 99.

[110] *Ibid.*, p. 124.

[111] *Idem.*

[112] "As of a Rushing," p. 106.

"Tongues Speaking" Among Non-Pentecostals

In recent years Pentecostalism has been gaining wider attention within the Christian world than ever before, not so much for its phenomenal growth as for the effect that its distinctive teaching—the baptism in the Spirit accompanied by *glossolalia*—has had upon mainline Protestantism. Once characterized as the religious experience popular among only the lower socio-economic strata of society, Pentecostal practices have infiltrated the drawing rooms of staid Episcopalians and Presbyterians[113] as well as the campuses of sophisticated academic institutions such as Yale.[114] Neither have the other traditional churches escaped the influence of "neo-Pentecostalism" or the "Charismatic revival," as it has been variously called.

"The charismatic movement," writes McCandlish Phillips in the *Saturday Evening Post,* "began on a tiny scale in the major denominations in about 1956, with perhaps 20 ministers openly involved."[115] As a definite movement, however, neo-Pentecostalism is traced to April 3, 1960, when Dennis J. Bennett, a rector of St. Mark's Episcopal Church in Van Nuys, California, informed his congregation of two thousand about his "Pentecostal experience," emphasizing "that the experience was 'enriching.' "[116]

The vestry asked Father Bennett to resign; Bishop Francis Eric Bloy of Los Angeles sent a new priest to St. Mark's and issued a pastoral letter in which he banned the recurrence of tongues speaking under church auspices.[117] Newspaper accounts of this and other similar outbursts of *glossolalia* drew the attention of the entire nation to the fact that a new Pentecostalism was emerging. In a short time, it was clear that "Pentecostal" practices had already penetrated or

[113] Jerry Jensen (compiler), *Episcopalians and the Baptism of the Holy Spirit* (Los Angeles: Full Gospel Businessmen's Fellowship International, 1964), 32 pp. Companion volumes dealing with the manifestation of *glossolalia* among Presbyterians, Baptists, and Methodists have likewise been compiled by Mr. Jensen.

[114] Cf. Harald Bredesen, "Awakening at Yale," *Christian Life,* XXIV (Feb., 1963), 32–34; and "Blue Tongues" in *Time,* LXXXI (Mar. 29, 1963), 52.

[115] May 16, 1964, p. 32.

[116] As reported in *Time,* LXXVIII (Aug. 15, 1960), 55.

[117] *Idem.*

would subsequently penetrate the American Lutheran Church, American Baptist Convention, Reformed Church in America, Methodist Church, Evangelical United Brethren, and the United Presbyterian Church (USA).[118]

Although these recent outbursts of the *charismata* within the traditional churches have been heralded as spontaneous movements of the Holy Spirit, I am inclined to agree with Russell T. Hitt's judgment that the neo-Pentecostal revival has been strongly influenced by "older" Pentecostal personalities and organizations. Especially significant, I think, have been the efforts of David J. duPlessis and the Full Gospel Businessmen's Fellowship International.

David duPlessis, who has been reared in Pentecostalism, so to speak, is a notable figure in international Pentecostal circles, primarily because of his role as Secretary of the World Pentecostal Conference. During the last decade, however, largely as a result of his being sponsored by John Mackay of Princeton, duPlessis has been a sort of roving ambassador among non-Pentecostals. He has addressed seminarians at Harvard, Yale, Union, Chicago, to mention only a few campuses. He has spoken at denominational retreats. He has attended conclaves conducted by the World Council of Churches. And in each place he has talked about Pentecostal Christianity. Doubtless scores "of neo-Pentecostals" are intellectually or experientially acquainted with charismatic phenomena like speaking in tongues because of duPlessis' witness.

The Full Gospel Businessmen's Fellowship International is the brainchild of wealthy California dairyman Demos Shakarian and the internationally famous Pentecostal, Oral Roberts. From the 21-member organization that was launched in Clinton's Cafeteria in Los Angeles back in 1951, the FGBMFI has developed into one with perhaps as many as 100,000 members.[119] It has conducted dinner meetings in nearly every major ballroom in this country and abroad, during which time laymen witness to other laymen, calling them back to God, "and telling them what the baptism of the Holy Spirit can

[118] Hitt, "The New Pentecostalism", p. 3.

[119] Morton T. Kelsey, *Tongue Speaking* (New York: Doubleday & Company, Inc., 1964), p. 88.

mean in their lives and in their witness for God. . . ."[120] Speaking of the success of the FGBMFI in reaching non-Pentecostals, president-founder Shakarian said a few years ago: "This full gospel movement is spreading. . . . Many ministers from various denominations have come into our businessmen's banquets and have received the baptism of the Holy Spirit through prayers of laymen."[121]

Also spearheading the movement for a charismatic revival among the traditional churches is the Blessed Trinity Society; however, it is not affiliated with the Pentecostal movement in any formal way. In addition to the efforts of the aforementioned David duPlessis, the activities of the Society are directed by Harald Bredesen, a Dutch Reformed minister from Mt. Vernon, New York, and Mrs. Jean Stone, editor of the Society's attractive quarterly, *Trinity*. This magazine features articles which "discuss not only questions such as the theological and psychological meaning of tongues, but also give many excellent case histories and news about those who are active in this ministry in the older established churches."[122]

To cope with the outbursts of the *charismata* among their clergy and laity, some denominations have created special commissions to study the problem. The Rt. Rev. Gerald F. Burrill, Episcopal Bishop of Chicago, appointed such a committee to visit meetings where speaking in tongues occurred, to study the phenomenon "in the light of the Church's scripture and history, and the living experiences of those who are engaged in 'spiritual speaking,'" and to recommend appropriate action.[123] The American Lutheran Church also had a Committee on Spiritual Gifts study *glossolalia* and prepare a report to be submitted to congregations and pastors for information and guidance.

Reactions to this Pentecostal penetration of the historic Christian churches has been mixed. Bishop Pike and his suffragan, Bishop Millard, issued a pastoral letter to be read in their diocese on May 5, 1963, in which the clergy were warned that tongues speaking was

[120] William C. Armstrong, "A Decade of Divine Destiny," *Voice,* XII (Oct., 1963), 4. Such a meeting is colorfully described by John L. Sherrill in *They Speak with Other Tongues* (New York: McGraw-Hill Book Company, 1964), pp. 132–41.

[121] *Ibid.,* p. 7.

[122] Kelsey, *Tongue Speaking,* p. 97.

[123] Atter, *Third Force,* p. 233.

"heresy in embryo"; they were admonished further "not to take part in the movement to nurture and spread the practice of speaking with tongues and not to invite visiting preachers or speakers who have this purpose."[124] Elsewhere, at the First North American Reformed and Presbyterian Youth Assembly which convened in 1962 at Purdue University, a United Presbyterian minister, who had come forward to ask the youthful gathering to repent and receive the Holy Spirit, was restrained and escorted out of the auditorium by a campus policeman.[125] Dr. William Culbertson, president of Moody Bible Institute of Chicago, one of the oldest Fundamentalist schools in America, allegedly warned his entire student body against praying in tongues.

On the other hand, Rev. Samuel M. Shoemaker, writing in *The Episcopalian* (May 15, 1962), advised his readers:

> Whatever the old-new phenomenon of "speaking in tongues" means, . . . I do know it means God is trying to get through into the Church, staid and stuffy and self-centered as it often is, with a kind of power that will make it radiant and exciting and self-giving. We should seek to understand and be reverent toward this phenomenon, rather than to ignore or scorn it.[126]

Dr. Philip E. Hughes, editor of the Anglican theological quarterly, *The Churchman,* was of the opinion that the outburst of tongues speaking among Episcopalians in California could be attributed to "a flirtation under the hot California sun with the extravagances of Pentecostalism."[127] However, after he had visited the Coast and had observed the phenomenon, he modified his view, saying: "The breath of the living God is stirring among the dry bones of the major, respectable, old-established denominations and particularly in the Episcopalian Church."[128] Even Billy Graham in commenting on the "Charismatic revival" advised the historic churches

> to learn once again what it means to be Baptized with the Holy Spirit. In the main denominations we have looked a bit askance at our brethren

[124] Reprinted in *The Living Church,* CXLVI (May 19, 1963), 12.

[125] Frank Farrell, "Outburst of Tongues," *Christianity Today,* VII (Sept. 13, 1963), 3.

[126] Cited in Sherrill, *They Speak,* p. 68.

[127] *Ibid.,* p. 69.

[128] *Idem.*

from the Pentecostal churches because of their emphasis on the doctrine of the Holy Spirit, but I believe the time has come to give the Holy Spirit His rightful place in our churches.[129]

The penetration of established denominations by Pentecostal practices has had a dual effect. One has been that dissension and strife in some areas have accompanied the outburst of *glossolalia.* A Minneapolis Evangelical Free Church, for instance, split over the issue;[130] so did St. Mark's Episcopal Church in Van Nuys.[131] Moreover, all too often some overzealous practitioners have made disquieting, patronizing statements to those who, they felt, had not yet experienced "the Pentecostal blessing."

But there has been a wholesome effect too: Biblical scholars, theologians, ministers, and laymen have been sent scurrying to their New Testaments and church histories to probe the evidence for the *charismata,* especially speaking in tongues, whereas only a few years ago, as one writer noted, "these same people showed relatively little interest in the subject despite a half-century of aggressive promotion on the part of the Pentecostal movement."[132]

Influence of Pentecostalism Acknowledged

Until lately, most observers were inclined to regard Pentecostalism as a temporary and passing phenomenon, not worth much attention. Then in 1958, Dr. Henry P. Van Dusen wrote an article for *Life* in which he censured the traditional churches for disdainfully dismissing a movement like Pentecostalism as a "fringe sect," overlooking the fact that its growth and activity is one of the phenomenal developments in modern religious history.[133] Since that time, books, magazine features, and newspaper articles—Protestant and Catholic, secular and religious, American as well as foreign—have been written about Pentecostalism.

[129] *Idem,* citing the Jan., 1961, issue of the Full Gospel Business Men's magazine, *Voice.*

[130] Farrell, "Outburst," p. 3.

[131] "Closely Guarded Secret," in *Living Church,* CXLIV (July 10, 1960), 5.

[132] Farrell, "Outburst," p. 3.

[133] "The Third Force," June 9, 1958, pp. 122–24.

For example, in *Christian Sects,* Konrad Algermissen, the noted German Catholic theologian, applauds Pentecostalism for initiating

> a revolt not only against modern, soul-less, mechanized, presumptuous humanity, but also against the rationalized, superficial, sophisticated Christianity of the Churches which spend much effort on everything but the one thing necessary; namely, a continual deepening of faith and a sacramental and moral life based on this deepening faith by the imitation

An article in *Time* describes Pentecostalism as the fastest growing religious movement in the hemisphere,[135] while Dr. Nils Bloch-Hoell, editor of the Norwegian *Tidsskrift for Teologi of Kirke* and an authority on the history of the Pentecostal movement in Norway, thinks that it is the greatest ecstatic movement in the history of the Christian Church.

Thus, while a few years ago Pentecostalism was regarded as a suspect religious movement, today it has achieved widespread recognition. In terms of percentage of growth, it has spurted ahead of the traditional Protestant denominations, "burying last year's statistics under a mass of new adherents, new churches, new territories,"[136] and forcing observers both of the American and of the international religious scenes to coin such new phrases as "the third force in Christendom" when referring to its influence within and upon contemporary Christianity.

In 1963, Daniel J. O'Hanlon, S.J., advised the readers of *America* that the phenomenal growth of Pentecostalism all over the world and the extraordinary appeal that it has had for the kind of people with whom the Lord especially concerned Himself demanded that they shed their "squeamish bourgeois prejudices and take a long hard look at it."[137] To this challenge *Pentecostalism* has addressed itself.

[134] P. 114.
[135] Vol. LVI (Nov. 2, 1962), 56.
[136] Edwin S. Gaustad, *Historical Atlas of Religion in America* (New York: Harper & Row, 1962), Fig. 101 on p. 121.
[137] "The Pentecostals and Pope John's 'New Pentecost,'" CVIII (May 4, 1963), 634.

of Christ.[134]

Selective Bibliography

Books marked thus [*] *are written by Pentecostals*

1. Pentecostal Faith and Practice

*ATTER, GORDON. *The Third Force.* Peterborough, Ont.: The College Press, 1962.

*BRUMBACK, CARL. *What Meaneth This?* Springfield, Mo.: Gospel Publishing House, 1947.

*CONN, CHARLES W. *Pillars of Pentecost.* Cleveland, Tenn.: The Pathway Press, 1956.

*CROSS, JAMES A. (ed.). *Healing in the Church.* Cleveland, Tenn.: The Pathway Press, 1962.

CUTTEN, GEORGE B. *Speaking with Tongues.* New Haven: Yale University Press, 1927.

DAVIES, HORTON. *Christian Deviations.* London: SCM Press, Ltd., 1961.

FULLER, REGINALD H. "Tongues in the New Testament," *American Church Quarterly,* III (Fall, 1963), 162–68.

*GEE, DONALD. *Concerning Spiritual Gifts.* Springfield, Mo.: Gospel Publishing House, 1937.

*HORTON, HAROLD. *The Gifts of the Spirit.* London: Assemblies of God Publishing House, 1962.

KELSEY, MORTON. *Tongue Speaking.* New York: Doubleday & Company, Inc., 1964.

*LEMONS, FRANK W. *Our Pentecostal Heritage.* Cleveland, Tenn.: The Pathway Press, 1963.

*MACDONALD, WILLIAM G. "Glossolalia in the New Testament," *Bulletin of the Evangelical Theological Society,* VII (Spring, 1964), 59–68.

*MCPHERSON, AIMEE SEMPLE. *The Foursquare Gospel.* Los Angeles: Echo Park Evangelistic Association, 1946.

———. *This Is That.* Los Angeles: Echo Park Evangelistic Association, 1923.

MILLER, ELMER S. *Pentecost Examined.* Springfield, Mo.: Gospel Publishing House, 1936.

*NELSON, P. C. *Bible Doctrines.* Enid, Oklahoma: Southwestern Press, 1936.

*PAULK, EARL P., JR. *Your Pentecostal Neighbor.* Cleveland, Tenn.: The Pathway Press, 1958.

*PEARLMAN, MYER. *Knowing the Doctrines of the Bible.* Springfield, Mo.: Gospel Publishing House, 1937.

*RIGGS, RALPH M. *The Spirit Himself.* Springfield, Mo.: Gospel Publishing House, 1949.

SHERRILL, JOHN L. *They Speak with Other Tongues.* New York: McGraw Hill Book Company, 1964.

*SQUIRE, FRED H. *Divine Healing Today.* London: Victory Press, 1954.

VIVIER, LINCOLN M. "Glossolalia." Johannesburg: University of Witwatersrand, 1960. Unpublished M.D. dissertation.

2. Antecedents of Modern Pentecostalism

*DALTON, ROBERT C. *Tongues Like as of Fire.* Springfield, Mo.: Gospel Publishing House, 1945.

DEWAR, LINDSAY. *The Holy Spirit and Modern Thought.* New York: Harper & Brothers, 1959.

DRUMMOND, ANDREW L. *Edward Irving and His Circle.* London: Clarke & Co., Ltd., 1937.

HAYES, D. A. *The Gift of Tongues.* New York: Eaton and Mains, 1913.

*KENDRICK, KLAUDE. *The Promise Fulfilled: A History of the Modern Pentecostal Movement.* Springfield, Mo.: Gospel Publishing House, 1961. Treats the eight largest American Pentecostal groups.

KNOX, R. A. *Enthusiasm.* Oxford: Clarendon Press, 1951.

MACKIE, ALEXANDER. *The Gift of Tongues.* New York: George H. Doran Co., 1921).

MARTIN, IRA J. *Glossolalia in the Apostolic Church.* Berea, Ky.: Berea College Press, 1960.

*PALMA, ANTHONY D. "Glossolalia in the Light of the New Testament and Subsequent History." New York: Biblical Seminary, 1960. Unpublished S.T.B. thesis.

SHAW, P. E. *The Catholic Apostolic Church.* New York: King's Crown Press, 1946.

VAN DUSEN, HENRY P. *Spirit, Son, and Father.* New York: Charles Scribner's Sons, 1958.

WALKER, DAWSON. *The Gift of Tongues.* Edinburgh: T. & T. Clark, 1906.

3. The United States: Birthplace of Twentieth-century Pentecostalism

*BARTLEMAN, FRANK. *How Pentecost Came to Los Angeles.* Los Angeles: Privately Printed, 1925.

BLOCH-HOELL, NILS. *The Pentecostal Movement.* Oslo: Universitetsforlaget, 1964.

*BRUMBACK, CARL. *Suddenly from Heaven.* Springfield, Mo.: Gospel Publishing House, 1961. The authoritative history of the Assemblies of God.

*CAMPBELL, JOSEPH. *The Pentecostal Holiness Church.* Franklin Springs, Ga.: The Publishing House of the Pentecostal Holiness Church, 1951. A comprehensive analysis of one of the oldest Pentecostal denominations.

*CONN, CHARLES W. *Like a Mighty Army.* Cleveland, Tenn.: Church of God Publishing House, 1955. A well-written, meticulously documented history of the Church of God.

*FLOWER, J. ROSWELL. "Birth of the Pentecostal Movement," *Pentecostal Evangel,* XXXVIII (Nov. 26, 1950), 3.

*FRODSHAM, STANLEY. *With Signs Following,* rev. ed. Springfield, Mo.: Gospel Publishing House, 1941.

*GOSS, ETHEL A. *The Winds of God.* New York: Comet Press Books, 1958.

**A Historical Account of The Apostolic Faith.* Portland, Ore.: The Apostolic Faith Publishing House, 1965.

*KENDRICK, KLAUDE. *The Promise Fulfilled: A History of the Modern Pentecostal Movement.* Springfield, Mo.: Gospel Publishing House, 1961.

*OTIS, ADDIE M. "The Apostolic Faith Movement." *Word and Work* XXIX (Feb., 1907), 51.

4. Pentecostalism Becomes an International Movement

*BARTLEMAN, FRANK. *Around the World by Faith.* Los Angeles: Privately Printed, n.d.

———. *Two Years Mission Work in Europe.* Los Angeles: Privately Printed, n.d.

BLOCH-HOELL, NILS. *The Pentecostal Movement.* Oslo: Universitetsforlaget, 1964.

*FRODSHAM, STANLEY. *With Signs Following.* Springfield, Mo.: Gospel Publishing House, 1946.

*GEE, DONALD. *The Pentecostal Movement.* London: Elim Publishing House, Ltd., 1949. Best treatment of the origin and development of Pentecostalism in the British Isles.

———. *Upon All Flesh.* Springfield, Mo.: Gospel Publishing House, 1935.

*HOOVER, WILLIS C. "Work in Chile," *Word and Work,* XXXIII (July, 1911), 220 f.

*RAMABAI, PANDITA. "Showers of Blessing at Mukti, India, 39 Years Ago," *Pentecostal Evangel* XXXIV (May 4, 1946), 1, 12–13.

*STEINER, LEONHARD, *Mit folgenden Zeichen.* Basel: Verlag Mission für das volle Evangelium, 1954.

"The Tongues Movement," *Independent,* LXVI (June 10, 1909), 1286–89.

5. Causes for the Initial Success of Pentecostalism

BOISEN, ANTON. "Religion and Hard Times," *Social Action,* V (Mar., 1939), 8–35.

BRADEN, CHARLES S. "Sectarianism Run Wild," *Protestantism: A Symposium.* Nashville: The Methodist Church, 1944.

*BRUMBACK, CARL. *Suddenly from Heaven.* Springfield, Mo.: Gospel Publishing House, 1961.

SWEET, WILLIAM WARREN. *Revivalism in America.* New York: Charles Scribner's Sons, 1944.

———. *The Story of Religion in America.* New York: Harper & Row, 1939.

6. Pentecostals Encounter Violent Opposition

AIKMAN, DUNCAN. "The Holy Rollers." *American Mercury,* XV (October, 1928), 180–91.

*BRUMBACK, CARL. *Suddenly from Heaven.* Springfield, Mo.: Gospel Publishing House, 1961, 282–93.

*CAMPBELL, JOSEPH. *The Pentecostal Holiness Church.* Franklin Springs, Ga.: The Publishing House of the Pentecostal Holiness Church, 1951.

*CONN, CHARLES W. *Like a Mighty Army.* Cleveland, Tenn.: Church of God Publishing House, 1955, pp. 29–33.

*GEE, DONALD. "Why Is 'Pentecost' Opposed?" *Pentecostal Testimony,* X (Nov., 1929), 16.

HAAVIK, O. L. "Pentecostalism or the Tongues Movement," *Lutheran Herald* (Oct. 23 and 30, 1934), pp. 935–37; 959–63.

*"Mob Attacks Pentecostal Evangelist," *The Pentecostal Testimony,* XVI (Mar., 1935), 13.

*"Persecution of Pentecostals," *The Pentecostal Testimony,* XIX (May, 1938), 11.

RICHARDSON, ROBERT P. "Pentecostal Prophets," *Open Court,* XLII (1928), 673–80.

STOLEE, HAAKON J. *Speaking in Tongues,* rev. ed. Minneapolis: Augsburg Publishing House, 1963.

7. Pentecostalism Menaced by Dissension

*BARRATT, THOMAS BALL. "An Urgent Plea for Charity and Unity," *Word and Work,* XXXIII (April, 1911), 104–7.

*BARTLEMAN, FRANK. *How Pentecost Came to Los Angeles.* Los Angeles: Privately Printed, 1925, pp. 69, 146–50.

*Brumback, Carl. *God in Three Persons*. Cleveland, Tenn.: Pathway Press, 1959.

———. *Suddenly from Heaven*. Springfield, Mo.: Gospel Publishing House, 1961, pp. 58 f., 98–106, 159 f., 192 f.

*Gee, Donald. *The Pentecostal Movement*. London: Elim Publishing House, Ltd., 1949, pp. 72–88, 106–8.

*Goss, Ethel A. *Winds of God*. New York: Comet Press Books, 1958, pp. 166 ff.

8. Varieties of Pentecostalism in America (I): The Oldest and the Most Prominent Branches

Bach, Marcus. *They Have Found a Faith*. New York: Bobbs-Merrill Company, 1946.

*Becker, Raymond. "The Church of The Foursquare Gospel," *The Foursquare Magazine*, XXVII (May, 1954), 15.

*Brumback, Carl. *Suddenly from Heaven*. Springfield, Mo.: Gospel Publishing House, 1961.

*Campbell, Joseph. *The Pentecostal Holiness Church*. Franklin Springs, Ga.: The Publishing House of the Pentecostal Holiness Church, 1951.

Clark, Elmer T. *The Small Sects in America*, rev. ed. Nashville: Abingdon Press, 1959.

*Conn, Charles W. *Like a Mighty Army*. Cleveland, Tenn.: Church of God Publishing House, 1955.

*Courtney, Howard P. "International Church of The Foursquare Gospel," *Pentecostal Evangel*, XLV (Aug. 11, 1957), 22.

*Gause, R. H. *Church of God Polity*. Cleveland, Tenn.: Pathway Press, 1958.

**A Historical Account of The Apostolic Faith*. Portland, Ore.: The Apostolic Faith Publishing House, 1965.

Hall, Gordon L. *The Sawdust Trail*. Philadelphia: Macrae Smith Co., 1964.

*Kendrick, Klaude. *The Promise Fulfilled: A History of the American Pentecostal Movement*. Springfield, Mo.: Gospel Publishing House, 1961.

Mathison, Richard. *Faiths, Cults and Sects of America*. Indianapolis: Bobbs-Merrill, 1960.

Mayer, F. E. *The Religious Bodies of America*, 4th ed., revised by Arthur Piepkorn. St. Louis: Concordia Publishing House, 1961.

*McNeill, Noel. "As of a Rushing Mighty Wind: An Assessment of North America's Pentecostal Movement." Typewritten.

Mead, Frank S. *Handbook of Denominations in the United States*, 4th rev. ed. Nashville: Abingdon Press, 1965.

*Moore, Everett LeRoy. "Handbook of Pentecostal Denominations in the United States." Pasadena: Pasadena College, 1954. Unpublished Master's thesis.

NEVE, JUERGEN L. *Churches and Sects of Christendom* (Burlington, Iowa: The Lutheran Literary Board, 1940).

*UNITED PENTECOSTAL CHURCH. *What We Believe and Teach.* St. Louis: Pentecostal Publishing House, n.d.

WINEHOUSE, IRWIN. *The Assemblies of God: A Popular Survey.* New York: Vantage Press, 1959.

9. Varieties of Pentecostalism in America (II): The Regional, Ethnic, Small, Cultic Groups

CLARK, ELMER T. *The Small Sects in America,* rev. ed. Nashville: Abingdon Press, 1959.

COLLINS, J. B. *Tennessee Snake Handlers.* Chattanooga: n.n., 1947.

EDDY, G. NORMAN. "The True Believers: Some Impressions of American Deviant Religions." Typewritten.

FAUSET, ARTHUR H. *Black Gods of the Metropolis.* Philadelphia: University of Pennsylvania Press, 1944.

*FIORENTINO, JOSEPH. "A Summary of the Italian Pentecostal Movement in the United States and Abroad." Typewritten.

FRAZIER, E. FRANKLIN. *The Negro Church in America.* New York: Shocken Books, 1963.

**Introducing Bible Standard Churches.* Des Moines: Inspiration Press, n.d.

**Introducing the Church of God of Prophecy.* Cleveland, Tenn.: White Wing Publishing House, n.d.

LABARRE, WESTON. *They Shall Take Up Serpents.* Minneapolis: University of Minnesota Press, 1962.

PREECE, HAROLD. *Dew on Jordan.* New York: E. P. Dutton Company, 1946.

REID, IRA. "Let Us Prey," *Opportunity,* IV (Sept., 1926), 247–78.

*TOMLINSON, A. J. *Answering the Call of God.* Cleveland, Tenn.: White Wing Publishing House, n.d.

———. *God's Twentieth Century Pioneer.* Cleveland, Tenn.: White Wing Publishing House, 1962.

*TOMLINSON, HOMER. *The Diary of A. J. Tomlinson.* New York: The Church of God, World Headquarters, 3 vols., 1953.

WHITAM, FREDERICK L. "New York's Spanish Protestants," *Christian Century,* LXXIX (Feb. 7, 1962), 162–64.

WHITING, ALBERT N. "The United House of Prayer for All People: A Case Study of a Charismatic Sect." Washington, D.C.: The American University, 1952. Unpublished Ph.D. dissertation.

WOMELDORF, JOHN A. "Rattlesnake Religion," *Christian Century,* LXIV (Dec. 10, 1947), 1517 f.

10. A Survey of Pentecostalism in Other Lands (I): North and South America, The Near East, Africa, and the Far East

*ATTER, GORDON. *The Third Force.* Peterborough, Ont.: The College Press, 1962.

BAINTON, ROLAND. "Mission in Latin America," *Christian Century,* LXXVIII (Jan. 11, 1961), 41–44.

BROWNING, WEBSTER E. *The West Coast Republics of South America.* New York: World Dominion Press, 1930.

CONN, CHARLES W. *Where the Saints Have Trod.* Cleveland, Tenn.: The Pathway Press, 1959.

DAMBORIENA, PRUDENCIO. "The Pentecostals in Chile," *Catholic Mind,* LX (Mar., 1962), 27–32.

FERRY, ANTHONY. "Oh, Sing It, You Precious Pentecostal People!" *Maclean's,* LXXV (Nov. 3, 1962), 20–23. A popular survey of Pentecostal growth in Canada.

*FRODSHAM, STANLEY. *With Signs Following,* rev. ed. Springfield, Mo.: Gospel Publishing House, 1941.

*KULBECK, GLORIA G. *What God Hath Wrought.* Toronto: The Pentecostal Assemblies of Canada, 1958. The definitive history of Canada's largest Pentecostal organization, The Pentecostal Assemblies.

LATOURETTE, KENNETH SCOTT. *The Twentieth Century Outside Europe.* Vol. V, Christianity in a Revolutionary Age Series. New York: Harper & Row, 1962.

MCGAVRAN, DONALD. *Church Growth in Mexico.* Grand Rapids: Eerdmans, 1963.

NORTHCOTT, CECIL. *Christianity in Africa.* London: SCM Press, Ltd., 1963.

*STEINER, LEONHARD. *Mit folgenden Zeichen.* Basel: Verlag Mission für das volle Evangelium, 1954.

TSCHUY, THEO. "Shock Troops in Chile," *Christian Century,* LXXVII (Sept. 28, 1960), 1118.

11. A Survey of Pentecostalism in Other Lands (II): The European Continent

*ATTER, GORDON. *The Third Force.* Peterborough, Ont.: The College Press, 1962.

*BJOERKQUIST, CURT. *Den Svenska Pingstväckelsen.* Stockholm: Forlaget Filadelphia, 1959.

BLANKE, FRITZ. *Kirchen + Sekten.* Zurich: Zwingli Verlag, 1959.

BLOCH-HOELL, NILS. *Pinsebevegelsen.* Oslo: Universitetsforlaget, 1956. Masterful study of Pentecostalism, especially of the Norwegian revival.

CHÉRY, H. CH. *L'Offensive des Sectes.* Paris: Les Éditions du Cerf, 1954.

CONN, CHARLES W. *Where the Saints Have Trod.* Cleveland, Tenn.: The Pathway Press, 1959.

DAGON, GÉRARD. *Petites Églises et Grandes Sectes.* Paris: Société Evangélisation, n.d.

*Dawidow, W. "Kosciol Chrzescijan Wiary Ewangeliczney." (Warsaw: Warsaw University, n.d.). Unpublished Th.M. thesis.

*Edsor, Albert W. *George Jeffreys: Man of God.* London: Ludgate Press, Ltd., 1964.

*Gee, Donald. *The Pentecostal Movement.* London: Elim Publishing House, Ltd., 1949.

Hutten, Kurt. *Seher, Grübler, Enthusiasten.* Stuttgart: Quell-Verlag Der Evang. Gesellschaft, 1958.

**Introducing the Elim Church.* London: Evangel Press, n.d.

**Kalendarz Jubileuszowy.* Warsaw: Prezydium Zjednoczonego Kosciola Ewangelicznego, 1963.

Kolarz, Walter. *Religion in the Soviet Union.* London: Macmillan & Co., Ltd., 1961.

*Krust, Christian H. *50 Jahre Deutsche Pfingstbewegung.* Altdorf bei Nurnberg: Missionsbuchhandlung und Verlag, n.d.

Latourette, Kenneth Scott. *The Twentieth Century in Europe.* Vol. IV, Christianity in a Revolutionary Age Series. New York: Harper & Row, 1961.

*Steiner, Leonhard. *Mit folgenden Zeichen.* Basel: Verlag Mission für das volle Evangelium, 1954.

Wilson, Bryan R. *Sects and Society.* London: William Heinemann Ltd., 1961. A sociological study of the Elim Church in the United Kingdom.

World Council of Churches. "The Pentecostal Movement and the Swedish Baptist Union," *Bulletin,* VI (Spring, 1960), 9–12.

12. Pentecostalism Since World War II: Significant Trends

**Abundant Life* Magazine, 1962–1964.

Arlt, Augusto E. F. "The Significance of the Chilean Pentecostal's Admission to the WCC," *International Review of Missions,* LI (Oct.. 1962), 480–82.

Barnhouse, Donald G. "Finding Fellowship with Pentecostals," *Eternity* (Apr., 1958), p. 8.

Bennett, Dennis J. "Speaking in Tongues," *The Living Church* (Jan. 1, 1961), pp. 12–13.

Blikstad, Vernon M. "Spiritual Renaissance," *Christian Life,* XXVI (May, 1964), 31.

Carter, Richard. "That Old-Time Religion Comes Back," *Coronet* (Feb., 1958), pp. 125–30.

*Chinn, J. J. "May We Pentecostals Speak?" in *Christianity Today,* V (July 17, 1961), 5.

*DuPlessis, David J. *Pentecost Outside Pentecost.* Dallas: Privately Printed, 1960.

*Farrell, Frank. "Outburst of Tongues," *Christianity Today,* VII (Sept. 13, 1963), 3–6.

*FISCHER, HAROLD A. "Progress of the Various Modern Pentecostal Movements Toward World Fellowship." Fort Worth: Texas Christian University, 1952. Unpublished Master's thesis.

GILBERT, ARTHUR. "Pentecost among the Pentecostals," *Christian Century,* LXXVIII (June 28, 1961), 794–96.

*GEE, DONALD. "The Pentecostal Churches and the WCC," *Pentecostal Testimony* (June 1964), pp. 8–9, 35.

———. "Pentecostals at New Delhi," *Pentecost,* No. 59 (Mar.–May, 1962), p. 17.

HITT, RUSSELL T. "The New Pentecostalism." Philadelphia: Evangelical Foundation, Inc., 1963. Reprinted from *Eternity*.

JACOBS, HAYES B. "Oral Roberts: High Priest of Faith Healing," *Harper's,* CCXXIV (Feb., 1962), 40.

*JENSEN, JERRY (comp.). *Baptists and the Baptism of the Holy Spirit; Episcopalians and the Baptism of the Holy Spirit; Methodists and the Baptism of the Holy Spirit.* Los Angeles: Full Gospel Businessmen's Fellowship International, 1963–1964.

*LINDSAY, GORDON. *Bible Days Are Here Again.* Shreveport, La.: Privately Printed, 1949.

———. *William Branham, A Man Sent from God.* Jeffersonville, Ind.: William Branham, 1950.

MUELDER, WALTER G. "From Sect to Church," *Christendom,* X (Autumn, 1945), 450–62.

O'HANLON, DANIEL J. "Pentecostals and Pope John's New Pentecost," *America,* CVIII (May 4, 1963), 634–36.

**Pentecost,* 1950–1964.

PHILLIPS, MCCANDLISH. " 'And There Appeared to Them Tongues of Fire,' " *Saturday Evening Post* (May 16, 1964), p. 31.

PIKE, JAMES. "Glossolalia," *The Living Church,* CXLVI (May 19, 1963), 11.

RICE, ROBERT. "Charismatic Revival," *Christian Life,* XXV (Nov., 1963), 30–32.

*ROBERTS, ORAL. *Oral Roberts' Best Sermons and Stories.* Tulsa: Oral Roberts, 1956.

———. *The Fourth Man.* Tulsa: Oral Roberts, 1960.

———. *My Own Story.* New York: Summit Book Company, 1961.

SHERRILL, JOHN L. *They Speak with Other Tongues.* New York: McGraw-Hill Book Company, 1964.

STEGALL, CARROLL. *The Modern Tongues and Healing Movement.* Atlanta: Carroll Stegall, n.d.

STONE, JEAN. "What is Happening Today in the Episcopal Church?" *Christian Life* (Nov., 1961), pp. 38–41.

Trinity, 1961–1964.

VAN DUSEN, HENRY P. "Third Force in Christendom," *Life,* L (June 9, 1958), 113–24.

**Voice,* 1962–1964.

Index